NATHAN RICHENDOLLAR

SIC SEMPER RES PUBLICA

*The Political Ramblings of a
Disgruntled Midwestern Teenager*

P 146   EEZ - Exclusive Economic Zone

200 miles off shore. country Have judicial jurisdiction. Can prosecute any law breakers. Regulate trade. Extract resources.

SIC SEMPER RES PUBLICA

The Political Ramblings of a Disgruntled
Midwestern Teenager

That's why the ship captain Phillips commanded was just 200 miles off shore instead of the safer 600 miles. The U.S. was able to try and jail the sole surviving pirate (Somali

Law of the Sea Treaty passed by U.N in 1945

NATHAN RICHENDOLLAR

WestBow
P R E S S
A DIVISION OF THOMAS NELSON

WestBow Press books may be ordered through booksellers or by contacting:

WestBow Press
A Division of Thomas Nelson
1663 Liberty Drive
Bloomington, IN 47403
www.westbowpress.com
1-(866) 928-1240

ISBN: 978-1-4908-0768-3 (sc)
ISBN: 978-1-4908-0769-0 (hc)
ISBN: 978-1-4908-0767-6 (e)

Library of Congress Control Number: 2013916204

Printed in the United States of America.

WestBow Press rev. date: 09/12/2013

Table of Contents

Acknowledgements

T his book is the product of years of experience in the most volatile period of human history thus far, my personal observations during my sixteen years on this planet, and the dedication of my parents in raising me, especially my mother for encouraging my love of the natural world. It is also due to the real-world economic experience that this recession has given me via the housing market and observing the public school system. Speaking of that system, at least one hundred pages of this book might as well have been written by my history teachers since the seventh grade. My brother also helped me along the way by providing comic relief and a few of the many puns in this book. The memories of Milton Friedman, Ronald Reagan, Margaret Thatcher, the Roman Republic, and my great-grandfather, in addition to my living relatives and the recollection of an American Republic forgotten compelled me to write this book as I observed the ignorance, discord, and craziness that pervaded the past few years. This book was written over six months in our basement while I listened to Gordon Lightfoot, Stevie Ray Vaughan, Garth Brooks, Bruce Springsteen, and Blue Highway to a repetitive extent while pushing my loyal canine companion Noble away from my dinner plate without success, prompting my self-interest analogy.

The many trips to Appalachia that my family has been so kind as to take with me enlightened me on the environmental and heritage front, and I owe a debt of gratitude to my very knowledgeable, benevolent environmental science teachers, in addition to my father for providing much of the information that wrote the environmental chapter. The sarcastic comments and sheer ironies of this book were made possible by the stupidity and hypocrisies of the socialist governments of Europe and the U.S. Government. Last but not least, the great team from West Bow publishing helped me move this book along after it was written.

This book is dedicated to my beloved family, the memory of an America forgotten, liberty, those who fight for it, and the Appalachian wilderness.

Introduction

I'm a 16-year-old from the suburbs of Southeast Michigan. I love Ronald Reagan, nature, and my family. I'm a conservative who is forced to see the consequences of union busting, as my dad is a public school teacher. I go to school with him, and ride in with my father every day. I also see the problems with union strangleholds, and despise liberal and Keynesian economics. I'm a believer in Reaganomics for a simple reason: because it works. My mom stays home to raise her family, and I admire her for that. She has a common nerve disease known as multiple sclerosis.

When I look at the glitches in the government safety net, and the unsecured, untrustworthy, unfunded Social Security Trust Fund, I believe my family is being punished for their decision to put more emphasis on the next generation than personal career goals. My family took out a mortgage on a $200,000 home in 2001, and like most people then, was tricked into thinking that this was the best investment possible, and that home values would never go down; that the bubble's surface tension was infinite. But Barney Frank and Chris Dodd were wrong, and my family is paying the price in three ways: through bank mortgage payments, taxes that go to bailouts and quantitative easing, and falling home values. My family is a microcosm of the American story from 2000 to 2013; boom and bust, surplus and shortage.

We currently live in a time that is eerily reminiscent of the sinking Titanic. We have a $17 trillion national debt which increases by

6 to 7% yearly; three times as fast as our GDP does according to the Bureau of Economic Analysis (BEA). Currently, we live under monopolized rather than free markets. We can't come to an agreement on anything dealing with the budget, we're engaged in conflicts all over the world, we have a crumbling infrastructure system, home values are in the gutter, and there is no end in sight. We are currently following the path which has lead every republic that has ever existed, save ours (so far), into extinction, whether it is into oligarchy, dictatorship, takeover by a foreign power, or collapse of the civilization. This is the story of a great dying republic and its predecessors; the fading into the pages of history of a behemoth of idealism, though every element of doom can be averted by the efforts of a nation re-enlightened.

CHAPTER 1

The American Nightmare

E ver since the vast expansion of the Department of Housing and Urban Development (HUD) in the 1990s, the federal government forced big banks to make extremely risky home loans, now known as subprime loans. These loans were often made with zero money down and required no background check. In the 1990s through 2007, if you were unemployed and filed the proper paperwork with HUD, you would probably get a house you knew you could never hold onto for greater than a few years. Most politicians told us that this didn't matter—that the number of subprime loans was minimal. They said that the U.S. economy was too strong and vibrant to ever correct, that the growing population—and, thus, the demand for housing—would boost the economy enough for us to outgrow the national debt and the loans given to the unemployed. But they were wrong, as all politicians are at least once, and this subprime mortgage blunder was a doozy.

The cheap credit that Washington DC pumped into the housing market led to the biggest housing bubble in American history, if not world history. The driving factor that pushed this housing bubble was the artificial demand for housing that government capital made it look like was present in the marketplace. In truth, nearly one-third of the people buying houses around the turn of the millennium had no business buying the houses that they bought. When demand goes

1

up, prices go up, exponential growth is expected, speculation takes over, and the rest is history. The members of government should have known, along with the people themselves, that in a nation where the birth rate is not enough to replace the population, housing prices probably shouldn't march north at any considerable rate. But because the economy had been vibrant for nearly sixty years, and because the government and large institutions were relatively trustworthy for those sixty years, the people (especially the middle-class people) bought into the ideas of "buy as much house as you can!," "go king," and "go big or go home."

The government, along with a complicit private sector, gladly led us over the cliff. Although I will briefly talk about the housing crisis and focus on our current downward spiral, if I want you to get one thing out of this book, it is the suspicion of large institutions and government-business collusion that we have recently lost, along with a sense of empowerment in a free-market economy and a rugged sense of individualism. Thomas Jefferson and James Madison ingrained in themselves these innate senses to preserve our liberty from both the private and public sectors.

The government wasn't alone in creating this massive housing bubble; however, it was well aided by a banking system that was eager to make as much money as possible on a growing consumer economy version of America. Traditionally, when someone took out a mortgage, it was mandated by law that the loan owner and servicer were listed directly on the title to the house. However, there was a fee of between $40-100 to register a title or title change with the county clerk. When banks were mandated to make risky loans in the 1990s, they came up with what they thought was a foolproof scheme to avoid the inevitable housing crash's brunt: they would sell the rights to collect on the loan multiple times. However, banks did not want to be stuck paying the $65 fee for filing the change over and over at the county courthouse. If you do the math by assuming that the average mega-bank made about ten million home loans between the mid-1990s and 2007, if each bank tried to change each title twice, the cost incurred by the bank would be well over $1 billion. So to remedy the problem and start issuing loans at the fastest pace possible, the largest banks got together to create an all-encompassing body called MERS.

Virtually every bank in the United States is a member of an organization called Mortgage Electronic Registration Systems (MERS). MERS is a mortgage tracking service that converts the title and mortgage to a Mortgage Identification Number (MIN) by which the organization alone can track the information on the mortgage, including the identity of the owner and servicer. When a bank is part of MERS, it technically turns over all of the titles and notes it has to MERS, and by osmosis, every single other bank in the nation. That way the bank can deny showing anybody the "blue ink" copy of their original mortgage title and sell the mortgage as stock on the market, technically voiding the entire agreement with the homebuyer. My family got a taste of this runaround when we attempted to get a refinance in 2011.

We were denied a refinance, we were told, because the owner of our second mortgage note refused to consent. We called who we currently make payments to on our second mortgage and asked them to send us the original copy of the agreement, and they referred us back to the previous holder. That holder said that his institution did not own it and that Citigroup had it. When we called Citigroup, a representative said that the bank had no record of our note passing through the institution. The person said that the bank didn't have the note, and finally told us that MERS had it. Every single institution we talked to was technically right, because they all belonged to MERS; they all owned the mortgage note.

At that point, out of sheer curiosity, we decided to investigate where our primary mortgage note was. When we called our mortgage servicer, Seterus, for the blue-ink copy of our title, an employee stated that the company didn't have the mortgage note;

it was just the servicer. Fair enough. The individual that we spoke to also referred us to Citigroup, who referred us to Di-tech (now a defunct company), whose employees referred us back to MERS. For those of you who think that you can just contact MERS, think again. Although it is based out of a small Delaware town and has fewer than 100 employees, MERS handles nearly every mortgage in the United States and makes mortgage-backed securities sellable via the MIN.

As if that weren't strange enough, your mortgage company sells the right to collect on your mortgage. For example, a $30,000 second mortgage could be sold to another mortgage company for $35,000 if the loan is expected to bring in $20,000 in interest over its full term. The original lender would make a quick $5,000, and the next lender would expect to make money. So the original lending company probably does not have much faith in the economy overall, because it wants to unload its liabilities as quickly as possible, and the buyer is usually very bullish about the housing market.

Sometimes a massive institution like Citigroup or JP Morgan will see the storm clouds coming before they actually arrive and will look to sell its mortgage-backed securities in bundles. This essentially turns the mortgage market into a high-stakes game of hot potato (or hot potatoe, as Dan Quayle would play it). The better the housing market gets and the higher interest rates go on adjustable arm secondary mortgages, the more money a bank can make by selling the right to collect on a mortgage. However, if you're the one left holding the subprime bag when the music stops, it's off to the poorhouse with you, and off to bankruptcy court with your company.

Although MERS exists to circumvent the county courthouses, there is one thing that the banks can't get around in continually pawning off collection rights: your signature. That's no problem; the banks just robotically sign your name (or robo-signs). Who robo-signs your name? MERS does. That way, no one bank is responsible for breaking the law, and they can all point fingers at the other banks or just flat-out deny that they broke the law. The individual who really holds the original note is entirely untraceable for most people in America.

What does that mean? Someone collects money from you with no proof of his or her right to collect money from you except an agreement with the previous holder of the rights to collect. The original proof is entirely gone—lost to some trader on Wall Street who bought up a multitude of mortgage-backed securities during the housing bubble's peak. This also means that any bank within the vast MERS system could claim the right to collect on your mortgage if it wanted to, which happened to a woman in Florida. The Floridian had already paid off her mortgage in its entirety and had the paperwork to prove it. However, Bank of America claimed the right to collect payments on the mortgage, because it held the agreement to collect.

The Florida woman won the case in court, but the bank would not stop sending her threatening letters and notices, at which point the court stepped in, and let the woman foreclose on the local Bank of America branch along with a few law enforcement agents, until the bank gave up its case. Upon the plaintiff actually carrying out that act of irony, the story hit every national news networks within a few days, and I vividly remember watching it with the rest of my family intently.

When a mortgage is sold as a stock, it is technically supposed to be nullified for the previous holder of the note, meaning that it is against the rules to just hire someone to collect for you as a condition of a stock sale. However, the pressure in the early 2000s and late 1990s to make as many loans as fast as possible made these rules and the tradition of the county clerk's office all but obsolete.

These loans began to default at a massive rate in 2006. This year saw housing values climb to an all-time peak in summer before falling off of a steep, rocky, unstable cliff. This left those who took out *legitimate* mortgages with falling housing values. Even after 2006, traders and politicians continued to deny that the banks were in major financial trouble. By 2006, most smart traders on Wall Street had noticed a trend in the housing price graphs, when adjusted for inflation. From 1920-1990, with the exception of the Great Depression, housing values stayed close to a constant price when adjusted for inflation—around $100,000 in today's money (just take housing values in any year and adjust based on overall inflation). But after 1990, prices rose artificially an exponentially. This happened because America's Depression generation retired and died off. That generation understood that a house was just a box to shelter them from the elements and that without usable land, it was not worth an exorbitant amount of money.

In 2008, the stock market crashed like a Japanese zero at Okinawa. The banks had to admit they were in trouble, and the taxpayers had to pony up the dough, so to speak. Now the middle class was paying in two directions, not only in falling values, but also in taxes toward trillions of dollars ($10,000,000,000,000) in federal bank bailouts. But here's the kicker. Perhaps like yours, my family borrowed that $200,000 with interest, and in 2001, interest was around 7%. 7% per year times 30 years of paying is equal to 210% interest. In other words, a $200,000 house in 2001 actually cost $620,000 over 30 years. So, as a 16-year-old, I look at my family's situation and responsibility as compared to that of the banks that preach financial responsibility, and it isn't even close. In fact, this can be compared to someone like John Edwards who says he's for "family values," having an affair. Like many of the families in America, here's my family's situation; we now have a house worth $125,000 that we still will pay $620,000 for over 30 years, and we improved it with $50,000-$60,000 before the crash, not to mention that we're paying the bank through taxes. What do those banks do to thank us? They still want $620,000 for a $120,000 house, and they deny us for any refinances or modifications because the middle-class "makes too much", and "isn't in imminent danger of default."

One day, a man from the PNC Financial Services Group (PNC) called our house to see when my family would make the payment on our second line of home credit. When my mom asked him about why the bank still wanted so much money for such cheap houses, he said "everyone wants to blame the banks now, we are huge target; no one wants to admit that it is the people that are walking away from their mortgages that are the problem." How arrogant and pompous. If you take five times the worth of a house from a person and create a budget shortfall that forces the government to cut defense and meaningful investments on Capitol Hill, it should not be a shocker that your popularity is lackluster and people are defying you like a persistent six-year-old.

This is how I think the system should work: if the bank makes a loan and housing values go down, the bank must cut your principal debt to that amount. If you fail, you fail, don't come looking for Uncle Sam when you made bad decisions in a free market. By the same token, the government should not be able to force banks to make any risky loans, for any purpose or cause, under any circumstances. This system would encourage responsible lending to people who can actually afford houses, which would translate into stable housing prices and reduced inflation, not to mention the lack of economic Armageddon every now and again.

As a Reagan conservative, I tend to favor big business over big government. But I realized that the "free market" is a relative term when talking of big banks with representatives of the Federal Reserve Board. If the policy of the bank is pure capitalism, don't whine and cry because you lost. Lump it; because in life, there is a winner and loser. Just because you were once a CEO, it does not guarantee you millions for life. We are being manipulated by a dangerous collusion of business and government called the Federal Reserve. Thomas Jefferson once said "I believe that banking institutions are more dangerous to our liberties than standing armies". He was right. For the hard-working members of the American middle class, those who only know extravagance and luxury and think they are entitled to wealth are very dangerous indeed.

This battle has been playing out since the 1830s, with Andrew Jackson going against Nicholas Biddle (to be expounded upon later); the hard-working part of the country versus the New England elite. The score is currently Federal Reserve: 1, everybody else: zero. So the cycle will go on, and by 2070, my generation will retire, taking with us our fear of risky lending (if we have any, most of my generation is too preoccupied with its facebook status to bother taking in what's going on around it). If there is an America, or an American economy, by 2080, it will be in another housing crisis. We must pass on these lessons to posterity to avoid falling prey to more Barney Franks, Chris Dodds, and bank CEOs in the future. However, as this crisis has already played out in the 1830s and 1920s, and every time we seem to choose short-term profits, I'm not holding my breath. The bailout was also made possible by the many lobbyists that the banks hire; a subject for subsequent chapters.

CHAPTER 2

Inflation: That Ballooning Feeling

W hen the Mongol Yuan Empire collapsed and left China, it left behind an economy that was just discovering credit and the concept of buying without precious metals. The dynasty that took over China after the Yuan was the Ming Dynasty. When the Ming Dynasty discovered credit, many people began to buy without any precious metals on their person. This caused a boom in the consumer credit economy in China in the 1500s. However, when the Spanish began sending their silver through Asia and not straight to Spain, the value of the credit buying notes of the Chinese people was seriously devalued. In addition to natural resource depletion, and the lack of energy, the Ming now faced the serious risk of an economic collapse. To mitigate the problem, the emperor thought that the best way to deal with the situation would be to create more paper currency, which the Mongols had tried earlier in both Russia. The result was horrendous.

After some years, people began to see through the non-value of the paper currency. After a while, goods became very expensive in China. The government had to print ever-larger bills to keep up with hyperinflation. In addition to famines brought on by the Little Ice Age and floods of the Yellow River (brought on by lack of infrastructure maintenance, to be discussed later), the cost of living in China became outlandish. The government lost all control of the economy, and all trust of the people. The hyperinflation that took place in the Ming Dynasty was one of the factors that propelled China into another Dynasty, the Qing Dynasty. It was an experiment in economics gone horribly wrong that the people of China would not soon forget. The scariest part is not that the Ming went through hyperinflation and collapsed, it is the manner in which it happened. Before hyperinflation set in, the boom was in the consumer economy, similar to the American economy in the 20th and early 21st centuries. The Mings began using up their source of energy (wood) at an ever-faster pace to support their credit-based economy. When the credit-based economy collapsed, and people did not have the precious metals to back up their promises, the government took it upon itself to try to rescue the floundering economy with ever more currency for the creditors, much like the bank bailouts of 2008 and 2009 in the United States.

China was not the only place where hyperinflation was experienced. Early Russia under the rule of the Golden Horde of the Mongol Empire also experienced hyperinflation. Russia under the Golden Horde and in its early years as an independent nation experienced hyperinflation due to an infusion of silver from the Spanish Empire. In combination with fewer goods on the market due to the Little Ice Age and the multiple Russian famines of the time, more silver on the market meant much higher prices for goods, and, thus, hyperinflation. In lieu of a better system, Russia began to print paper money. In fact, many Russians had never seen paper money before, and didn't know what to call it other than a stamp (denga). The cost of living shot through the figurative roof, and the Russian economy collapsed. Such was the effect of this experiment gone wrong in economics that today the Russian word for money is still denga, or stamp.

Although printing money to fix a down economy has failed everywhere it has been tried, our brilliant government and the Federal Reserve have decided to print over $10 trillion in the wake of our financial crisis in a mad dash to fix our economy and give money to none other than creditors. If this is all sounding familiar, it should be. What we're doing right now is exactly what was tried by the Ming Chinese dynasty approximately 500 years ago. From 2000 to 2009, the United States more than doubled its money supply (M2, total, M1, any way you slice it), and we are slated to triple the amount of M2 (money in banks accounts and raw circulation) that was in circulation in 2000 by 2016 according to the Federal Reserve. However, hyperinflation will be slower to hit the United States than other nations that have tried printing money because we are currently the World Reserve Currency. What that means is that investors flock to our currency in bad times. However, when you lose the trust of the people who carry your currency and the people who invest in your currency, you'll probably lose your status as the World Reserve Currency. When you do, all of the printing that you did while you were the World Reserve Currency will catch up to you very quickly. Your economy will suddenly be in a state of collapse, goods will suddenly be 2 to 4 times as expensive as they were before, and everybody is left wondering what the heck just happened. As much as it pains me to say it, the United States will soon go through this cycle. Since the mid-1900s, America has increased its money supply almost tenfold. When we eventually cannot make all of our debt payments because our economy is not vibrant anymore or we hit an economic slump that may be the size of the one we are currently in, we will no longer be the World Reserve Currency. That means that interest rates on the loans we take out will go up very quickly, and all of a sudden it will be very hard to finance our national debt, let alone pay for Social Security, Medicare, Medicaid, or defense. We will probably lose our status as the World Reserve Currency within the next 15 to 20 years. However, our excessive printing at present may lead to hyperinflation before that point (well before that point).

For those of you currently saying, "It's been four years since we started printing, and no inflation yet, so your theory is wrong," let me lend a little bit of wisdom here. The classic Austrian economics definition of inflation is "too much money chasing too few goods." Clearly, when you increase your money supply by around 100% (a lot more than that if we factored in M3), you've got the money side of that equation down pat. Yet, with a 100% increase in the money supply, prices have only gone up around 2% per year. The reason for this is that the money is there, but it's not chasing any goods. The economy is so anemic that printing all of that money can only keep us at equilibrium as far as prices go because the level of buying is so low. When consumer spending comes back and banks take the cash that they have been keeping on the sideline into the market, hyperinflation will hit with or without us losing our World Reserve Currency status.

There is a way to stop this, however. We do not have to print money and give it to the banks. Call me crazy, I think that if we never bailed out the banks in 2008, smaller banks would have taken their place and expanded, employing many of the people who lost their jobs when the larger banks closed. If we do not continue printing money, if we stop quantitative easing, if we let the market truly hit bottom, and we let the economy go and recover on its own, it would come back vibrant, and hyperinflation would be no immediate concern. In the end, we must realize that our currency has to be backed up by some sort of precious metal, or something of value. It could even be corn, wheat, or soybeans. Many towns and villages in the 1800s ran their entire economies based on a currency of some sort of cash crop or food, and only used paper currency as a backup. I'm not saying we have to go back to the 1800s; that would be completely crazy, but, trying to print your way out of a recession like so many nations have done before us and having a currency entirely built on thin air and what the government says it's worth is crazier; it's absolutely nuts. In addition, we need to audit the Federal Reserve to make sure it is not spending money that it is not telling us about or printing more or less than it is telling us, or buying or selling stocks to manipulate the market.

If we are to truly have an open free market system, a national bank is completely unacceptable. The largest banks in America all have representatives that sit on the Federal Reserve Board. The Federal Reserve is the entity that prints money for the United States government. In addition, the Federal Reserve has bought up most of the United States' debt. This may sound like a conflict of interest, and in my book it is. How much power are we willing to give an entity, and how naïve are we, that an institution in a free society should have the power to print as much money as it wishes, shielded from the public eye, and, in secrecy, buy up the stock of the money it prints, while collecting interest on the debt monthly? Isn't it shocking that in the freest and most open nation on earth (allegedly), such an institution, completely unaccountable to the public, should be handling such large sums of money belonging to the public? In addition, the Federal Reserve has the power to buy up stocks with the cash and currency it holds in order to bolster the market, or sell the stocks that it already holds and send the market into a downward spiral. We need to abolish the Federal Reserve in its entirety. I will discuss at length in subsequent chapters the debate in the early years of our country on the existence of a national bank and other national banks throughout the world in history.

CHAPTER 3

Guessing Isn't Always Right: Speculation

C urrently, the United States has a very centralized economy based on banking, industry, financial services, and to a very small degree, agriculture. If you watch any cable news, you no doubt know that on the New York Mercantile Exchange (NYMEX) floor, people speculate on the price of oil, natural gas, and other commodities. You may think that we are living in the first period of human history in which speculation has played such a large role. Well, if you thought that, you're wrong. Speculation has been tried many times before. The Romans, the Tokugawas in Japan, and no doubt other examples that have been lost to the pages of history, have collapsed due to speculation running their respective economies.

Without a doubt, crude oil is currently the product that we need more than any other; it powers our lives every single day. In the 1970s and 80s, according to testimony on crude oil speculation given on the House floor by an oil industry expert, the oil market on Wall Street was made up of about 20% speculators and about 80% oil transporters and purchasers. Right now, however, the balance of power on Wall Street has flipped. According to the same expert's testimony, at least 60% of the oil market is now made up of speculators, and less than 40% of the market is now made up of those who actually ship the finished oil and natural gas products. For those of you who do not know what a speculator is, let me quickly explain.

A speculator is someone who does not buy the product, but rather buys a share that shows that they have an interest in the price of the product. They have absolutely no interest in the delivery or transport of the oil, and the sheer act of them buying the piece of paper pushes the price of the raw material up, because it shows that people are demanding to be in that market, that demand is up, that the product is thought to be profitable in the future by some smart people on the NYMEX floor in New York. If speculators *presume* that the price of a product is going to go up, they may get into a bidding war for the piece of paper that says they have an interest in the price of the product. For example, if the price of oil is $80 a barrel, and a Wall Street firm projects that the price of oil will go to $100 a barrel, it may attempt to buy the oil stock at $85 a barrel. When another Wall Street firm sees that Wall Street firm by the oil stock at $85 a barrel, it may bid it up to $90 a barrel. When all is said and done, the firm may be content to take only three or four dollars a barrel profit if it thinks that the price is going up. Therefore, the consumers pay the price that they should have been paying two or three years in the future. The result is that the price of a barrel of oil is $15 a barrel higher than it would be in the traditional supply and demand system. Literally, you are paying the price that should exist in the future because someone bet that they could make money on that raw material. This is how every speculation market in the world works.

You can speculate on every single commodity on the NYMEX floor; you can speculate on crude oil, natural gas, cows in Oklahoma, pigs in Missouri, corn in Nebraska, wheat harvests in Russia, sugarcane harvests in Haiti, raw beef, heating oil, gasoline, and coffee beans from Columbia. The consumer pays more than they have to by sometimes 10 or 20 or 30% due to speculation on these products. But, in the end, it's a free market. Therefore, we, the consumers, decide the price of product. If we don't like the price, we shouldn't pay; we should demand lower prices. The businessmen aren't fools; they won't go bankrupt and make zero money on a product to spite the consumer; the speculators will just be priced out of the market.

For those of you who are currently saying, "Right, but I don't see any example there that would tell me that speculation could bring down a nation," let me lend a few examples. In the early days of the Roman Republic, it was common for men to go off to war against some barbaric tribe in the north of Europe or some tribe in Spain or Asia. Thus, women were left home on the land while their men were away at war. Traditionally, the Romans grew wheat and other foodstuff crops, and were very self-sufficient in their food production. However, when the men were away at war, speculators from the big cities of Italy would go out into the country looking to buy up property for the production of cash crops. Since the men were away at war, the women were easily intimidated into giving up their land for the fair market value or just under the fair market value. The investors would then grow cash crops such as olives and grapes (for wine). Since wine and olives were so rare in other parts of the Eastern Mediterranean world, they were very valuable. Due to this, investors from Roman cities would buy up as much land as they could to grow cash crops on.

The problem was that within a few centuries, most of the Rome's farmland was in the hands of the investors. These investors were not growing any food that could be eaten inside the republic, there were trading away all their food to other parts of Europe and Asia for huge profits. In no time at all, the Romans did not have enough food for their own country. Due to this, Rome had to start importing its wheat and other food crops from other areas inside the Mediterranean trade route. As people moved toward the cities and were displaced from their farms, the middle class in Rome became more urbanized. The Romans lost touch with their heritage and the republic's beginning ideals. After a while, competition ran out in the investing market for farms. Much of the new urban middle class went to work for the firms that controlled most of the farmland in the country, or went to work for traders to trade goods throughout the Mediterranean Sea. Still others went to work for investing firms that *speculated* on the price of goods in trade. By the end of the republic, and the beginning of the Roman Empire, almost none of Rome's common people lived in rural areas. They were clustered in the cities, and almost all of them worked for very large groups. By urbanizing, water and food became scarcer, crowding became a problem, disease became a problem, and crime became a problem (much of it due to people losing their jobs in times of a down market or a bad buy). Speculation on a raw material started the ball rolling.

If this is all sounding eerily familiar, it's supposed to be. The story above is the same one that the United States is currently in the final stages of right now. In the 1700s and 1800s, most of America's economy was built on small farms and an agrarian society. Although we did have much manufacturing, it was mainly done in what were called "cottage industries", or shops run out of somebody's house. These cottage industries were very small, and banks did not play a very large role in early American society; the middle class in America was not urbanized at all. Most of America's land was owned by a large share of the people, almost everybody owned a little bit of land (mostly because land in the New World was so cheap for the first few centuries). But, the bankers concentrated in one area of the country (the large cities of the Northeast in the Mid-Atlantic) began to buy up farmland and *speculate* on the price of farmland. Their speculation made them enormous amounts of profits until the bubble finally burst for the first time in American history in the year 1837, which precipitated the "Panic of 1837."

In the late 1800s, in the midst of the Industrial Revolution, manufacturers began to employ more people than ever before. As a result, more money could be made if someone moved to a large city.

America went through a period of rapid urbanization, and investors began to hold more and more land. This process continued all throughout the 20th century, and, currently, corporations hold over 90% of U.S. farmland. For the first time in American history, more people live in an urban or suburban setting than live in a rural setting. Most young Americans are more familiar with the logos of their favorite corporations than they are with birds, or species of trees, or species of reptiles and amphibians in their area. Most of us cannot even recite one Founding Father's quote, and do not know in what state the majority of our Founding Fathers lived. In short, we are losing touch with our heritage. The middle class today in the United States lives mainly in the suburbs and in urban areas. You are living in a Roman-style situation right now, only about 2000 years later.

Today, 83% of the American jobs are created by the service sector according to a Georgetown University study; with miniscule numbers of people working in farming, mining, and manufacturing, where things are actually produced. America has gone through an astounding transformation over the past 200 years. It is one in which most of our middle class citizens work for financial firms, investing giants, banks, tax servicers, retailers, national franchises, and accounting firms. A plurality of those who do not participate in these professions are public employees, who make their living on the taxes generated by the private sector, and are thus subject to the whims and fancies of every investing mistake that someone may make. As to the farming aspect, most of our farmland in the United States is now held by just a few corporations. Food production is now carried out on an industrial scale, and our crops are incredibly un-diverse. I will never forget when I was riding down U.S. Route 30 in Ohio between Mansfield and Interstate 75 on October 10, 2011. After doing a bit of nature walking and seeing a Long-tailed Salamander, my family was driving back to Michigan under the light of a full moon. Along U.S. Route 30, near the town of the Bucyrus, Ohio, farmers were harvesting wheat, soybeans, and corn in anticipation of the coming frost. I expected to see small tractors or farmers out with their families harvesting crops before winter set in, but what I saw was an industrial-scale operation. For 10 miles down Route 30, I could see giant combines driven by no one, robotically operated by one person in a control room, with corporate logos on them, going down the rows in perfectly straight columns, and harvesting acres upon acres of staple crops. It was one of the saddest sights I've ever seen, knowing that once, this little stretch of Ohio housed hundreds and hundreds of farmers who participated in small community government, and local control, and federalism, knew the land intimately, and were in touch with their natural world. Now that stretch of Ohio houses combines of perhaps Archie Daniels Midland (ADM), or Cropland, or Golden Harvest, and the members of the old families that once inhabited this land have gone to the cities of Ohio (or of other states) to work for investors, or accounting firms, or large corporations, or to be public servants.

That's not the scariest part. The most striking similarity between the Roman debacle and our current situation is that due to the growing of cash crops on their best land, the Romans had to import their food crops. As Rome had to import all of its food crops, it became "vulnerable to price shocks in the market". That should sound pretty familiar. When a famine or drought in some foreign land pushed the price of wheat, barley, or rye up, it became harder for the middle class citizens in the cities to get their hands on food. When food became scarce, people resorted to becoming criminals or demanding money from the government dole. Right now, America uses much of its land to either grow cash crops (like tobacco in the South), or grow food crops to feed the nations of Asia. We import some of our food right now. Currently, we are extremely vulnerable to price shocks in the market. Just take a look at crude oil. If a Sheikh in Saudi Arabia decides he wants to have tuna fish instead of the chicken sandwich for lunch (I'm exaggerating a little bit here), the price of oil can rise two dollars a barrel, the price of gasoline can go up $.20 a gallon, somebody cannot afford to go to work, an investor loses money because he was betting on oil prices falling, and we slip into a recession if that investor was from Goldman Sachs instead of a 50 year-old guy trying to get a retirement fund going. I'll provide more examples of our similarities later, but for now it will suffice to say that we are simply Rome two thousand years later. For the last 100 years, our middle class has been mainly urban, and we've been living in a world where a bad wheat harvest in Russia can push the price of wheat here in the United States up by 20%, even if our harvest is completely unaffected. In short, we're living in a world that is very, very vulnerable to foreign price shocks.

The next example of speculation bringing down a nation is one that hits very close to home. The Tokugawa Shogunate prospered in Japan approximately 500 years ago. Their society was entirely based on war. The main organizing principle in Japan was that of the samurai society. The Japanese and the Chinese always looked down upon merchants as less worthy citizens, believing that they were not willing to give up their life or their livelihood for the good of the country in war. The entire Tokugawa economy was based on the trade of rice. When the samurai warriors were not at war, but were at home in peacetime, they became members of the consumer economy of Japan. The merchants saw an opportunity to make a lot of money off of this trade. These merchants began to *speculate* on the price of rice. When the Warriors did not have enough cash in rice to buy a product, merchants would allow them to take out loans, however, the interest rates were ridiculous. The merchants figured that because the price of rice would keep going up, their speculative measures would pay for any defaults that might happen on the debt. They also assumed that the high-interest payments they were getting would serve as a hedge, just in case the price of rice did collapse. The merchants didn't see the high-interest loans as risky, they saw them as a moneymaking measure, and therefore, tried to make as many loans as possible. Eventually, the price of rice became so high from speculation, that the consumers needed all of their money and all of their loans just to buy food. The ventures of merchants in high interest loans collapsed. Once the consumer economy was gone, and the middle class had collapsed, the price of rice fell off a cliff, and the entire nation was in ruin. The Tokugawa Shogunate collapsed shortly after the bubble had burst, and the entire nation was in a slump for at least 200 years. All of this happened because of speculation on the base need of a society.

The previous paragraph should ring a bell as well; American retailers from the mid-1990s to 2008 offered as many promotions and as big a credit line as possible to the customers to attempt to get high interest, short-term loans on their books as profit. High-interest loans were very, very common in the mid-2000s, as retailers thought that the price of everything would keep going up along with wages, the economy would stay vibrant, and they would be able to easily get their payments for the high-interest loans. Many investors speculated on the price of oil, sending the price of that product so high that people needed much of their money just to buy gasoline, and it became one of the factors that pushed America into the recent Great Recession. Speculation in the market pushed oil and natural gas prices up to a ridiculous amount, so high that no one could ever be expected to pay them. At one point in July of 2008, oil was up to $147 a barrel, and if the recession had not hit, gas would've topped five dollars a gallon by the end of summer. After this lesson was temporarily learned, retailers stopped their lines of credit, and buying things on credit or charging them became much more difficult for average consumers. Have you ever heard the saying "Tulips are blooming in Holland?"

In 17th century Belgium, tulips became all the rage. People began using them for everything, from medicinal purposes to gardening purposes and decorative purposes. In the early 1600s, merchants began to see an opportunity to make money on the trade of tulips, and began a market to trade tulips publicly, and offered stock that showed that someone had interest in the price of the tulip. People began to invest their entire fortunes in the trade of tulips. *Speculation* was underway. In the 1630s, when prices were at their absolute peak, brokers on the stock market began to offer stocks that could be bought on "margin". People could buy stock in the tulip commodity for less than the value of the actual stock, and a promise was signed to pay the total later from the profit of the stock. This was the introduction of "margin buying," which is still in place today. When the price of tulips hit its peak level in 1637, people were investing their money like crazy in the price of tulip bulbs. When the price inevitably fell, the brokers issued "margin calls," and people could not meet them. People went bankrupt from their purchase of leveraged tulip funds, an issue that would seem to be confined to the 20th and 21st centuries in the minds of most present-day people. However, this example shows us that speculation on prices of goods, both necessary (like crude oil, wheat, rice, and corn), and unnecessary have been happening for many, many centuries. Needless to say, the Dutch economy was in the dumps for a very long period of time after the tulip crisis. Most of the middle class was investing in tulips at the time of the market collapse in Holland. The economy of Belgium collapsed for least a few decades, and the prestige of the Dutch Trading Empire never recovered.

So, I hope it is now plainly clear how speculation can bring down an entire civilization. It starts with somebody getting a bright idea that they can make money by betting that the price of something will go up and not delivering or transporting something. Then, when the price keeps going up, the people who are buying the product want to hedge themselves against the rising price, and they themselves begin to speculate. This increase in speculation and supposed demand for the product creates a bubble in the market, and the product reaches its peak price before crashing. After a while, everybody will figure out the emperor's "wearing no clothes" in any one of these given situations; that the price of the product is entirely built on air; on pomp and circumstance.

As for the United States, we currently speculate on everything that can possibly be traded. We speculate especially heavily on those products which we need for everyday life, and this will probably eventually be the downfall of our economy once again, as it already has been in this Great Recession. The cycle of speculation will continue probably without end, as humans are greedy and short-sighted by nature. In addition, no nation that has had its economy based on banking and financial services has ever survived or even prospered for any long period of time; it has prospered for a short period of time, and then collapsed very rapidly due to the volatility of its trade. America is currently a financially-based economy, and will probably soon (when I say soon in speaking in the context of world history, I mean in the next 50 years) experience another rapid decline, partly due to speculation, and partly due to a lack of an agricultural and manufacturing base. We ultimately control our economy, because no one forces us to buy anything, but for now, you're paying about $.50 more gallon than you should be.

CHAPTER 4

That Line in the Sand:
Illegal Immigration

merica now has greater than 13 million illegal immigrants inside her borders, according to most sources, and most of us think that this is the first time in history when such a problem has occurred for a nation. However, one nation before us, the Roman Republic, had this problem. The Southwestern United States has a major problem with illegal immigration. People can cross our borders illegally with only a minimal chance of Border Patrol being present to stop them. Drugs are run across our borders, criminals run across the border, and people just looking for jobs run across our borders. If you go to Arizona, California, Texas, New Mexico, or any area of the Southwest, you will see many illegal immigrants (by illegal immigrant I do not mean Hispanic; I mean anyone who has come across the border illegally; many people from Asia and Europe have tried to cross our southern border illegally to get into the United States; in my book, an illegal immigrant is someone who has broken the laws of the United States and crossed over a border without permission). Most of the narcotics in the United States come across our southern border illegally, and many of the crimes perpetrated in America's Southwest are perpetrated by illegal immigrants. Illegal immigrants often can't pay for their health care, and when they get healthcare from doctors, the doctors charge the price of the healthcare to the taxpayers. Illegal immigrants often go to emergency rooms to attain free treatment. Some states are on the verge of bankruptcy due to the influx of illegal immigrants, along with the burden on the healthcare system, the educational system, the welfare system, and "sanctuary cities."

Another issue that comes with illegal immigration is, "anchor babies," which are children born to illegal immigrants inside the United States that automatically become United States citizens. This happens due to the Fourteenth Amendment of the Constitution, which says that all people born in the United States are United States citizens. The Fourteenth Amendment was passed just after the Civil War to ensure that former slaves could not be deprived of their citizenship. This was passed to ensure that a repeat of the *Dred Scott* case would never happen, in which Chief Justice Roger B. Taney ruled that Dred Scott (a slave arguing that he was unlawfully made to be a slave in a free state by his master) could not file a lawsuit because he was not a United States citizen. However, the amendment was originally intended to fight discrimination efforts in the South; it established that former slaves born in the United States or the children of former slaves born in the United States were United States citizens, and had the same rights as everybody else.

Illegal immigrants generally hold low-paying jobs, such as farmhands or construction workers. The common argument heard on the liberal talk shows and MSNBC is that Americans "won't do these jobs". That's completely false. We currently have an unemployment rate hovering near 7.5%, and Americans would love to have those manual sector jobs. In down economic times, Americans will do anything to keep their family alive and stay afloat financially. Our great-grandfathers and great-great-grandfathers worked on the Transcontinental Railroad in negative temperatures, and in the searing heat in the Nebraska plains. They also mined in West Virginia, Virginia, and Tennessee; getting Black Lung from it. Our ancestors cut trees in the North Woods and slept in lumber camps by night. They operated dangerous machinery, and worked through 120°F in Carnegie's steel factories and Rockefeller's crude oil refineries. Excuse me for thinking that an American can pick a watermelon or take an order at a restaurant. I would do either one of these things for a decent wage. But another common argument is that the restaurant business would "collapse," without illegal immigrants' cheap labor. If the restaurant business can't stay alive without cheap illegal immigrant labor, maybe it shouldn't be in business. The industry should just have to take a little bit out of its profit margin to hire Americans citizens, or increase its prices.

First off, let me establish that when I say illegal, I don't mean all immigrants, I just mean illegal immigrants that break laws of the United States. *Legal* immigrants built this country in the 1800s and early 1900s. Irish immigrants built the Erie Canal, immigrants from Germany, Southern Europe, and Eastern Europe built the cities of the East and Midwest. Legal immigration is just fine; immigration is not the problem. The problems are people that don't respect our laws and people that come here because they committed crimes in their home country and don't want to go to jail. I know it must come as a shock to some of the far left-wingers, but most conservatives are just fine with immigration as long as it's legal immigration. The Know-Nothings have been gone for 150 years, and they were mostly a Northeastern elitist party that valued English heritage above all things; they were centered in the liberal industrial heart of the country. I know Rachel Maddow will be devastated to hear that what she's been told is a lie, because illegal immigrants didn't build the cities of America in the 1800s.

I was born in Kingsville, Texas. That is a city in Kleberg County, in South Texas, less than two hours from Mexico. My mom and dad paid over $10,000 in medical expenses for my birth. Other American families must pay similar amounts of money for childbirth services. Meanwhile, illegal immigrants cross the border to have children for free! This happens because it is illegal to deny anybody emergency-room care when they come into the hospital even if they don't have any money or insurance. You may be wondering, "Who foots the bill?" You foot the bill. Your state and federal taxes pay for tens of millions in illegal immigrants' healthcare costs. Personally, this is infuriating. Even though I don't agree with free healthcare for anybody, if we should give it to anybody, it should be people who took their education and their life seriously, not people who, well, jumped a fence. But, no, we give it to people with no background check, people who are not U.S. citizens. Pure genius. We are incentivizing people in Mexico to incur costs in the Bear Flag Republic, or the Lone Star State, or from Uncle Sam. One has to ask why?

As proof that illegal immigrants are damaging this nation, we don't have to look any further than California. In the 1940s through the 1970s, California was a bustling, growing state with a great economy. Powered by tourism, natural resources, abundance of land, Ocean-front property, and robust agriculture, California's economy roared onto the world stage by the early 1970s. California before the 1980s was a bastion of growth and unlimited opportunity for fresh capital to be invested. Starting in the 1970s, illegal immigrants started pouring in over the state's southern border with Mexico, predominantly near San Diego, California. Through the 1980s, California's economy still roared for the most part, and the state politicians and national representatives from California figured that it was affordable to help the illegal immigrants, to take charge of the unpaid hospital bills of illegals, and to set up sanctuary cities. Today, California pays its public employees in IOUs, has more bankrupt cities than any other state in the nation, has a bankrupt state government, has one of the highest crime rights in the United States, and is quickly using up the rest of its resources. California is also a major trafficking point for narcotics, and has one of the highest drug use rates in the nation. That state has quickly falling home values and a dismal economy. This is not entirely due to illegal immigration, but it is largely due to illegal immigration. California had the biggest economic advantages of any state in the nation, and it squandered them hopelessly. For those reading this book 45 years old and up, you probably remember Ronald Reagan's biggest blunder: his amnesty program.

Reagan once famously said "Latinos are conservatives, they just don't know it yet," obviously conveying that because most Latinos are strict Roman Catholics, they're pro-life, anti-gay marriage, and generally pro-Christian values. Reagan's thinking was that if he could make the illegal immigrants here support the GOP and help them become more financially sound, he would lock up millions of new votes for Republicans in future elections; and, thus, make a Democratic tidal wave election nearly impossible. When the dust settled, the Republicans in the 1980s had lost their gamble. What *actually* happened was that the giant flow of illegal immigrants grew, due to the incentive of amnesty and the promise of their becoming United States citizens. The immigrants did not use the assistance to better their situation, but, rather, most of them remained on welfare and continued to vote Democratic despite their conservative social beliefs. The GOP invited in millions of Democratic votes, and ticked off their conservative base to the point of giving them Lyme's Disease.

The United States is the most powerful nation on the planet right now and, yet, we give extremely lax protection to our own borders, and give half the troops to the Border Patrol that it says it needs. Speaking of the federal government shirking its responsibility, this brings me to my next point of federal versus state power in the immigration issue. The federal government is the purveyor of all international crossings, commerce, ports, and immigration, as enumerated in the U.S. Constitution. However, the U.S. Government is not doing its own job, in my opinion, as illustrated by the existence of sanctuary cities.

A sanctuary city, for those of you who don't know, is a city that harbors illegal immigrants knowingly, and gives them housing, healthcare, and welfare against federal immigration law. As the Constitution clearly states in Article 6, the Constitution and federal law shall be the *Supreme Law of the Land*. However, when the causes are liberal, the federal government doesn't seem to abide by the so-called "Supremacy Clause," of the Constitution. Currently, the Department of Justice under Eric Holder is turning a blind eye to the blatant transgression of federal immigration law. Yet, when a state such as Arizona, in 2010, tries to help enforce federal law by identifying and deporting illegal immigrants more efficiently, and obeys the vast majority of its constituents, the full power and fury of Eric Holder and the Department of Justice comes crashing down on them like a landslide in the Federal District and Circuit Courts. One must ask: why the obvious double standard? I believe there are two main reasons for the Department of Justice's double standard, and two for the lack of legislative action against illegals.

To the conundrum that we call the Department of Justice, I'd say that it tends to recruit great trial lawyers who happen to be from Ivy League or Pac-10 schools with left-wing law professors. Also, the Department of Justice is an extension of the presidential administration, and it does not want to give the perception of being the party in power against Latino immigration. I believe that the federal government should preside over immigration policy, however, states and municipalities should be able to help the federal government enforce the national policies. The sanctuary cities of the West Coast and Southwest should be punished for disobeying the Constitution and federal law, in addition to interfering with and hindering the enforcement of federal immigration policy. States are allowed to have specific gun laws that only pertain to their respective states, and are also allowed to have specific laws pertaining to speech. Both of these matters are clearly mentioned in the Constitution, and states and municipalities do have a legitimate place in helping the federal government to enforce the law more efficiently.

As far as Congress not cracking down on illegals goes, it receives very heavy lobbying from large corporations that want to keep their ridiculously cheap labor, such as the restaurant business, and large agricultural corporations (ADM, Cropland, and Golden Harvest). The second reason is that the prevailing wisdom of GOP politicians in the 1980s is still around today, as illustrated by Dick Morris's opinions on the subject in his book *Catastrophe*. Morris is a GOP strategist who believes that amnesty is the way to go to lock up votes. The same applies for Congress controlled by either party. If one party were to shove through legislation to enforce the law of the land, it would lose the vast majority of the Latino vote. Latinos are currently 14% of the USA's population according to the Census Bureau. This group is growing much faster than any other ethnic group in the United States. I don't mean to sound too blunt on this point, but, any party that enforces the immigration laws forcibly gives up political power in the Southwest within a decade, and would probably be nationally feeble within 30 or 40 years (in lieu of some economic miracle under that party's leadership).

As for businesses saying that they rely on illegal immigration, I think that is despicable. Are agricultural businesses and other sectors really making the argument that breaking the law of the land is the only way that they can make money? Preposterous I say; hiring American workers rather than resident illegal immigrants would only minimally reduce profits in an era of rising inflation of crop prices. Corn recently topped out at nearly eight dollars per bushel. Restaurants and agricultural businesses are making more money than ever. Businesses that hire illegal immigrants should be fined at least $25,000 per year per illegal migrant worker to make sure that hiring Americans is more economically sound than breaking the law and hiring illegal migrant workers. Such a fine would push illegal immigrants back across the border due to the lack of jobs in the United States for them. For those of you who don't think that illegals would move back, let me cite a statistic; before the recent and arguably ongoing recession, Arizona was home to over 550,000 illegal immigrants. In 2010, due to fewer jobs, Arizona only harbored 360,000 immigrants according to the Department of

Homeland Security (DHS). In two years, almost 200,000 immigrants left because of Arizona's illegal immigrant crackdown law (recently struck down in court) and a lousy economic climate. In fact, in 2010, several reports came out saying that Border Patrol agents were so bored in 2010 that they were playing solitaire and texting! Border crossings have dropped by approximately 72% since 2000, again, according to the DHS and Border Patrol. In 2000, border crossings were occurring at the rate of 1.6 million crossings per year. In 2010, border crossings dropped all the way to 448,000 crossings per year. Just relying on the down economy to keep illegal immigrants out is not a feasible solution, because the economy will not stay stagnant forever, and we will need to increase Border Patrol presence to deal with the increased amount of illegal crossings when the economy inevitably improves.

For all labor-intensive (get it) purposes, let's assume that such a large crackdown on businesses hiring illegals cannot be passed due to the congressional gridlock in Washington and the Department of Justice lawsuits against states that enacted such laws. You'd at least assume that the money illegal immigrants earn would stay in the United States and contribute to our overall Gross Domestic Product (GDP). You would at least assume that illegals in the United States would help the economy with consumer spending, right? Wrong; most illegal immigrants send a good portion of the money they earn back across the border to their families in their home countries. Let's say the average illegal migrant worker in an agricultural job makes four dollars an hour for 12 hours a day, 325 days a year (Southwestern California in areas has nearly endless growing seasons). That means that they make approximately $15,600 a year. Most immigrants would send $5,000-$6000 of that back home; so the real contribution to the GDP of the USA is only $10,000, and if an American was hired for that job, that American would have to make at least minimum wage, and he or she would be making $29,000 if he or she worked 325 days a year, 12 hours a day, and it would all stay in America. That's a difference of $15,000; give or take a few thousand. Now take into account that 13 million illegal immigrants live in the United States, and about 10 million of them work. If all those workers were placed by American workers, it could result in a growth of up to $2 trillion, with a T, in the GDP of the United States. A much more healthy, vibrant economy with a much lower debt to GDP ratio would be produced by replacing illegal immigrant workers with American workers; and the effect of eliminating over $100 billion in welfare checks, and adding 10 million new workers no longer collecting unemployment checks could mean over $450 billion in new revenue for the federal government.

Additionally, there are limited records to judge who we are letting into the nation illegally. Some studies suggest that as many as 40% of illegal immigrants were either involved in a crime south of the border or in the United States other than an immigration infraction. Many illegals are involved in the vast U.S. drug trade; as over 90% of the narcotics in the United States are imported illegally via the United States-Mexico border. In Juarez over the past few years, there been thousands of confirmed murders related to drug trafficking and the all-powerful drug cartels. Arguably, illegal immigrants earned Phoenix the temporary title of, the "kidnapping capital of the world," in 2008 and 2009. But, surprise, surprise, as illegal immigrant numbers went down in 2009, and chiefly in 2010, the crime rates in Phoenix dropped sharply, and by 2010 the term was only used as a buzzword by state and national politicians (they seem to be really good at that, finding stuff out two or three years after it was actually important). Another added danger of not properly protecting our borders is terrorism. In some sleeper cells' (terrorist cells) plans that we have discovered, the method of weapon delivery is to sneak biological or nuclear warheads across the Mexican border and detonate them in large southern cities.

You're probably wondering when I'll get to what other empires had a problem with borders. Near the end of the Roman Republic, the Visigoths, tribal barbarians in the area today known as Germany, Poland, Romania, and Northern France, were slowly but surely gaining strength. When the Romans expanded, they always put up walls. The first expansion that Rome experienced in Europe was to the Alps Mountains in the north. To expand past the Alps, the Romans had to defeat various barbarian tribes in Europe, notably the Visigoths. When the Roman Republic became impoverished at a later date, it could not maintain its internal infrastructure. As the Romans attempted to conquer the Middle East and North Africa, their infrastructure in Europe was collapsing. Little by little, the Visigoths retook territory north of the Alps, and terrorized the towns at the border of the Roman Empire. Within a few centuries, Visigoths had crossed the Alps Mountains, and were bearing down on the northern mainland of Italy. Because the Romans could not maintain their northern walls, or secure their northern borders, the Visigoths eventually sacked Rome (for a loss of the whole nine yards). This new threat, which drained the treasury, and created an entirely new theater of combat, was a contributing factor in the decline of Roman civilization.

We are in the same situation as the Romans were 2000 years ago with respect to immigration. On our southern border, a violent and barbaric civilization is slowly creeping across our Southwest, in the same fashion as the Visigoths 2000 years ago. We also have problems in attempting to erect a wall, just as the Romans had trouble trying to maintain their border walls. We still have not built the continuous border wall, and at this point, we probably never will.

In addition to the punishment for those who hire illegal immigrants, we need to secure our border with a fence and increased Border Patrol. If we do not secure our border, we will not be able stop those who are not looking for jobs in the United States from crossing the border. We will probably need to double our Border Patrol in order to secure the border, and if we stop the flow of illegal immigration into the country, we can then start to deal with the illegal immigrants already inside the United States effectively. In order to enforce the penalty on the employers, we need a system of national identification cards. This card should probably only contain your picture, your birthday, and very, very basic information. The national ID card should not become the subject of George Orwell's *1984*, whereby the national government obtains a bio print of every citizen in the United States (including DNA, fingerprints, personal information). The fact that our government cannot set up a national ID card system to effectively deal with illegal migrant workers without making it something straight out of a Jesse Ventura episode should be telling.

That said, we do need an easier way to become a legal United States citizen. Legal immigrants have enriched our economy and culture for hundreds of years. Many of the people in our country illegally are not here of their own accord, and do not deserve to be kicked out. If this is so, they can have a pathway to citizenship provided that they learn English, have not committed a crime, are active members of their community, and pay a minimal fine (15 million people paying $100 or $200-$300 each could raise a substantial amount of money for the government). I believe that after all the reforms are implemented, about one-third of illegal immigrants will remain in the country because they are not criminals, did not have a job, or were deeply rooted in the USA. These people could be given a pathway to citizenship if the above requirements are fulfilled, and our rule of law would be intact. Within a few decades, these people would become productive members of society.

Although some of you may be skeptical, take, for example, the early 1800s, when people thought that American society should be almost entirely of English descent. Americans in the early 1800s formed what we call today the "Know-Nothing party", which was dedicated to a nativist platform. The party's members were scared that immigrants from Southern and Eastern Europe, not to mention Ireland and Scotland, were inferior. They were soon proven wrong when these groups successfully integrated into American society and enriched its traditions. The bottom line is this: we need to stop illegal immigration at the border, we need to have an effective way to crack down on employers that hire illegals, we need a national ID card system that is not straight out of East Germany in 1980 (I'm referring to the brutal regime of communism that did intelligence work on its own population), we need to drive most of the illegals here back across the border, we have to stop believing the lie that Americans won't do low-level jobs; state, national, and local governments have to cooperate to effectively enforce immigration laws, we have to prosecute states that harbor sanctuary cities, we have to respect our rule of law, and for the few productive members that remain, we need an easy path to citizenship provided that illagals pay a fine and learn English.

CHAPTER 5

BCA, 123: Public Education

O dds are that your child goes to a public school. My dad is a public school teacher in a close suburb of Detroit. As a teacher's son, I get to see firsthand the problems with the system, and the reasons for unions. The first major problem with education that I see is continuing education. The public school teachers that you are paying through your tax dollars must take days off every five years to register for college courses in order to stay certified. Once registered, teachers must write 3 to 4 major essays per week. The essays are on such subjects as the globalization of education. If you disagree with the opinion that the UN should regulate the education of youths all over the world, you can be marked down or failed, perhaps losing your certification and your right to teach. These essays tire teachers for the day, and, in some cases, force teachers to spend time away from students. Teachers pay thousands of dollars to take these classes. Here's the kicker. You're paying universities via the Department of Education to make teachers take the classes. You're probably thinking that there are exceptions, but there aren't. A 45-year-old teacher with a Master's Degree or PhD still has to pay for propagandist college courses. My father is a physics teacher, and due to these classes, I found myself editing the essays of a 45-year-old physics teacher regarding the subject of the United Nations globalizing the entire educational system, to which my dad was strongly opposed, as am I. But here's the problem: he's a physics teacher. Why does he need to learn about elitist theories of education?

Here's an obvious solution: pay teachers to teach kids instead of paying teachers to teach teachers about subjects they don't need to be taught about with tax dollars. How unthinkable to those who see local or state control of an issue as a cardinal sin. Do you know why we can't eliminate that horrible system (We actually can; only currently, there is no political attention being paid to the issue)? Because thousands of bureaucrats at the Department of Education who do absolutely nothing all day but think up ways to subject teachers to "diversity training" and the like and vote Democratic in the state of Virginia (swing state; what a coincidence) would lose their jobs. What a tragedy.

The next major problems with public education today are the people I refer to as four-hour educators. Four-hour educators are people who have one or two out of five or six hours as prep periods. Four-hours teachers are normally older, do not put in any extra effort, do not coach, but, rather, go home after teaching three or four class segments. There are two types of educators in the public school system, in general. The first type of teacher is the four-hour teacher, which I have already described. These teachers are the targets of the political right in general, and politicians of all stripes. These teachers will collect large pensions from the state as seniors, and have large salaries for just teaching three or four hours a day for 182 days per year if they can stick it out for 20 or 30 years. This type of teacher is protected by the general teacher's union.

The second type of teacher is the extracurricular teacher. These teachers coach sports, help kids get into colleges in their spare time, run clubs, tutor after school in difficult subjects and classes, and make an actual difference in the child's life. The bulk of four-hour teachers should be fired because they are not the best people for the job. These teachers are normally older, and are protected by the union rules of seniority. The common sense solution to this issue is simple: pay teachers based on the amount of time that they spend with students, not by how long they've been in the system. This leads me to my next point: the problems with the proposed "merit pay," system.

In many states in America today, the state government is considering "merit pay" systems for its teachers. These systems will determine teachers' pay through how well their students perform on standardized tests. This seems like a logical plan until you delve deeper into the issue. First, if the system were to be enacted, every teacher would want to teach the best students and the best classes that don't need much help, but would mean good pay. What happens to the teacher stuck with the special education class or with the C and D students? The teachers who have to put in the most time and effort could be getting paid the least. No teachers graduating from college would go teach in Detroit or the Bronx; they would apply to teach in Malibu or Bloomfield Hills, and those who need the most educators in the system would be facing a serious shortage of teachers. If a merit pay system were to be enacted, a bonus or tax credit would have to go into effect as well to reward going into tougher districts, or teaching subpar classes. The quality of the children coming into the classroom would have to be accounted for before a valid merit pay system could be enacted.

The second problem with the merit pay system is a doozy, and one my family has firsthand experience with. The issue is the ease of tests. If teacher pay is determined by how well students do on a final exam, teachers can simply make the test simple. My dad gave his second trimester final exam, which showed average student improvement of 30 to 40%, with 65% of the test correct; up from 25 to 35% upon students entering the class. However, aware of the possible impending merit pay system, fellow undisclosed staff changed the tests to make them incredibly easy to show higher overall scores, even though the level of knowledge gained by the pupils was not reflected by these numbers. If this system were to become widespread, it would pose the threat of a new generation that was passed through the system but cannot compete in the new global economic setting. Speaking of students who are not prepared to compete in the global economy, that leads me to charter schools.

All over the United States, charter schools are popping up and advertising their education as much better than that of the public system. However, all they are really doing is taking the best students and saying that they are doing a great job by showing good results. This should come as no surprise; if you take the best tanks, the best airplanes, the best trained infantry, and all the bio weapons in the world, and fight the Falkland Islands, you'll probably win. That doesn't necessarily mean that you have better generals, and if the war is even close, the other side's generals are probably better. Such was the case in my home district, where a charter school had popped up across from the administration building. The charter school recruited mostly A and B students out of the district's middle schools. Although the charter school would have higher test scores than the public middle schools, the children at the charter school would sometimes come back to the public school a year or two later, and they would be a full year behind in subject matter. Charter schools do not have to take the same standardized tests as public schools. In most charter schools, the teachers are paid next to nothing, don't have to be certified, and sometimes know little of their subjects. The charters get away with this because they recruit the best students, and they are able to show high test scores, and, thus, retain public funding. I have a friend in Texas who is currently attending a private school. He's taking AP chemistry, and hopes to become a doctor. He's having trouble at the private school because the AP chemistry teacher there doesn't know much about chemistry. However, this private school in Texas recruits the best kids from all around the county, and frequently pulverizes the local public schools in test scores. My friend is now considering transferring to a public school because the AP chemistry teacher at the public school knows his subject very well, and is spoken of very highly by professors at local colleges. So you see, charter schools aren't necessarily better because they have higher test scores; that would be like saying that General Ulysses S. Grant was a better general than Robert E. Lee because he beat a few militia members with shotguns handily. Until both systems have equal students (which will be never), we may as well compare Bolshevik revolutionaries to the bourgeoisie.

The third problem with the "merit pay" system is straight up, good old-fashioned cheating. Not many teachers would contemplate this desperate technique. However, the teachers that would choose this route would seriously alter the numbers. The bottom line on merit pay is that the teachers will find ways around the system to retain their salaries, and that less intelligent children, or those pupils who do not try as hard and need motivation will not get good teachers. In my opinion, the merit pay system is a ploy to get every teacher one bad class at least once. Every teacher in a school district will get at least one class full of rock-heads that won't be able to pass the test. When this happens, the school district will be able to fire the most senior teachers that are making the most money, whether they are good teachers or not, and improve its bottom line.

In my opinion, the elite and the state bureaucrats will never figure out what every youth learns on a field or a court: discipline and good old-fashioned competition. My dad coaches a high school football team, and I wrestle and play football. On the field, coaches instill discipline and the principles of economic competition into the next generation. In many school districts, when tough times hit, sports are the first targets for budget cuts. Coaches around the nation, except for football coaches in the great state of Texas get a minimal stipend for their time. We should decrease pay to those teachers who do not coach or run a club or after-school activity of some sort, because their average child contact time is lower; about five hours per day. For having a 12-hour workday, there should be major incentives to coach, and bonuses to staff that help students in their off time. I support a teacher pay scale of about $9,000 an hour of child contact time per year. The system would pay average teachers $45,000 a year, four hour teachers $36,000 a year, and coaches right around $105,000 a year. Although those numbers may jump off the page at you as being too high, you must remember that most teachers start at about $35,000, but build seniority until they make $90,000-$100,000 just to work five hours a day before retirement. The majority of teachers do not coach or run clubs. The real bank-breakers for states are long-term obligations for teacher pay and pensions. In this system, no steps or seniority would be available; you just get consistent pay commensurate with your contact time with children. Since only 15 to 20% of staff members are coaches in the average district, it would be a budget cut for most states; and if it weren't, it would mean a huge expansion of extracurricular activities that add to the value of an education. Either way, it's a plus. In addition, this new pay system would incentivize the teachers who are not coaches to spend time after school with kids tutoring, and would bump their pay slightly into the $40,000 range. But to do this, you would have to battle some of the most powerful organizations in America: teacher's unions.

Although I see the importance of unions, I also see some major problems. The unions, of course, are necessary to make sure that teachers are not working for peanuts. Looking back to the days of the Gilded Age and JD Rockefeller, it's hard to imagine the USA without unions. However, teachers' unions, I believe, have overstepped their bounds in many areas. Even though my family is conservative, the union takes $400 a year of our money, and donates it to the campaigns of liberal Democrats without fail. The seniority system in teacher's unions is damaging to the education of youth for one reason; if a good, energetic, coaching teacher, and a 65-year-old, unmotivated teacher are in competition for one job to hang onto, under the current system, in most states, the 65-year-old teacher keeps his or her position because of union seniority. There is no doubt that seniority and tenure are detrimental to the education of students. Tenure is a state of employment given after a teacher is in a school district for a given amount of time. This tenure virtually assures teachers their job for as long as they want it, barring that they commit a serious crime. My dad tells me of the teaching system in Texas, where I was born and remained until I was eight months old. There is no tenure in Texas (at least there wasn't when my father was teaching there), and barely any unionization. Though my dad coached three sports, and was energetic as a young teacher, he made less than $30,000 each year (private school). The system in Texas, while it encourages relating to students and being involved in extracurricular activities, sets the pay per hour of contact time too low to attract quality teachers. Texas now has one of the most diverse and vibrant economies in United States, and has withered the recession untouched. However, with high-paying private sector jobs plentiful, Texas faces a teacher shortage (surprise, surprise). It is no coincidence that the state with the least tenure and seniority is now one of the most successful. However, the failure of Texas to pay their teachers better is now costing them dearly. Bottom line: tenure and seniority have to go, but good teachers and coaches cannot make a pittance.

The next problem with public education is federal and state control. In the 1970s and 80s, education was a purely local issue. The individual community decided how much emphasis it would put on education through bonds, millages, and city taxes. The communities that decided to put more of a premium on education attracted people from all over, especially those people who had the cash to pay the bonds and taxes and had children. This obviously raised the housing prices in those communities dramatically. But in the 1990s, most states in the union switched to state run education (including my home state of Michigan). This allowed the states to impose the onerous regulations of continuing education and state tests. Although there must be some standardized testing, as it is necessary to measure student progress, determining funding based on tests, as some states do, makes teachers "teach to the test," or focus only on the material that would be on the standardized test. In the end, education is about instilling knowledge and values for the next generation.

Teaching only how to give the illusion that you have learned enough to do well in life isn't teaching. This, like merit pay based on testing, poses the danger of creating an economically uncompetitive generation that does not understand what is really important. Now there are calls to make education global via the United Nations. I've got a better idea: how about we make education local again. Kids in Alaska don't need to learn about multicultural diversity because it's a waste of money and time. If we give control back to the communities, they can once again decide whether or not to make long-term investments in their own towns and cities; they know better what their kids need to learn for success than a state, overreaching federal, or even global government. I think about education like a lesson that was taught to me in physics class once. Thomas Edison preferred to send electricity through direct current, or DC electricity. In DC electricity, the further the electricity is sent, the more friction is in the wire, and the more energy is lost. Due to this, under Edison's system, you need a power plant every mile or two. It's the same way in education, or money in general. If you send the money to city hall, there is virtually no friction, because the money is not moving very far, and the people you're sending it to know your needs well. If you send the money to the state capitol 200 miles away, all of a sudden, that money has a lot of friction on it. You now don't have your needs met as well, and you lose much of the money to state bureaucrats. This effect is amplified when you send the money all the way to Washington. The money that you send goes even farther, and you lose even more money to a larger set of bureaucrats, and the extra distance it travels requires people to move the money along the way, who have to be paid. Now imagine sending that money all the way to the United Nations. So you see, the rules of physics do apply, even to economics.

Speaking of city control of education, there is an experimental education program being tried in some of the cities in my home state of Michigan. In Kalamazoo and Hazel Park, there's a program called "The Promise" being tried. The Promise is a program that gives any student that has been in the district from kindergarten to 12th grade, first grade through 12th grade, or second grade through 12th grade full tuition to a four-year in-state college. This program costs about $1 million per year in communities with 30,000 to 35,000 people and a 25% rate of high school students going to a four-year college. The cost is $300-$1000 per taxpayer to begin, which gives the city enough money to run the program for 9 to 12 years. If the money is put in a bank CD with an interest rate of 9-12%, the fund never runs out of money. This program would attract new home buyers, who would drive up the home values in the community.

In the first quarter of 2011, home values fell 10.8% in Grand Rapids, Michigan while values in the Promise town of Kalamazoo only fell 2.3% (2011 was not a great year for home values in the Great Lakes state). Community control of education, in my opinion, is the conservative solution to our education issues, and models the conservative economic philosophy. You're free to succeed, and free to fail, but, if you fail, no one is going to save you with public cash, get back on your feet. Until the 1980s and 1990s, control was purely local in most states. This system is not new, much to some people's surprise. Public education was set up in the Midwest with the Northwest Ordinance under Thomas Jefferson. One part of each township was to be set aside for township-run education in the plan, because it would be in everyone's best interest. That brings me to the subject of community business incentives.

I know, this education chapter is dragging on like the Pacific theater of World War II after Okinawa, but we're in the final section. Businesses would take well to the Promise idea. For $600-$700, the businesses could attract a new market of hundreds of families. The businesses would actually have a vested interest in the Promise program, and may lessen the burden on the taxpayers. The businesses would all want better schools, because in the long run, all the establishments need a skilled workforce that has an education. In addition, the hundreds of families that the Promise program attracts would be new customers for the businesses, pushing up those businesses' profits.

Now for the wrap-up: teachers have to be paid a living wage of some kind, or you get a teacher shortage. Unions are necessary, but cannot have the vast power that they currently enjoy to keep senior teachers onboard and influence elections. "Merit pay," won't work because there would not be an incentive to teach those who need teaching the most. It's a very effective way for the state to dispose of senior teachers before they can reach retirement. Four-hour teachers must go. Coaching discipline and competition on a field or court is supremely important. Communities must have control over education, not the national government or the UN. As Thomas Jefferson once put it, "Government closest governs best."

CHAPTER 6

The Harbingers: Factions

Our Founding Fathers were decently shrewd men overall. They were attempting to draw up the outline for a republic that would preserve individual liberty, although they were not very confident that it would last very long. Most of the Founders felt that they were exercising an experiment in self-government. They warned us of many things in the beginning; Washington, Madison, Jefferson, and Adams all made comments to suggest that some things may be too great for the republic to withstand in the future. Among their greatest fears were political parties, factions, an urban proletariat, and a nanny state. Currently, we have all of these elements present in our government and society. Without a doubt, these things continuing are the harbingers of the end of the republic. That may sound a bit melodramatic, it may sound a bit odd, but if you go back through world history, and to our Founding Fathers, you'll realize that the time that you are now living in is one in which America is transitioning from a republic built on the rule of law and constitutionalism to something entirely different; whether it is an oligarchy, a socialist democracy, or something else, that I don't know.

George Washington was a brilliant man. Although he accidentally started the entire French and Indian war, he had wisdom beyond his years. Upon his death, he freed all of his slaves, an act that was both uncommon and reprehensible to many in 18th century Northern Virginia. After he successfully commanded the American Revolution, he had to focus on how to build a new nation that was not divided along boundaries of occupation, geography, or ideology. The threats he saw as being greater than all others were political parties. At the Constitutional Convention, and at all the sessions of the Continental Congress, there were no political parties present. There were only men representing their states, who brought their own personal ideas, experiences, and ideologies. They did not have a speaker or a whip to lead them; they exchanged ideas freely as Americans, and as individuals fighting for a common cause. These periods in American history were incredibly productive in terms of the ideas that came to the forefront of the national debate.

When George Washington was the president, he saw divisions among the country clearly emerging within the House of Representatives, the Senate, and the population at large. We were dividing along lines between farmers and small manufacturers, and bankers, merchants, and traders. Although Washington tended to lean toward one side, and he did not see conflicting ideas as a threat to democracy, but rather as a tool to enrich the debate; he was strongly opposed to political parties on the grounds that the parties would become corrupt and start to silence some peoples' ideas and greatly centralize the government. He thought that political parties would eventually undermine the will of the people, and bow to special interests. In the latter years of his Presidency, the debate between the two sides intensified rapidly. Washington was worried that the nation would soon split into two rival camps that would have formal organizations instead of being a united nation with differing viewpoints that could come out on the floor of the legislative body, or through the citizenry. He worried that people would begin to have goals not for the nation, but for their own political parties. Such was the worry that Washington had that, in his final farewell speech, when he stepped down from the Presidency after eight years to show that America could not have a king, but had to have a change of leadership every so often, he focused on warning the nation about the dangers of political parties. John Adams was chosen by the American people to succeed George Washington to the presidency, and when George Washington died in 1799, as if on cue, political parties immediately formed.

Thomas Jefferson and James Madison were on one side, transforming the anti-Federalists into the Democratic-Republican Party, Alexander Hamilton and John Adams were on the other side, and the old Federalist movement became the Federalist Party. Just before Washington's death, his worst fears for the republic were realized. The Adams administration passed the Alien and Sedition Acts, which required immigrants to wait 14 instead of seven years after becoming United States citizens to vote (new immigrants were voting heavily Democratic-Republican at the time), and placed heavy restrictions on criticizing the government in the press. One New Hampshire anti-Federalist man, who formally wrote for an anti-Federalist newspaper, won a seat in Congress from his jail cell. The bill was passed for no apparent reason, except to better the political outlook of the Federalist Party. Due to the bill's blatant violation of the First Amendment of the Constitution, Kentucky and Virginia tried to nullify the law in their state houses, creating a constitutional crisis. It had not been half a decade since George Washington's farewell address when his advice had already gone unheeded and a political party had done things for its own benefit instead of the good of the country, and divided the nation, almost causing secession. What a slap in the face that must have been for George Washington.

Trouble with political parties in the United States continued, and in the 1840s and 1850s, both parties straddled the fence on slavery even though large portions of the population in the North were demanding abolition. This was because the higher-ups at the heads of both parties felt that slavery was a divisive issue; that arguing for abolition, or even against the expansion of slavery, would lose them votes in one region or another more than it would gain them votes in one region or the other; forget the fact that it was morally right. It took an entirely new party, the Republican Party, to bring the abolitionist platform to a national stage.

Later, in 1876, after a very close election, where a few electoral votes that were to decide the election were disputed, the Republican Party chose to make a bargain with the Democrats. The Republicans' presidential candidate, Rutherford B Hayes, would receive the disputed electoral votes, but reconstruction efforts in the South would end. The Republican Party, by this point, had been around for 20 years, and was beginning to corrupt. Even though the entire Republican platform at the time was based on making sure that former slaves in the South received justice, that they were not the victims of southern hatred, and that they got their economic freedom, the Republican Party chose to have its man be the president and abandon all principles that it had by letting the South run itself a mere 11 years after the Civil War.

In the 1880s and 1890s, both parties were looking to realign with the new Industrial Revolution. Senators got in bed with Standard Oil under JD Rockefeller, U.S. Steel under Andrew Carnegie, and countless other large corporations (such as Vanderbilt and his railroads). This time in American history had so much corruption in the Senate (and in the House) that a painting was created representing JD Rockefeller's Standard Oil Corporation as an octopus, with its tentacles stretching into every facet of Capitol Hill and the White House. Political parties at the time were known for printing out party ballots that allowed voters to only vote for members of one party (straight-ticket only), and having party workers fill out ballots. Voter fraud was rampant, and parties incentivized voting for them with money. The most infamous of these operations was the Tammany Hall operation, run by Boss Tweed. Parties in this era were at the height of their power. Parties would preach different platforms in different areas of the country in order to win the elections. The two political parties had virtually no real distinctions between them at the beginning of the 20th century.

Since that time, political parties have declined in influence, but interest groups have rapidly taken their place. If George Washington knew about interest groups, he would clearly think of them as even worse than political parties. Interest groups are not beholden to the public in any way, and are free to influence legislators and the governmental process in any way they see fit. Today, the United States government is overrun by interest groups and lobbyists, which have perhaps more influence than the parties themselves at this point. It is very hard for one individual, or one area of the country, to get its viewpoint out into the open due to the hierarchal system of Congress. Just take the recent fiscal cliff deal, for example. The Republican Party caved, not because it thought it was doing the right thing for the country, not because it thought that it was doing a noble deed, but because it knew that it would look absolutely horrible if it did not fold and let us fall over the "fiscal cliff". This runs contrary to everything that Republicans are supposed to think is good for America; the entire Republican platform preaches that tax increases contract economic growth and hurt the nation as a whole, and is based on free-trade, free enterprise economics. The Republicans did not get any spending cuts for their trouble (officially they got 15 billion in spending cuts but spread out over 10 years that's 1.5 billion a year, fewer than $1 out of every $3000 the government spends, and it was only a reduction in future increases). We did not have any substantive national discussion on how to grow the economy, what economic system is the best, or where or if we should cut government spending. We did not come to any consensus, learn anything new about the other side, compromise, or better the country. We signed a deal that was, frankly, pointless, to keep business as usual going and make sure that one party or the other did not look really bad.

Although I am an avid capitalist, I'd like to have a national debate about what economic system is best, I'd like to have a discussion about whether or not we should raise taxes, and where to cut government spending, instead of just rhetoric. The only reason you should have a view is because you think that you can win an argument due to the fact that you are right, morally or statistically. If you hold a view for any other reason, you shouldn't be in politics (just like everybody on Capitol Hill right now). Once again, we share similarity in this respect with our sister republic from 2000 years ago-Rome.

After investors had bought up most of the land in Rome's productive agricultural areas, they wanted ways to grow their power and hide their wealth from the ever-higher Roman taxes. In exchange for the military service of their slaves (Roman senators were judged based upon their military achievements), investors and landowners got advice from Roman senators and *former* Roman senators on how to hide their wealth from Roman taxes. This was known as a patron-client relationship. Former senators would also commonly work for wealthy citizens on their behalf, using their influence as a former member of the Senate to sway the way the current Senate voted. One of the biggest businesses in Rome itself became influencing the Senate and telling people how to hide their money in exchange for glory in war or money. If this is all sounding eerily familiar, it should be. This is nearly the same manner in which our congressmen are lobbied today.

Here in the United States, we have something called "K Street," in which former senators and congressmen in America commonly join the "consulting" business. In this business, former senators and congressmen get paid to tell corporations and other clients how to hide their money from federal taxes, using the ever-more complex, 78,000 page United States Tax Code. This is the fastest growing business in these United States, with billions of dollars in growth every single year. Consultants also use their influence as former members of Congress to sway the direction that the current Congress votes; and many former public servants get exceptionally rich from this business.

George Washington was not the only Founding Father with a strong fear of political parties and interest groups. James Madison was absolutely obsessed with the dangers posed by factions to the American Republic. Madison envisioned America as a large and diverse republic, while Jefferson envisioned America as more sectionalized. Madison, in his famous piece, Federalist number 51, said, "If men were angels, no government would be necessary. If angels were to govern men, neither internal nor external controls on government would be necessary." Madison thought that the primary danger posed to the federal government was not from some outside form of power, or from a political ideology; he thought the biggest danger to America's democratic system of republic would be a group of people with lots of power looking out for their own interests and controlling most of the government.

Madison viewed power in what can be called a "pluralist view," which preaches that many factions have to be present, and all have to have some power to balance each other out, allowing the will of the people to usually prevail. In order to achieve this, Madison set up, in the Constitution, a much decentralized republic. Although I cannot speak for James Madison's intentions, I think it is relatively clear from the Federalist papers how Madison wanted to avert the perils of factions. He wanted the government to achieve three coequal branches that acted separately, a concept known as Separation of Powers. The thought was that it is harder to corrupt hundreds of people who all must be in agreement to make someone's will public policy than it is to corrupt one or two individuals running government. He also thought that power would be spread around, and that the branches would almost never work together outside of final passage of legislation, lessening the effect of a planted idea from the "ruling classes" that Hamilton favored (I'll get to that later). He also wanted the Tenth Amendment of the Constitution to decentralize power.

When creating a new nation that is supposed to be free, you have to be extraordinarily paranoid and see every situation in which freedom could be taken away or the nation could be hijacked, and implement measures to try to mitigate those scenarios. The Founders' reasoning for adopting the Tenth Amendment was that power would be even more spread out, making it even tougher to control the government. Even if you implemented something against the peoples' will at the national level, or violated the Constitution in D.C., the states could nullify laws, and act as alternative interpreters of the Constitution. The idea was that power would hinge at so many points that it would be nearly impossible to pass anything that a good majority of the public did not agree on. The Tenth Amendment meant, essentially, that except for a few key topics, the decisions would be left to the states.

Some political science professors will tell you that our federalist, separated system encourages interest groups, gives them more power, and weakens the effectiveness of our political system, and that a more centralized and parliamentary system like those that exist in Western Europe would mean a more effective democracy and fewer interest groups. These political scientists would also tell you that the feeble state of our political parties here in America (especially when compared to European political parties) gives more power to interest groups seeking to influence the government. I would quite politely say to them that this is a bunch of Bolshevik.

The reason that interest groups have been so powerful in America as of late, in my opinion, is that we have removed many of the barriers to them, not that we have retained them. If we consolidate power at the national level by doing away with nullification and ignoring the Tenth Amendment (which we have), it is easier to force your will on the nation, because power is more concentrated. Now take into account that Separation of Powers is currently a joke (the branches work together before final passage constantly, and commonly meet, the power of the president has been steadily growing, the Constitution is readily ignored), and it is no wonder that Wall Street was able to shove through its bailout as soon as it realized that it was in real trouble.

Now is when that concept about weakened political parties becomes really important. Although George Washington despised political parties (and rightfully so), they can act as a secondary check on the power of interest groups and factions. If you have a strong party leadership that tells you to vote one way, or else your district is going to see a very well-funded primary challenge, you will not be very likely to vote on a bill the way a lobby wants you to just because it wants you to; you don't really need it or its campaign cash.

Once Federalism is removed, and Separation of Powers is nearly done away with, the only remaining check on the interest group is the political party. Don't get me wrong, I hate political parties, and most nations in Europe have high unemployment, ridiculous taxes, and a corrupted system that their centralized political parties cannot fix. If your political party leaders become corrupted in a centralized parliamentary system, the entire nation is going the way that a few very powerful people want it to go. The original federalist system is a much better system for containing interest groups. However, if that is gone, and a nation has weak political parties, the patron-client relationships are going to really, really prosper. That's the way it's going in America right now.

Thousands of consulting firms dot the streets of Washington, D.C., and the vast majority of them have sprung up in the past half-century. Madison's worst fears are being confirmed before our very eyes. The constituent is something to be manipulated, played for a fool, and ignored whenever possible, because the sources of campaign cash are more important and powerful factions can get anything they want done in D.C. In early America, many factions were present. Farmers in the South wanted us to kick out all the Native Americans from fertile lands, people in the Mid-Atlantic region wanted higher tariffs, and New Englanders wanted better relations with Britain and unfriendly relations with France (New England held extensive trade with Great Britain). Madison thought that the only way to preserve a republic under the circumstances was to have these factions balance out, and for their effect to be essentially neutralized, forcing them to only work on issues wherein they could find common ground and solutions. Madison thought that America would be a prime example of this type of republic, because we were large, diverse, and had many different economic and social interests.

This is what differentiated America for over two centuries from every attempt at a democracy or republic in Europe, Africa, or Asia. These small European and Asian nations that attempted republics and democracies had a limited number of factions, a common heritage, were very homogeneous, and had very un-diverse economies. Due to this, the differences between economic classes within that economy were exacerbated, and the system of civil debate was impossible to maintain. Thus, power in the European democracies for the last 100 years has always been very centralized, and locales have never had much power. The conflicts have never really changed, and one group holds most of the power. Because of this, the nation goes very far in one direction, and then very far in the other direction. In America, however, at least until the 1970s, no single economic interest had an inordinate amount of power. We were very diverse in our economy, and we still are, sort of. One faction did not hold so much power that it could change the government, or push the country a long way in one direction. In the last 40 years, however, all that has changed. The largest institutions in America, namely financial institutions and banks, hold so many assets that they can influence what the government does with amazing power. Who would've thought that a party that preached fiscal responsibility and pure capitalism for one century would vote to bail out the largest banks in America? We are no longer as diverse as we once were, and factions in America are very powerful, mainly due to the proliferation of interest groups. If politicians are more concerned with pleasing an interest group than pleasing the voters back home, the power of those factions becomes immense, and those factions can get almost anything they want done. In short, you're not living in the Founder's Republic anymore; you're living in a quasi-oligarchy.

Benjamin Franklin once said, "When people find that they can vote themselves money, that will herald the end of the republic." Benjamin Franklin was speaking of another common fear of the Founding Fathers in the 18th century: the urban proletariat. For the Founding Fathers, almost nothing was scarier than people with no stake in the political system participating in it and demanding gifts from the revenues brought in by taxes. In the Founders' day, over 90% of people in America lived in rural areas. Most of those who lived in suburban or urban areas were wealthy and worked in business. The urban poor were a very small minority at this time, but Ben Franklin saw it as a problem down the road. Benjamin Franklin was often a visionary; and such was the case in regard to the urban proletariat. Today, we have more people living in urban areas than we do in rural areas.

Of our federal budget of almost 3 3/4 trillion dollars a year, much of it goes to entitlement programs (when I say much, I mean well over 50%) according to the Congressional Budget Office (CBO) and other agencies. True, some of these programs are not for the poor, but for the elderly (Medicare, Social Security). But, we do have a problem with too many people being in what the Founders would call the urban proletariat. These people do not pay any income taxes (although they do pay sales taxes), yet they draw from the public dole, allowed by the revenue that comes in from income taxes. Over 45 million Americans now receive food stamps according to the U.S. Department of Agriculture (USDA), the highest level ever (in terms of the percent of the society, not just raw population). Ben Franklin saw this as a problem 200 years ago; how does somebody who doesn't pay into a system at all draw money from that system, and not have a conflict of interest? Of course, many of the people who are poor in our country are not there of their own accord. People slip through the cracks sometimes. However, when you start getting free money from the government, you slowly lose your incentive to support yourself. People start demanding more and more things of the government, and, at some point, people who *are* supporting themselves by working begin to question why they are doing it, and the pool of people not working grows and grows.

Such is the nature of all life on earth. You will never see a deer run a longer distance than it has unless it is evading a predator, never see a salamander move from under its log unless it is going to breed or catch food, and you will never see a cheetah sprint at 70 mph just for the novelty of it. Organisms are lazy by nature; all organisms. This is just a product of the nature of life on earth; we all act in our own self-interest, much like my dog Noble does when he relentlessly begs for treats. Except in rare cases, we only do what we can gain something from, whether it is money, food, recognition, etc. So, the Founder's idea two hundred years ago was that you could only participate in the political system if you paid taxes, because people would vote for their own self-interest if they had the option, regardless of the consequences for the nation as a whole. The Founders did not come up with this idea out of disdain for the poor, or because of a passing whim, or for the sake of strict social classes; they came up with this idea because of their common sense and examples from times past. Ben Franklin actually lived in poverty for a while and had the utmost respect for the working poor, remarking, "Having been poor is no shame, but being ashamed of it is." Once again, you can probably guess the empire (republic for the first part of its existence) that tried the same thing. If you said the Roman Empire, surprise, surprise, you got it.

As previously mentioned, the Roman middle class became more urbanized as farmland became owned by investors. When displaced from their farmland with cash on hand, middle class and lower-middle class citizens would flock to the Roman cities where they could work in trade, finance, or in the government. During tough times for the investors and businessmen (tough times meaning that rich Roman citizens could only have 50 instead of a 100 slaves, or they could only afford to buy up 1000 acres of farmland that week for a vineyard), employees were laid off. Being in such close proximity to the government outposts in the big cities, unemployed citizens began to demand money from the government treasury, which was then sitting on a heap of cash at the height of the Roman Republic.

Little by little, the majority of citizens became more and more dependent on government to support their lifestyle. All of a sudden, people did not care what the tax rates were, didn't care about foreign affairs, didn't care about the moral questions of the day; they cared about who was going to give them bigger gifts from the public treasury. As a result of the welfare state, little by little, the sums of money the public treasury was sitting on dwindled, and money had to be diverted from infrastructure projects and wars to pay for the needs of the urban proletariat. Although it was breaking the bank, anyone aspiring to power in Rome had to do it, because, the politicians that got elected to the Senate or the emperors that were most loved were always the ones who promised the best goodies. If the Roman politicians didn't deliver, mobs would have their head on a platter, not to mention that their political career would be over. So, every new Senate kept handing out goodies that they couldn't afford to hand out, and hoping that the new senators would fix it. To use a much maligned cliché, the Romans were, "kicking the can down the road."

Slowly, Rome's infrastructure collapsed, barbarians overran the borders, and the empire began to lose wars. But what did that matter? The majority of the citizens needed their benefits, and some silly Huns 1000 miles away weren't going to keep them from voting for "Santa Claus." Rome started to accumulate debt in the form of inflation. Eventually, the illusion couldn't be kept up anymore. But it was much too late. The figurative frog in the slowly heating pot was cooked. By the end, the government was God in Rome, the only concern of most voters was the nanny state, and, even though voters often agreed with other candidates on most issues, they almost always went with the big-government candidate. All for a couple of senators, whose names are now lost to history's pages, getting glory for a few short decades. Rome traded away its republic for dependency, but let us not forget how it started: with consolidation of assets, and the people losing touch with the land.

This should not be just sounding familiar; this should be sounding exactly like our situation today in the United States. In the recent 2012 elections, voters shot down a candidate with whom they agreed on most major issues. Mitt Romney was for lower taxes. 70% of Americans are for lower taxes for most people. Mitt Romney was for lower regulation. At least 65% of Americans are for lighter regulation on almost every industry. Mitt Romney campaigned on small government. At least 60 to 65% of Americans are for small government. He campaigned on more oil and natural gas drilling, on which 60% of Americans agree with him. However, he lost to a candidate, a sitting president no less, who was for larger government, higher taxes, more regulation, and less fossil fuel production. One has to ask, how is that possible? Some will attribute it to America's changing demographic situation (Latinos now comprise about 15% of America). Some will attribute it to high African-American turnout. Some will attribute it to Americans generally wanting higher taxes on the "1%." But, I don't like to qualify things by race or ethnicity, and the polls I just cited weren't excluding groups of people, or done by hyper-partisan pollsters. The truth is that this year's election was decided based upon welfare. For the first time ever, more Americans receive government assistance than do not. 47% of us (that number is old, by now it is probably 50%) do not pay any federal income taxes. Sure, some of those people are retirees, and some voted for Romney, but the vast majority will vote Democratic even if they are conservatives at heart. "Don't bite the hand that feeds you," as the old proverb goes. The reason that President Obama won this election is that too many people in America were dependent on government for anyone else to win. So, America's dependency state will grow and grow, barring some miracle. Undoubtedly, without action from the public, we will follow down the road to Rome; and only a few of us will realize where we're going. But, do not of think of this as our destiny. It is a changeable fate. It is one we must change. Thomas Jefferson once said, "The natural progression of things is for liberty to yield, and for government to gain ground." Mr. Jefferson there was prophetic as usual, but he can be proven wrong.

CHAPTER 7

It's Like Déjà Vu All over Again: Bubble Mania

For some reason completely lost on me, or anyone else, America seems to repeat the same exact recession about every 80 to 90 years. You may think that I am exaggerating, but I am not. The Panic of 1837, the Great Depression, and the Great Recession of 2008-present have all played out in the exact same manner.

In the 1830s, banks were speculating wildly on the price of land in the still wild lands of the Northwest Territories (today Ohio, Michigan, Indiana, Illinois, Wisconsin, and part of Minnesota), and the American economy was experiencing a boom based on easy-to-get loans. Banks also bet on the harvest prices of key crops grown in the Northwest. You can probably already guess where this is going, just from the opening. In 1837, it was discovered that the emperor didn't have any clothes, and that properties in the Midwest weren't worth nearly what the speculators had pushed the prices up to. The paper currency market collapsed, home values fell, and the ripple effect hit the entire economy. The problem was made worse by the fact that banks had been issuing bonds without the gold to back up the notes, hoping to make sufficient money to cover their risks with high-interest loans. Boy, this is like a Yogi Berra quote, "It's like déjà vu all over again." The middle class was crippled in the economic contraction, and a generation of America learned to be very wary of credit buying and risky loan practices.

That generation died off in the late 1800s and early 1900s, taking its wisdom with them. A new generation of American businessmen pushed products that had just come out in the 1910s and 1920s: vacuum cleaners, telephones for everyone, and cars. To sell more of these products to the masses, sales of these products on credit began in earnest in the early 1920s, after the end of World War I. Due to the credit buying en masse, the stock market soared, and everyone thought that it would keep going up indefinitely along with consumer spending. Brokers began to let clients, "buy on margin," and only pay part of a stock price to own it outright. The owner would often use the profits of that stock to buy more on margin, until he or she held thousands of shares, and owed over half of the share value. It was like house-flipping on the stock market. However, when people started defaulting on their loans, and stock prices stalled, everyone that bought on margin got "margin calls," asking for the rest of the money. When the shareholders didn't have it, the price of that stock fell through the floor, as people on the markets figured out that most people only paid half of the price for the stock. The Great Depression was on, and the poverty and pain lasted for a decade.

My great-grandfather was part of the Depression generation, and he took the lessons of those years with him for life. He always kept half a tank of gas in his car just in case. He never bought anything with a credit card or gave out personal information. That generation retired in the 1990s, the same decade in which the Glass-Steagall Act was repealed. The Glass-Steagall Act required the depositor and investor arms of a bank to be separate. When that act was repealed, banks were free to invest with your bank account for the first time since the Great Depression. I don't think it was a coincidence at all that this happened when the last of the Depression generation was departing the workforce. When this generation left the workforce, it took its fear of risky lending with it, in addition to its wariness toward credit buying. Throughout the first decade of the 21st century, credit buying and risky lending powered the American economy to new heights, and the Dow Jones industrial average zoomed past 13,000 points. However, eventually, the inevitable happened. Everybody figured out that the emperor didn't have any clothes on again. People during this latest Great Recession speculated on oil, houses, stock, and consumer products, driving the prices of these products way too high artificially. My great-grandfather predicted it all in my last visit with him in 2007. He told me that he thought America would enter another recession very soon; and when I asked him why, he said that all the signs were the same as when he was young man during the mid-1920s: the whole economy was built on people buying things on credit, and people were speculating on the price of everything. I guess old age and treachery really do conquer all. Thus, America has come full circle by completing its third in what is fixing to be a long series of nearly identical recessions.

This time, however, was different. It was not an entirely private-sector based recession (neither was the depression, but it was more private-sector based than this one). The government incentivized, and largely created the bubble. HUD housing, in the 1990s, by forcing banks to make risky loans on houses, artificially inflated the number of people on the housing market, and, thus, inflated the prices of houses. If you look at a chart of housing prices adjusted for inflation, they stick between $80,000 and $100,000 in 2009 U.S. dollars, except for the period of time after 1990. This is because government investment in the housing industry (which was largely to get politicians votes from those who got houses from the new zero money down government program; sounds like Rome) pushed the price up artificially. In addition to pushing the price up artificially, the government knowingly misled Americans into buying larger and larger houses. My parents bought under the impression that it was the best investment possible, especially after they heard multiple government officials say that it would help the U.S. economy if everyone bought as much as they could afford to buy, and that they would make hoards of money on their investment over time.

Your government had statements from Fannie Mae and Freddie Mac as early as 2003 and 2004 that showed housing prices were fixing to plummet, and that Fannie and Freddie were in trouble. However, Barney Frank, (D-MA) who spoke for Fannie and Freddie on the house floor, said multiple times at this point in time that the two institutions were financially sound. Government investment in products always increases the price. This is the case with every single product that the government invests in, from school lunches to tuitions to healthcare.

If you go to any McDonald's in America today, you can get two double cheeseburgers and an ice water that is over 40 ounces for $2.25, if you want to add apples to the order, it might cost you $3.00. However, that is not the story at my high school in suburban Lower Michigan, where the government runs the program. Some students who are in the lower-income bracket get free school lunch. However, most of us pay $3.00 for a lunch. That sounds fine, until you consider what the lunch is. The average lunch is just a milk (7 oz), a juice (4 or 5oz), and a burger (a small burger at that). It used to contain fries, until those were taken out for health reasons. Anybody could get the amount of food provided to us by the government at a fast food chain for half of the cost, and it wouldn't be any less healthy. The school food all around the nation is usually processed heavily, and the school "cooks" are really "micro-wavers."

The price of lunch in our school used to be about $1.50. However, when the government invests in a product, it gives the product to some for free, leading others to get in line to get it for free, leaving an ever smaller amount of paying members to pay higher and higher rates for everyone else. This is a good analogy of what is happening to the economy on a very small scale. If everybody just paid the same rate, the rate would be more affordable and much lower for everyone, (that's why I favor a flat tax as well) but government will never operate that way. The government's goal is not nutrition, or low prices, it is to get more votes next election, and to get more people dependent upon the government. It unintentionally creates a bubble in the process every time. Some schools now even have nutrition police. Not to get ahead of myself and into the nanny state chapter already, but a girl in North Carolina recently had her turkey sandwich confiscated in school, and was given a substitute of processed chicken nuggets and fries (before fries were banned) in addition to high-fat cow's milk (that's healthy . . . . not). What do you think the goal is? Thomas Jefferson once said, "If we let government decide what foods we will eat, and what drinks our bodies will consume, then our bodies shall soon be in such a sorry state as the souls of those living under tyranny." Speaking of living in a sorry state, let's get on to college costs.

Nearly all parents want their children to go to college. However, the cost of college has gone up over 400% in the last quarter of a century. Since median income has not even doubled in that period of time, you have to ask yourself why this has happened. It's very simple: the government has invested heavily in college loans. Starting in the early 1990s, the government began to give out financial aid like candy to anybody who qualified. The result was that the price of a college education started to skyrocket after the early 1990s. The reason that this happened is that when the government invested, the colleges knew that they could now charge what people couldn't ordinarily afford, because people could just borrow what they needed from the government, and the government would pay whatever the college wanted, because the politicians were doing it for the votes; to tell their constituents that everyone in the district could go to college.

However, when everyone goes to college, the degree that the students earn there loses much of its value. I hate to be blunt, but not everyone should go to college. Some kids can't understand Algebra 1, but have a knack for fixing cars. Forget college, go make

$70,000 a year as a mechanic; you don't need to know Voltaire and complex economics to turn a wrench. We'll always need people to work in factories, or on farms, or as firemen, or as soldiers. The newest craze of sending everybody to college will undoubtedly result in ruin soon. It is plain right now that the college market is a bubble. A piece of paper that doesn't even guarantee you a job, because everybody is supposed to have one, is not worth six years of starting salary or more. It will take many people until the end of their lives to pay off their college debt with interest. Without a doubt, people who couldn't afford the college loans taken out will soon begin defaulting in huge numbers, just like in the housing market. When that happens, the banks that held the debt (before the government took over the entire market in 2009) and the government will have serious financial trouble.

The way accounting works in Washington is a little bit backwards. I take that back; it's a lot backwards. When Washington DC loans out $100,000 for a college loan at 5% interest for 20 years, it is counted as the government making $100,000 at the moment the loan is issued, because the government is expecting $200,000 back over time. So, the government could inflate its revenue by 100 billion dollars if it made one million such loans in one year. This is the same way the banks operated before the housing crisis. The banks signed as many loans as possible, because those loans were counted as revenue-positive. Look where that landed our country.

The same thing is happening in the student loan business. The mentality is that we should give out as many loans as possible, because it is good for the next generation, and will make money for Uncle Sam. That is not what will happen. Once again, people will eventually discover that the emperor doesn't have any clothes. Some people who cannot handle the rigor of the college curriculum will be financially ruined after they cannot pay back their loans, others with jobs will spend decades just trying to get their heads above water. When college for four years gets to an average of about

$300,000, (it is currently about $125,000 and rising exponentially) the bubble will burst, because too many people will be defaulting to keep the process going, and 18 year-olds will start being much more reluctant to sign on the dotted line and resign themselves to serfdom. Until that point, colleges will keep charging more money, because they can get it; politicians won't stop the aid because it's a highly popular program. Loan-backed securities will be issued a few years before the crash at just below the overall value of the loans, a last ditch effort by the banks that hold the debt to make money, the largest financial institutions will sell the stock to inexperienced traders. The stock will be just like the mortgage-backed securities in the 2008 crash. That will be the warning sign that the crash is close, when people in high places start playing hot potato with billions of dollars in toxic debt. At the point of collapse, the Treasury will have a major problem, because the profit expected from the loans won't be there; it'll probably be facing losses. Just think about it this way, if everyone had a college degree, what's so special about it, and does it guarantee employment? Even if it does, is it really worth two houses' worth of debt to get? People will eventually see that, and the boom in the college market will be over. Government spending in a product will always push the price up exponentially just like it has done in the college market. So, what's the solution, you might ask?

The solution is the free market, sort of. If the government withdrew most of the funding for student aid, no catastrophe would ensue. The colleges would simply have to lower their tuition rates if they wanted to maintain a large student body. The college presidents aren't fools; they wouldn't keep the cost of tuition $300,000, and only have 5% of their current student body. Academic institutions would go bankrupt if they did that. Instead, the colleges would have to lower the rates to at least 50 or 60% of the population could afford to go. That would mean that the consumer-based free market economy would be at work, in which the consumer controls the price of a service, not a government with a seemingly endless power to borrow and print. At that point, four year college tuition rates would come down back below $100,000 for almost every single college (except the Ivy League and the Pac-10). College would be affordable for almost everybody, because every college would want to expand the number of students it could get. However, the government would have to maintain some financial aid for the poorest students. In addition, colleges would now have to compete on an open market where any college could drop its rates as low as it wanted, as opposed to a market in which the government negotiates. The government has an interest in loaning more money because it goes down as more revenue in time.

Having the government negotiate the price for you is a bit like having Vladimir Putin negotiate with Dmitry Medvedev to reduce Russia's nuclear arsenal. Colleges would be incentivized to help students find work under a free market, as those universities that did would get more business. Those universities would also be more inclined to incentivize students to come with a multitude of partial scholarships. So, we could have a giant bubble where college costs $500,000 over time, (including interest) where scholarships become more seldom, and the quality and value of the education itself decreases, where conflicts of interest run amuck, run by a government that never learns its lesson, or we can have cheaper college, more employment out of college, and less of a need to go to college for some of us in a free market. On a separate note, we need to stop continuing education; the universities are bleeding our economy dry. Although college tuition is currently in a state of impending bubble, it is not the biggest bubble that will soon implode on us.

We've all been told for years that healthcare is such a complex market that only professional bureaucrats can deal with the problem; and that we couldn't possibly understand it. Wrong. This market is much simpler than anyone could guess. It is only complicated right now because of insurance companies acting as the middlemen in the market. The cost of healthcare has been skyrocketing because of the need that insurance companies have to make a profit for their shareholders. Currently, premiums on quality insurance run from about $5,000 to $7,000 a year. Most Americans visit the doctor just a few times a year for minor problems and checkups. The raw cost of those visits is well under $500 for most of us (average doctor visit=$100 overall; average number of visits per year=between three and eight). No one can honestly say that this situation does not absolutely scream bubble. It would be much easier for the first 65 years of our lives to just pay for healthcare with cash.

The great dilemma of the healthcare industry is this: If a majority of buyers got more value out of their insurance than they paid in, the insurance company would not exist; it would be bankrupt. If most people put more money into the system than they got out in value, why did they buy insurance when they didn't get any benefit out of it? To illustrate my point a little more clearly, I'll use a couple of examples. Recently, I injured my back. I went into the Chiropractor, who charged us $10 up front for the treatment, and charged the insurance, BCBSM (Blue Cross Blue Shield of MI) $140; that's $150 overall for 15 minutes of treatment. Ten minutes after I sat down in the waiting room, a man from Kentucky, on vacation up North, came in with no insurance. He told the doctor that he had cash, and that he would pay the full amount up front. When he asked the cash price, much to my surprise, the doctor said, "$35 bucks." I was astonished, to say the least. What the doctor had just said had very profound implications, although he did not realize it. What he said meant that every person with insurance in his office was being bilked of $115. Multiply that by the number of customers the doctor has, and you're looking at a heist such that Bonnie and Clyde would be jealous. So, what was happening there was quite simple. My family (or my family's employer) pays $6,000 for insurance, then goes to the doctor, who takes advantage of that fact by charging four and a half times the rate he would if you had cash, knowing that the patient doesn't care; it's money the patient already put in to the insurance. The doctor may use the money to expand his practice, hire new secretaries that can push papers around, or buy himself a mansion.

To the same end, Fox News called a hospital in California out of curiosity to ask about the price of an MRI. The hospital said it would be $6,000. If you had insurance, the insurance company would negotiate it down to $4,000. But, if you had cash, it cost, wait for it, $255! In America, this is what we call a "growing profession," or at least we have for the last 50 years. Like the umpire in *Funny Farm*, I call 'em as I see 'em, and it's a bubble waiting to be burst. The health care industry consists of trillions in investments and incomes getting ready to evaporate forever. I say this because, eventually, people will discover how much cheaper paying with cash is (or employers will), and they will try to do it. Catastrophic insurance will be the new fad (insurance specifically designed for end-of-life and major incidents that is cheaper than traditional insurance, and lets the user pay cash for everything else). The government, however, is trying to block this move with a switch to Obamacare (Affordable Care Act, for those liberals who stop reading at the mention of its alternate name). Through a mandate, the government keeps the bloated insurance companies alive by telling people that they must buy insurance, or pay a penalty of a higher amount (individuals; employers pay less of a penalty than the premiums are). The Democrats will tell you that the sweeping bill that they passed "took on the insurance companies", when, in reality, the biggest lobbying for Obamacare came from health insurance companies. Basically, the government is forcing the people to support the shareholders of large corporations that are not necessary, and are detrimental to the majority of consumers.

Speaking of the Absolutely Clueless Act (ACA; otherwise known as the Affordable Care Act), I'm going to take a paragraph or two here to lambaste it. Obamacare had three basic principles that it was sold to the American people based upon: if you liked your doctor or your insurance, you could keep them. Premiums and health costs under Obamacare were supposed to go down, and everyone was supposed to have healthcare after the bill was passed. To the last point first, the CBO now estimates that 30 million of the approximately 40 million Americans that were uninsured in 2009 will still be uninsured after full implementation. That's 10 million people that got insurance, with a CBO estimated cost right around $3 Trillion. That's three million dollars per person that got insurance. That's one expensive policy. Why is this? Well, that goes to the fact that the second premise of Obamacare has not been fulfilled in any form or fashion. When premiums go up an average of 100%+ in the Midwestern states because of the ACA, not many people are going to be able to afford non-employer health coverage that is any good. By the estimates of any credible source, the additional demand that Obamacare will artificially put in the health insurance market will drive health insurance premiums up by at least 50%, on average, throughout the nation. That's not good for the middle class, especially when the amount and quality of care is going to inevitably go down. We were told, while the bill was making its way through Congress, that 'death panels' didn't exist; that they were just a figment of Sarah Palin's very active imagination. However, Howard Dean, the former Chairman of the DNC, and former governor of Vermont, recently called the Independent Payment Advisory Board (IPAB) a "rationing body" because it would inevitably set the prices of some treatments, deemed by bureaucrats to be too expensive, wasteful, or too helpful toward people that are no longer productive in society, so high that no doctor in his or her right mind would ever perform the procedure. So much for that "no death panels" thing.

To the assertion that Obamacare was a righteous piece of legislation directed at empowering the citizen over the insurance company, I would most sincerely argue the contrary. The tool that was supposed to protect the citizen from excessive deductibles and insurance company pocket-lining, the requirement that insurance companies spend at least 85% of their gross revenue on patient care, was unconstitutionally delayed. Before I get into what that means, I would like to take a minute to prove decisively that what President Obama did by unilaterally (how ironic; a Democratic president did something unilaterally) delaying measures of the ACA was unconstitutional. The legislative branch of government passed a law, which they funded. Thus, the President has to enforce the thing. His assertion is that he was "interpreting" the law as an executive when he delayed the provisions. That is simply ridiculous. If congress passed a law that said no dogs were to be allowed in Congress, the President could not just decree that the word 'no' had been delayed until 2014 even though the law said that it was to go into effect sooner. Changing a law is not interpreting a law; gutting a law is not interpreting a law; and acting as a tyrant is not governing a republic. To the practical implications of the suspension of that part of the ACA, it is very simple. Insurance companies are going to jack up deductibles to ridiculous amounts, they are going to hike their premiums, and they are going to be stingier than ever. This is because insurance companies are going to want to build up as much money as possible before Obamacare goes into effect, after which time, people will begin just getting insurance when they're sick because pre-existing conditions will be accepted, rendering the whole system insolvent. When insurance companies start charging so much for so little actual care and payout, people will begin to demonize them, rather than the government itself. At that point, people will begin filtering into the health care exchanges, giving the program enough capital to at least get off the ground. The other troubling aspect of Obamacare is the fact that the employer mandate (which was unconstitutionally delayed) has penalties for employers that are lower than the cost of insurance premiums. This inevitably means that most businesses will not provide their employees with health care, causing those individuals to go into the exchanges one the mandate takes effect.

Do you see the big picture yet? Serfdom is the big picture; you're being led into a system where your employer won't cover you because the penalty for not covering employees is less than the cost of insurance premiums, good insurance through a private company is unaffordable, and your only real option (unless you work in an exempted union or make a million dollars a year) will be to enter into the government-run system on the exchanges. The only mandate that isn't going to be delayed is the "individual mandate," the most peculiar tax in American history. The reason for not delaying that mandate is to make sure that you do not have the option of demanding lower prices and a free market with the leverage of being able to just not buy. You'll be forced to buy, and no one will want to cheaply cover you. When the cost of private care goes up because of the abandonment of the 85% spending requirement, the exchanges will look cheaper, that's where many will go, and Harry Reid's goal of single-payer will be reached. Thus will end the "how to" guide on how to dismantle the most advanced health care system on the face of the earth, where the patient and doctor cooperate directly without any outside influence. Just for your information, most credible polls (Rasmussen Reports, CNN, Reuters, Fox) showed that 90% of Americans had insurance that they were happy with before the ACA. Many liberal organizations that held similar studies counted people who didn't have insurance for a week while switching between jobs or moving to boost the number of uninsured Americans in their stats from 30 million to 45 million. In reality, Obamacare will get approximately zero people to get insurance for the first time, but it will ruin an entire system that people were decently happy with and keep children mooching off of their parents' insurance until they are fully 26 years old.

In addition, to the whole government investment point, now that the government is going to be heavily involved in the market and subsidizing much of it, premiums are skyrocketing (even though President Obama promised that Obamacare was going to cut premiums). Eventually, when we lose our status as World Reserve Currency, and when other welfare programs become so expensive that we cannot fund healthcare, the government will be forced to pull funding, and the charade will collapse, taking with it either over half of the workers in health care (which will be impossible due to the nurse and doctor shortage), or the wage levels of health care workers (we're talking over half of the salary, if not more). The profession will shed most of its record-keepers and secretaries. People will once again start directly negotiating with their doctors on price and paying what's affordable, which will be much cheaper than the current levels (once again, the consumer-based economy at work). Insurance companies will evaporate, and the amount of money flowing through the health care system will be reduced by at least two-thirds. That means that being a nurse or a nurse's assistant won't be very lucrative anymore.

We will basically be back in the early 1900s, as far as the system of paying goes, when the system finally collapses and people begin to pay for healthcare with cash again. The solution to our current healthcare debacle is simple but painful. Paying with cash and negotiating directly is really the only way to bring down costs dramatically. If insurance companies are to stay alive, we need to open up state lines so that they can compete (Some states in the West and South have much lower premiums than states in the Midwest and Northeast). This will bring down rates for most states, and drive average costs down, as companies from New York and California, Michigan and Minnesota, are forced to lower their rates to stay in business when competing with companies from Texas, Montana, and Wyoming. Tort reform is also in order; if doctors cannot be sued so easily, they will not charge as much for service, because the risk of having to hire an attorney in the future would diminish. Anyhow, either way it happens, the cost of healthcare will come down, and rapidly. When that happens, the years spent in school piling up student loan debt, will not be worth it to most of the workers in the field. Since the government is artificially keeping the bubble going and facilitating an exponential rise in the cost of healthcare, the bubble may not burst for 10, 15, or even 20 years. But it will happen. The lesson of all these examples is relatively simple. If I have one philosophy that is actually practical, it is the one taught to me by my great-grandpa, my parents from buying a house in a bubble, the Depression, the Panic of 1837, school lunches, and tuition rates. If people are telling you to buy something because the price is going up really fast, or to invest in something because the price is going up really fast, or get into a line of work or a market because its profits are going up really fast, run like a hurricane-force wind! Someone up at the top is trying to make a huge short-term profit and pass the buck off to some other poor sucker, usually the consumer (bank bailout, housing crisis, Depression).

Bubbles occur often in the private sector as well, with one major difference: the private sector can only persuade people to buy into a bubble; the government can *compel* people to buy into a bubble, through taxes, or through mandates. One infamous private-sector bubble of late was the 2008 crude oil bubble. Oil was about $100 a barrel at summer's beginning, but people began betting that the economy would grow, and that consumer spending would increase, a pretty dumb bet when you look back on the economic conditions in May and June of 2008. The gamblers, I mean investors, thought that the best representative of the still-strong American consumer economy was oil. These traders bought up oil futures like it was going out of style, and oil rose exponentially, as everyone was betting that the price would keep rising. This links in with the speculation chapter pretty well. The price of oil peaked around $147 a barrel. By that time, most people on Wall Street could plainly see that oil was in bubble mode, reinforced when bad numbers started coming in August. Bottom line: never buy an investment that is already going through the roof; it's coming back down soon. Judge things by their real value, and never buy just because other people are. When you're buying on credit to try to keep up with the Joneses, eventually, you wind up just trying to keep up with the debt collector instead.

The government has more power than a business to propel a bubble forward, because it has the power to print, borrow, and spend almost as much money as it wants. One other newly added power, in particular, makes the government exponentially more powerful in our lives: the individual mandate. The Supreme Court ruled this summer, by 5 to 4 decision, that nationalized healthcare was legal, and that the individual mandate was, too. Chief Justice John Roberts said in his decision that the government was just imposing another form of taxation, which the Constitution clearly gives it the power to do. This decision will be used as precedent by future generations again and again. I'm not really sure if Justice Roberts is aware of the beast that he let loose with that statement: the government now has the power to create commerce in order to regulate it, and can levy a tax that is really a penalty for not buying a specific product with a citizen's own money; it can tax a negative action.

That means that the government could tell you tomorrow that if you do not buy a Chevrolet car for at least $10,000, you must pay an $11,000 fine, and you still don't have a car. No fool would elect not to buy the Chevy. The free market, and freedom itself, are drying up before our very eyes. The U.S. Government could mandate the purchase of a certain type of food, a certain drink, a certain type of schooling, a certain brand of computer, phone, furniture, and it could come up with multiple reasons for the mandate: American-made products, protectionism, product safety, consumer protection, trade purposes, national security, collective good (common good), you name it. But, this all stems from the fact that a group of people in the Northeast and in Washington D.C. think that they are much smarter than everyone else, and that they must save America from itself as a moral obligation. Before you know it, you would be broke if you did not purchase every single product the government wanted you to buy, and you would be living exactly how the government wanted you to live. Mandates dont even work for the purpose of bringing down costs; the auto insurance mandate has only pushed the price of insurance higher because you don't have the option of not buying if the prices are too astronomical; the company would have to go completely bonkers on the price to ever get close to pricing itself out or causing such an uproar that the mandate would be a main campaign issue and be overturned. That system is not constitutionally sound whatsoever, because the government cannot tax you for not buying something, tax you for what you don't have, or tax you for negative property. Look out, because one day, you're going to wake up, and realize that our freedoms have become non-existent, and that the words of Thomas Jefferson's preamble no longer apply to the American Republic.

You may be thinking that the current time period is the first one in which governments have attempted to control a marketplace, but you'd be wrong. I'll give you a guess at which other republic tried to do the same thing. Once again, it's Rome. When in Rome, take notes on how a free society decays and take them forward 2000 years, as my saying goes. When that urban proletariat that we talked about earlier was getting government assistance and draining the treasury, well, the treasury eventually began to run dry. When this happened, the Roman government, in a flash of pure genius (not), attempted to control the prices of goods and services, essentially creating a government-controlled marketplace in all sectors. The government did this because of the rising costs of goods and services, and the result was awful. No one could make a profit, and some sectors evaporated. The government only contributed to keeping bubbles going, not bursting them. This all sounds a little reminiscent of what's going on today, does it not? Just in case this is not ringing a bell, let me take you back to our first experiment in this economic mentality.

Richard Nixon was president, and the price of oil was gaining ground quickly, and wages were stagnant. Inflation was through the roof, the precursor to the more virulent "stagflation" of later in the decade. To try to mitigate the problem, Richard Nixon and moderate Republicans began proposing "wage and price controls," which were marketed widely to the American people as perfectly congruent with a capitalist economy. The result of these policies, which were soon overturned and repealed, was a recession, the likes of which had not been seen since the Great Depression, and Jimmy Carter's infamous "golden malaise" speech. The only way America got out of this recession (still accompanied by stagflation) was to implement free market economics, and lower tax rates for everyone. "A rising tide lifts all boats," as John F. Kennedy once said. The wage and price controls failed horribly. The wages went up, but hiring and promotion rates went through the figurative floor, and prices stayed pretty much where they were before price controls went into place. The only effect of trying to curb inflation was to drive interest rates to all-time highs in the 70s, as everyone high-up began to make a mad dash for cash, anticipating an imminent government takeover of the economy. The only real effect was to make home ownership and car ownership even harder for most, and drive those sectors into the ground.

In short, mandates will not work. Mandates will merely perpetuate bubbles and cycles of exponential price growth, due to the fact that people will be forced into paying whatever the companies are charging, or else pay a higher penalty. As long as the penalties keep rising, companies can keep raising the rates as high as they want, until the system finally collapses. This is how the health care mandate will work: prices on premiums will continue to rise, the government will begin to subsidize premiums in an effort to mitigate the pain on average Americans, rates will keep rising, and we will either go broke, or the people will throw off the mandate. I can only hope that this cycle is completed before America mires herself in a series of mandates, and that the cycle ends in the latter of the two outcomes. What this all boils down to is very simple: someone

1000 miles away can control your life and make all the economic decisions, and bet the well-being of the entire nation on every decision the bureaucracy makes; or Americans can make their own decisions, and no one decision will have the power to bring down the entire economy (Pluralism applied to economics; James Madison's brilliance comes through again). The government will always make mistakes; just look at its predictions about the housing market only a few years before the crash. An individual mandate is just a way for a politician to guarantee his biggest donor a constant customer base or for government and business to collude to make the most money possible off of everyone else. Individual mandates presume that the consumer is too inept to make his/her own decisions, and that the government is a source of infinite wisdom in economics, because we all know how efficient government is (I'm being sarcastic). Elites think that we consumers are fools, and they have to direct the economy from Wall Street and Washington. That won't result in a good economy or stability, and, even if it did, that wouldn't compare to the loss of our liberty. Please, don't save us from ourselves; we're just fine if we control our own economy.

CHAPTER 8

2012: A Monet: The Art of the Mock Election

J ust a while back, we held a big presidential election that you probably remember. If you're at all like me, you didn't just pay attention to the general election, you paid attention to the Republican primaries in the winter of 2011-2012 and the spring of 2012. If so, you'll remember that Mitt Romney had two serious opponents for the nomination of the Republican Party: Newt Gingrich and Rick Santorum. Mitt Romney was criticized in the Republican presidential debates repeatedly for "waffling," and was described as a "Massachusetts Moderate" by Newt Gingrich.

What Mitt Romney actually stood for may never be known to the members of conservative America. He passed a system of socialized medicine in his own state of Massachusetts, called himself left of Ted Kennedy on gay marriage, and included abortion coverage in his Romneycare package in Massachusetts. He was in favor of the bank bailouts, although he was infamously opposed to the auto bailouts. No one really does know what Mitt Romney feels; where he is on economics, social issues, or the military. He was a man who made the same speech 100 times over, and made no bones about it.

Mitt Romney won the Republican primary for one reason: he had more money than anybody else. Newt Gingrich was outspent 20 to one in the early primary states of South Carolina and Florida, and after his defeat in Florida, he was no longer a real contender (barring his near comeback on Super Tuesday when he almost won Tennessee in addition to Georgia). He dwarfed every other contender in the Republican race in fundraising. That was his single strongest suit. With hundreds of millions of dollars in Super Pac money (mostly from large donations, whereas Santorum and Gingrich raised most of their cash from small donors), Romney beat the former speaker to smithereens, with seemingly no reverence for the speaker's accomplishments (negotiating a balanced budget with Clinton, Republican Stampede of 1994, aiding in the resurgence of free-market economics, and the Contract With America).

I was personally a Gingrich supporter during the primary season, and predicted, at the first GOP presidential debate, that Romney would lose if nominated. Mitt Romney was supported widely by the Republican establishment during the primary, on the grounds that, "He is the most likely to beat Obama." This was false right from the beginning. Mitt Romney was exactly the kind of candidate that could not win, even in a down economy. The truth was that Mitt Romney's non-stance on social issues, combined with his waffling on every single constitutional issue, made him unacceptable to much of the party's base, including me. If you look at where Mitt Romney lost the election county by county, he didn't lose it in swing counties.

He won Lake County Ohio, he beat 2008 margins in Volusia County, Florida, he closed tremendously in Macomb County, Michigan, he won Culpepper County, Virginia in a landslide, and he won King and Queen County, Virginia, which is usually a very good indicator of where the state as a whole is going. So, in hindsight, Mitt Romney lost the election in two places. First, he thought the urban turnout would never, ever, ever in 1 million to the power of 1 million years, reach the level that it did in 2008, and he was wrong. Obama got higher turnout in most urban counties than he did in 2008, although his margins went down.

The most crucial place in which Mitt Romney lost the election was in rural areas. Mitt Romney missed 2008 turnout marks in every rural county in Western Ohio, Southern Virginia, North Florida, and Western Iowa. He underperformed in these areas for the very same reason that he was nominated: he was a moderate with a lot of business experience. Someone should have told Karl Rove that a non-stance on abortion and gay marriage, coupled with dumb comments about money, and not being a fervent supporter of gun rights doesn't play well in Washington County, Ohio, Swain County, North Carolina, Highland County, Virginia, or Nassau County, Florida. When you look at who donated to the Mitt Romney campaign, it becomes perfectly obvious that Wall Street really didn't want Gingrich, Santorum, or Ron Paul to be the nominee. One must ask, then, how did Mitt Romney get the nomination for the Republican Party, and why did the Republican establishment support him?

It's a question I'm not sure I have the exact answer to. I can say that the powers that be would've been just fine with either Mitt Romney or Barack Obama as president of the United States. Either way, the banks would still get supported if they made too many bad loans and crashed again, the Federal Reserve would keep printing money like mad, we would stay in a stagnant economy, Mitt Romney would not return us to the days of Reagan because he's wasn't Ronald Reagan, the deficit would stay high, and we would have four more years in the direction we were going. We had a choice between somebody to keep going and someone from the other party to preside over the decline. In short, we didn't have a choice.

Mitt Romney and Barack Obama both thought that government spending was the best way to stimulate the economy. Call me crazy; if you listen to Mitt Romney's speeches (that were scripted and given to him by Republican operatives), you would never think that. What gives me the absolute confidence to say that about Mr. Romney is the press release that he gave about the "Fiscal Cliff" and the sequester when the super committee failed. Mitt Romney's campaign said that the sequester cuts were unacceptable because such a sharp and sudden decrease in government spending would jar the economy. I guess the real Mitt Romney came through there. That's the way Romney felt when he was in Massachusetts; he favored individual mandates at the state level, and didn't really trust the consumer-based marketplace. The only place where he trusts the free marketplace is when he's making money on it, when elites are in control of the market. In short, he's the last of a dying breed, a breed I call the Hamiltonian Republicans for a reason we'll get into later.

The only places where Mitt Romney promised to cut were deductions and loopholes, where you can't possibly balance the budget. Pres. Obama was worse; he didn't want to cut anywhere, and he wanted to raise taxes. But, the lack of fiscal responsibility in both parties, and the support that Mitt Romney received from the establishment is astonishing. It almost suggests a conspiracy to keep America from having a real choice between liberal and conservative, or moderate to conservative and moderate to liberal. I'll tell you what, I think I'm a pretty honest person, but if I was running Goldman Sachs, and I was making 50 billion dollars a year as a corporation, I might think it was a great idea to invest a billion dollars every four years to make sure that the status quo didn't change, and that no real free-market conservative, constitutionalist, or any ultra-liberal could ever win the election. In fact, I would have a vested interest in making sure that we get deeper in debt, because that means that the Federal Reserve keeps printing money, and the former head of my corporation now controls another Trillion dollars in debt, and the right to collect interest on it. It's a really powerful faction.

The financial establishment is a faction that has become a wing of the government unto itself. That faction has a vested interest in making sure the nominees of both parties are as elitist and anti-free market as possible, especially in down economic times when those factions might need government assistance. Romney would not have governed as a conservative, and would have been elitist in his economic viewpoint, even if subconsciously. Neither candidate was where 42% of America is in every credible poll: in the conservative column.

President Obama let General Electric pay $0 in taxes during 2010 (fair share in practice), and got a good deal of his 2008 and 2012 campaign contributions from Goldman Sachs, General Electric, and other large Wall Street firms, and Mitt Romney got most of his donations from the exact same people, with the exception of oil companies. Wake up, America, there was not a choice last year, and America would have headed down basically the same path, no matter which way the election went. You were choosing between Liberal and Liberal-light. Hold onto your hats, because the entire Republican Party establishment is vying for the party to nominate a candidate even more moderate for the 2016 elections, and think that we have a huge "demographics problem." I've got news for them: look at the county map, you lost it in rural areas, the conservatives didn't show up; you have an elitist problem! We've nominated two moderates in a row now, and lost twice. The definition of insanity is trying something over and over and expecting a different result. So, I can safely say that some of my party is insane if we think our way to victory in 2016 will be paved by a moderate. The Republican establishment can't possibly be that stupid, they must be in on the plot to deprive America of choice. The members of GOP establishment don't want conservatism; they want oligarchy, permitted by a polarized electorate voting on social issues in an election with two nearly identical candidates on economics. The Hamiltonian elites in this country win no matter which candidate hits 270 that first Tuesday after the first Monday in November. Eventually, the GOP will move so far to the left that the party splits in half, with about 80% of us on the right side (the new party), and about 20% loyal to the party label. It will be just like the emergence of the original Republicans in the 1850s. It is the only way to make sure that a plurality of America gets its voice heard, and that we have real choices in elections, and an open, deliberative, and honest debate. For now, the game goes on.

CHAPTER 9

Ayatollah Ya' so: Defense

Since September of 2001, the United States has found itself locked in a bloody conflict with radical enemies 5000 miles away, galvanized by their belief, and completely off of their rockers. We have spent a few trillion dollars, a few thousand lives, and 11 years now fighting in the Middle East. We can't seem to beat them, because it is very difficult to beat an enemy without a uniform that is not fighting because of the military incentive. It is also very difficult to fight enemies and beat them on their own turf; on ground they know very well. Britain had to learn this lesson when it was a great empire by fighting the American Revolution, in which the British lost to an enemy galvanized by common morals and radical beliefs, entrenched in its homeland, under attack from a great world power. You may think that we are the first nation to fight a war in the Middle East against radicals, or even to have a general radical problem, and you'd be wrong. Surprise, surprise, Rome did the exact same thing.

Of all the enemies that Rome had on the European mainland, the one that it couldn't seem to shake was the resistance effort put forth by the Spanish. The Romans took over France (then called Gaul) rather quickly, disposed of barbarians like there was nothing to it in Eastern Europe, the Balkans, Greece, and the Alps region. But, when Rome ran into Southern Spain in the south and the Rhine

River in the north, it was brought to an abrupt halt in its spread to the west. The fight against the rebels was costly to the empire; it began to drain the treasury of much-needed funds for infrastructure at home, as the Romans built infrastructure farther and farther to the west. In fact, the Romans built extensive infrastructure everywhere they went, sometimes gaining the favor of local populations when they did.

The Romans kept sending wave after wave of military offensives after the Spanish rebels, but they could not be defeated. As soon as it seemed that the enemy was defeated at long last, a new generation of radicals would rise up, and begin to make up lost ground to the north until another legion was sent by the Senate or emperor. The cycle went on like this for centuries, slowly sucking the life out of the Roman economy, and causing constant budget deficits (along with internal factors in Rome). Eventually, Rome could pay no longer for the fighting in all theaters, and the rebels built up strength, moving east slowly, terrorizing Roman settlements in Western Gaul (France), and formerly conquered Eastern Spain with guerilla tactics. Their strategy for the entire war was simple: wait out the big, powerful country, and let them spend as much as they want on the war. Hide, use guerilla tactics, and make the war expensive, awkward, and difficult for Rome by not fighting conventionally. Drag the war on by creating generation after generation of radicals through the established customs, making it impossible to snuff you out. Take the infrastructure projects that Rome wants to construct for future settlement, and use them to your advantage in the future. Let the war drain the Roman economy, at which point the Romans would be forced to divert money from their increasingly unpopular and costly war. The rebels' strategy eventually worked, and they brought down (with plenty of help from Rome itself and Visigoths) the greatest empire the world had yet known. The same thing happened to the Romans when they tried to take over North Africa and push ever further into Palestine and the Middle East. The empire was fighting a group of people that were not nearly as advanced as they were, had a very simple economy, but had a very strong motivation that could not be beaten on a military battlefield, because they didn't fight like a conventional military.

The same exact thing is happening to us 2000 years later. Although we may win short-term battles, we will never completely eradicate radical Islam through military means; it's impossible. You'd think we'd figure that strategy out by now, seeing as we invented it! Think back to the Revolution. George Washington used strategies that were though of at the time as "improper" like hiding behind trees to fight, ambushing, and using guerilla tactics in cities that the British had already taken by conventional means like Charleston. We were fighting the most powerful nation on earth at the time, and used the familiar territory to our advantage with surprise attacks, reminiscent of how the Islamic radicals are conducting their war right now.

Like them, the American revolutionaries of the 1700s were united by a common ideology that did not necessarily pervade the society, but that was deeply rooted, and invoked passion. It is estimated that about one-third of Americans in 1775 were Patriots, one-third wanted to remain loyal to the King, and one-third didn't care one way or the other. The same thing is happening to us.

The Islamic radicals are not in the majority in most Middle Eastern nations, but their numbers are nothing to be sneezed at either, and their main binding is the rigid ideology that they share. The same strategy was employed 40 years ago by Hoh Chi Minh to win the Vietnam War. The idea is that you are not fighting to win; you are fighting to tie. In the irony of all ironies, Ho Chi Minh studied George Washington's tactics to fight us in Vietnam.

Although I agree with staying in the Middle East because the best defense is a good offense, at some point, we won't be able to keep up our presence. When this happens, even if it is just for a small amount of time, the radicals can re-strengthen their ranks, and a new generation will come of age to fight. The radicals will use all of the infrastructure that we left to their own advantage, and, before you know it, we've lost. We are currently replicating Rome's mistake with infrastructure as well.

In the recently ended Iraq War, we started off with all soldiers in Iraq to march on Baghdad and take down Saddam Hussein, the original objective of the mission. When we got Saddam Hussein out of power, the objective became to snuff out insurgents. Everybody knew that this kind of war would be long and drawn out. With this prospect, military contractors saw an opportunity to make a huge profit. Part of this would be providing service for the troops (substandard service at that), another would be building infrastructure in Iraq. We hoped that if we helped the Iraqis develop their economy, they might be grateful (sort of like the Romans thought that helping Palestine and North Africa would improve Rome's standing with those people). KBR-Blackwater and Halliburton sucked up hundreds of billions of dollars in tax money to build Iraqi infrastructure from 2003 to 2011, money that would have been spent at home, or left in the American economy.

Personally, I am not attacking George Bush's war strategy at all. If you think that an enemy of yours, especially a radical dictator who oppresses his own people, has a nuclear or biological warhead, take them out. I even agreed with the decision to stay in Iraq, because insurgents were still there. However, it should not have been U.S. policy to build Iraqi infrastructure with tax money. We probably should have known that this gesture wouldn't help any; after all, Ronald Reagan tried the same thing with the Afghanis when they were being attacked by the Soviet Union, arming the Taliban with assault weapons. We all know how well that worked out; the Afghan rebels turned the guns on the United States and its allies. We should also have been intellectually honest with ourselves at the outset of the anti-insurgent war. We should have admitted that it would be a long and costly war, and accepted the obligations of it. But, we chose to kid ourselves, and say that we would win in no time, because we were the biggest superpower on earth, just like the Romans did two millennia ago. We were not prepared for the cost and lingering time, and we have pulled out.

Here's another striking similarity: part of those price shocks that I talked about the Romans being vulnerable to earlier happened because of the Middle East. When the Romans started growing cash crops in huge numbers as I mentioned earlier, they had to import all their grain. Due to this, much of Rome's grain started coming from the rich growing areas in the "Fertile Crescent," of Turkey, Syria, and parts of Lebanon, in addition to the Nile River Valley of Egypt. Anytime a conflict broke out in a rebellious province of the empire (usually Judea or an adjacent province), merchants drove up the price of grain coming from those regions, which, in time, became nearly all of Rome's grain.

As a result, Rome's military activities became very closely related to the price of essential products for the Roman homeland. Rome's cost of living became dependent on a bunch of rebels in a province 2000 miles away, and the cost of living rose steadily, sometimes going through periods of exponential growth. The Roman military suddenly found themselves defending strategic grain-producing areas in the Middle East, and using much funding from the public treasury to do so. Along with many other factors, this instability in the grain market helped to bring Rome's economy down, and erode the trust the citizens had in their existing institutions. The "barbarians" figured out that they held an inordinate amount of leverage over the most advanced, richest nation on earth, because they produced a product that Rome did not want to produce at home. The irony of it all is that Rome could have solved at least one of its problems by producing its grain at home; Rome had enough fertile land to feed itself by a country mile.

The same thing is happening to the United States right now. Oil is a product that we depend on to carry out our everyday lives. Yet, we find ourselves in a constant fix with nations in the Middle East that are hurdling headlong into the 1st century, that have discovered that they have leverage over the most advanced, most prosperous nation on the face of earth. Even though we have been able to overcome against all odds and become a world superpower, we are at the mercy of squabbles in the Middle East. The oil spike of 2011 (March and April) was largely driven by fears of conflict in the Middle East and the emergence of the "Arab Spring," conflicts in Southwest Asia and North Africa. In the spring of 2011, oil went up from $90 a barrel in mid-January to over $119 at its late April peak. Gasoline prices shot up from $2.90 to over $4.20 that spring at my local gas station. Every penny that gas rises, a billion dollars is taken out of the United States economy. That means that over 130 billion dollars ($130,000,000,000) was taken out of the economy that spring. Who do you think is winning?

Among Al Qaeda plans discovered in sleeper cells, one popular one is to defeat the United States by bringing down our economy, raising gas prices with constant small attacks in strategic areas, and eroding America's morale and freedoms. Uh-uh, TSA; sorry; I had something in my throat there. Like the Romans, our military is forced to spend great sums of money to defend strategic positions in the oil trade when we could just produce the product ourselves. However, we don't want to produce the product ourselves, for different reasons than the Romans, of course. We're worried about the environmental consequences of oil drilling, even though oil incidents are very rare, and we could attain energy independence for about fifteen years if we developed the Bakken shale area, Alaska, and the Gulf at full potential. But no, we would rather have our cost of living be dictated to us by a sheik or an Iatola. Eventually, every addict's day of reckoning comes, as ours inevitably will. If we don't break our addiction to Middle Eastern oil soon, it will bring us down. Canada will sell most of its oil to the highest bidder, which will soon be China, not us. The Canadians are not going to save us; we're the only ones that can save ourselves. For now, it's scary how volatile our markets are, and for the same reasons that Rome's were. Price shocks in grain and price shocks in oil are the same thing with two different products in two very different time periods.

This past year was one of the most dangerous ever in Iraq. The radicals are returning in force, Iran is starting to make its presence known in Iraq, and a new generation of insurgents is emerging. In addition to Iraq, we have problems in Iran, Libya, Syria, Turkey, Israel, Gaza, Egypt, Sudan, Somalia, Yemen, Pakistan, and Afghanistan. You could find a less volatile climate on the surface of Venus (not really). For the most part, if you point to a point on the globe between Greece and India, there's a strategic threat that America faces from that area. Every one of these problems is fixable, but not easily. Taken together, along with this administration's horrendous foreign policy and defense department appointees, we're probably not going to tackle them in my lifetime. In fact, these problems are probably going to tackle us. Let's try to take them one at a time, shall we?

The first nation we have a major issue with right now is Egypt. We obviously have not learned from our mistakes, as Pres. Obama remarked in the "Arab Spring" of 2011 that Egypt would be a new democracy, reminiscent of other Western democracies in the Middle East. We can all see how well that worked out. Egypt's majority party in parliament, before the most recent revolution, was the Muslim Brotherhood, and Egypt is currently governed by Sharia law in most areas, only getting relief from a popular military. For a while, the United States considered giving backing in the form of arms to the rebels when they were attempting to take down the regime of Hosni Mubarak. That would've been a disastrous idea. We would've literally given the Muslim brotherhood some of the most advanced weapons on earth, and the military would have had a much tougher time taking down the brotherhood. My favorite history teacher says, "If we've learned anything from history, it's that we haven't learned anything from history." That holds true in the Middle East, and especially with the Obama administration.

Ronald Reagan tried to give arms to Afghan rebels in the 1980s; and they used the weapons against us. The weapons we gave the Iraqis to defend themselves, and the Afghans we've trained in Afghanistan are already turning against us. It should come as no surprise that a nation where over 70% of the citizens in a poll just before the revolution wanted "strict Sharia law" (somewhat strict; as the recent revolution has demonstrated, about 70% of Egypt is on the side of the secular military rather than the brotherhood) has had such a tumultuous period, in which Coptic Christians have had their churches burned. This would be no cause for concern, if Egypt did not control the Suez Canal, where most of Europe's oil supply passes through, along with some of North America's. The Germans and the British fought extensively over the little strip of land in Northern Egypt, with the battle finally culminating in the defeat of Erwin Rommel at El Alamein. Those two behemoths were not fighting over this little piece of the Sahara desert for grins and giggles; Hitler knew that if he could get the oil supplies of the Middle East, or even cut off the British oil supply coming through the Suez Canal from the Brits' Indian and other Middle Eastern colonies, he could effectively shut down the British war effort.

Egypt is a pretty important nation in the Muslim world. In this case, the U.S. Government gives Egypt approximately $1.3 billion every year in military and foreign aid. Most people don't know why we give other nations foreign aid, and in this case it is pretty unique. Following the Yom Kippur war in the mid-1970s, in which Israel took the Sinai Peninsula and defeated both Syria and Egypt simultaneously, the world looked to peace negotiations. Jimmy Carter was the head of the negotiations, which culminated in the Camp David Accords. Although hailed as Jimmy Carter's greatest accomplishment (which isn't saying much), the deal essentially boiled down to the United States giving foreign aid to Egypt, as their economy was in ruins, in exchange for relatively friendly relations toward Israel, in a general agreement that the Egyptians would not attack Israel again. We've increased our foreign aid multiple times since then to the Egyptians, as world inflation has gone ever faster. Currently, we're faced with an interesting debacle. If we pull out the money, there is the very real prospect that a desperate Egypt (the inflation in Egypt equates to $30 loaves of bread) will roll every tank it has across the Sinai Peninsula to attack Israel to unite the nation, and a state that is staunchly anti-Israel and anti-Western will control the Suez Canal. If Egypt attacked Israel from across the Sinai, there is no doubt that Syria would immediately join in from the north and east, essentially repeating the Yom Kippur war, only this time, Israel already has insurgents in the Gaza Strip and the West Bank, Iran is a larger factor, and Turkey might also come in on the radical Islam aside.

Israel is a very small strip of land in the Mediterranean Sea area, and doesn't have a very big fuel supply. If the United States and Europe were unable to get fuel to the Israelis through Turkey, Syria, or Lebanon, the Israelis might run out of fuel for their jets and tanks readily. Israel would not have the same advantages that it had in the 1970s; it would be a much bigger underdog in this sort of Middle East conflict. Unless the United States or Western Europe came down solidly on the side of the Israelis, there is a very big possibility that the Israelis could lose all of their territory. That's not the distressing part.

The distressing part is that we didn't show any sign (at least from the White House) of retracting our foreign aid to Egypt when they had a Muslim Brotherhood-run government, we didn't seem to be thinking about an embargo, we didn't seem to be thinking about economic pressures, and we certainly didn't seem to be thinking about reestablishing a military presence in the Middle East at a time when it's politically popular to pull out. However, now that the Egyptian people have thrown off their radical regime; one that was disobeying religious freedom and its own constitution, we *are* considering retracting all of our foreign and military aid. If there were ever a time when we should be giving somebody other than Israel foreign aid, it would be right now in Egypt. There is a good reason why President Obama is not appreciative of what the Egyptian military has done for its people.

The radical Muslims took power by way of a popular election, in which they campaigned on moderate Muslim principles, rather than secular rules, governing the country, and a revision of the economy. When in power, the Muslim Brotherhood began subverting and changing the constitution in ways that the people did not approve of, causing demonstrations in the streets. When the Brotherhood continued to pursue a radical agenda, the military of Egypt stepped in, knowing that the United States would probably not back the Brotherhood, even though it was democratically elected. Taken in perspective, what the people of Egypt are doing is the most patriotic and Jeffersonian thing that they could possibly do. They are throwing off a tyrannical government that relinquished its right to call itself democratic when it violated the constitution and the people's popular sovereignty. When Leeland Vitter, a correspondent for Fox News in the Middle East, reported on the Egyptian violence recently, he reported that citizens, in the early morning hours, were preparing to fight the Muslim Brotherhood demonstrators right alongside the government forces. Those Egyptians that support the military, the Rule of Law, and their own sovereignty, are patriots; carrying on one of Thomas Jefferson's most frightening quotes, "The tree of liberty must be refreshed, from time to time, with the blood of patriots and tyrants." When 70% of the nation is on a side contrary to its present government in an armed government, it is not a coup, it is a righteous revolution. However, President Obama does not see it this way, largely because he does not even respect our Constitution, why should he respect Egypt's? Our President believes in a government that can pass anything with a majority vote between elections, whether or not it complies with existing law; a democracy in which the State acts in what is deems as the citizens' best interest, only curtailed by the occasional election.

While Egypt's Muslim brotherhood government was in power, we agreed to give them thirty F-16 fighters and 300 M1A1 Abrams Main Battle Tanks (MBTs) capable of inflicting serious damage on Israel. However, now that sane, moderate people are temporarily in control, we have stopped our shipment, apparently waiting for more radical Muslims in disguise to win the next election. Why would we give radicals that have, as their stated goal, to persecute Coptic Christians in Egypt and destroy Israel weapons of war? We could stump Aristotle with this one! As Lewis Black would say it, "It kind of makes you dizzy." This is one of those things where you have to agree with what Donald Trump has been telling us for a decade: that other countries are laughing hysterically at us. What nation would borrow money to give their enemies weapons? Well, us, obviously.

Iran has been adversarial towards the United States ever since the 1970s, with the Iranian hostage crisis. Although the Iranians have always been somewhat unfriendly to the West, they've never really had any leverage, because they didn't have much oil, and because they didn't have a very big military. But, nothing is quite as apt at persuading other nations to care about you as a threat of a thermo-nuclear warhead. Iran is currently hurtling toward having nuclear weapons, and estimates range between the next six months and five years as to when the Iranians will have enough enriched uranium to make a bomb and have the missile technology to put that warhead on a missile and send it to an enemy nation, depending on which source you choose to believe.

Although we are pursuing sanctions against Iran, it doesn't think that the military option is on the table. Regardless of their religion, their radicalism, their craziness, or their ambitions, our enemies are not idiots; they know that America will never engage itself in another war within the next couple decades, because it's politically unpopular. Our enemies are also well aware that the only thing backing up America's threats and sanctions are more threats, words, and sanctions. Iran's last president, Ahmadinejad, was certifiably insane, and said multiple times that he wished to bomb Israel back into the Stone Age, and viewed America as the great Satan. Iran recently got a new president, President Hassan Rouhani. Rouhani campaigned as a moderate to court the vote of younger Iranians, but has had extensive ties to radicals in the past (that sounds so familiar). Rouhmani played a key role in the overthrow of the American-installed Shah, has been good friends with the Ayatollah Khamenei (a radical), and wrote his doctorial thesis about how Sharia law would govern the nations of the Middle East forever. Some moderate. Underneath Rouhmani's electable exoskeleton is a man that is every bit as radical as his predecessor, and probably just as dedicated to the vision of a nuclear Iran.

As radical as Rouhmani probably is, the Iranian people are much more sensible (at least a plurality of them). In order to win the last mock election, I meant election, in which he participated, Ahmadinejad had to commit massive voting fraud and intimidate young voters in the urban provinces. Iran's economy is in the dumps. Unemployment is sky-high, so is the cost of living, and living conditions are abominable. The people of Iran are not happy at all with their Ayatollahs or radical leaders. The majority of Iran is against the development of nuclear weapons, because they know that it will bring more sanctions and less economic development from the Western world. Most members of the Islamic religion are not radicals like Ahmadinejad or Rouhmani. That would be like saying that most Christians are like Jerry Falwell.

For now, the centrifuges keep spinning, despite attempts at economic sanctions. Stopping Iran's nuclear ambitions has to be a two-part strategy: first, we have to further cripple Iran's economy and get every possible investor in Iranian oil (Russia, China) to line up against them; second, we have to convince the crazy Ayatollahs that are not deterred by anything economic that the United States is well prepared to take military action in Persia. To do that, we frankly need a new president. The Obama administration is continually warning and scolding other nations, but no real threats of military force are ever made. I am not a war hawk by any means, but peace through strength is the only realistic solution to many of our problems. During Ronald Reagan's Presidency, most of the world feared the power of America, although they knew that we would not be the aggressor. They knew the consequences of going rogue. America's power was projected throughout the globe as a peacekeeping force.

President Obama was directly asked by Bill O'Reilly whether military force was on the table, and he said that we had to keep all of our options open. When asked for a yes or no, he dodged the question. When President Obama spoke in Cairo, Egypt and toured the Middle East, he said that America had been arrogant and overpowering in the past. If Iran doesn't think that America is prepared to back up our rhetoric with force, they won't succumb to sanctions, they'll wait them out. Military force should always be the last resort, but it should always be an option. The bottom line is this: on Iran, we have to make our presence very strong in the Persian Gulf. We need to always keep a fleet in the Indian Ocean area, and we need to have troops and aircraft in the area. We need to re-adopt a policy of peace through strength to make known to the world that we will not hesitate to use military force when appropriate. We have to apply tighter sanctions on Iran, putting internal pressure on the Iranian government, and use our $16 Trillion GDP to leverage our will (better use it now; we won't have it for long). We need to tell the Chinese and Russians that if they don't stop investing in Iranian oil (they are currently keeping any harsh sanctions from passing the UN Security Council), we will stop buying their goods (We are the biggest customers of the Chinese). For the Russians, we could threaten their European natural gas monopoly by telling them that the hoards of new natural gas that America produces from hydro-fracking could be liquefied and sent to Europe cheaply, rather than staying in North America and Latin America for even less. Something tells me that trillions will outweigh a few hundred billion for the Russians. However, if we don't get the Russians and Chinese on board, a horrific scene could play out as a result of a small conflict in the Middle East.

Imagine that the Israelis estimate that Iran will have a nuke in about three months, and decide to launch a pre-emptive strike without U.S. assistance. When the Israelis attack the Iranians, they knock out the vast majority of Iran's military infrastructure and buildings, but not all of it. Iran knows that it cannot fight off the Israelis if it engages in a long war, but that it still has some underground nuclear facilities too far below the surface for the fighters to destroy. The Iranians decide to leverage their investments, and tell the Russians and Chinese that if they do not give Iran military assistance, the Russians' and Chinese's hundreds of billions (possibly trillions) in oil investments would dry up as Iran descended into anarchy and the government lost control. China is perhaps the most aggressive oil-investing nation on earth right now; it needs the oil to power its rapid economic growth. China is attempting to buy up reserves all over the planet right now, because that's its one weakness. East Asia has virtually no fossil fuel reserves. This issue caused the Japanese to attack Pearl Harbor to keep their war effort fueled, and plagued the Japanese in the later years of World War II. The Chinese and Russians would probably not be too happy to see hundreds of billions in oil dry up overnight.

Now picture that the Russians and Chinese jumped in to fight the Israelis, launching a naval fleet into the Persian Gulf/Arabian Sea/Suez Canal area, with the Russians deploying a fleet into the Black Sea and Mediterranean. All of a sudden, the U.S. ships in the Persian Gulf are surrounded by two superpowers, and the Israelis are under attack by two of the most powerful militaries on earth. The Israelis appeal for help, and we accept. All of a sudden, alliance systems kick in across Europe, and World War III is reality. Only this time, nuclear and biological weapons (like smallpox mutated for 90-95% lethality rates) are unleashed all around the planet. I don't want to sound like a zealot, but this would sound a lot like Revelation 6:6 (Great Bear, Dragon, and False Prophet all descend on Holy Land). If America does not jump into in this conflict, Israel is wiped out, and we lose our only ally in the Middle East. If we lose Israel, the entire Middle East will be united in its struggle against America. Add to that the growing Islamic influence in Europe, and this is not a pretty picture. So you see, we had better get Russia on board before anything breaks out.

Libya is a different beast entirely. Even though Muammar Gaddafi was a tyrannical dictator who needed to go anyway, that's not why we attacked Libya (and violated the Constitution by not having Congress declare war, "presidential actions" are only supposed to be allowed to last 30 days without congressional approval). We attacked the Libyans because Gaddafi wanted to set up an African currency that would make it easier for Libya's oil reserves to produce more internal profits for them (along with increasing ease of trade across Africa, cutting down Western profits in the region).

Currently, crude oil must be paid for in U.S. dollars anywhere around the world, making it rather difficult for oil-producing nations to turn a large profit on their own product. Why we intervened is not entirely clear aside from the former point. Muammar Gaddafi was not accused of holding nuclear weapons or chemical weapons, we knew that his military was relatively weak, and Libya is not a strategic position in the Middle East. Yet, without the approval of Congress, or a majority of the American people on board, the president spent billions of dollars firing cruise missiles into Libya, and sending ground troops into Libya. The Constitution allows for the president to send troops anywhere without Congress's approval for thirty days.

However, after a scathing critique of George W. Bush by the Democratic Party for sending troops into Iraq without a declaration of war (Congress actually voted its approval on that one) violating Iraq's sovereignty, going in pointlessly, and spending taxpayer money, President Obama sent America into Libya, a place that we knew didn't have any advanced weaponry, unlike Iraq, and kept troops there for over three months, clearly violating the Constitution for no apparent reason, other than that hanging around in the Sahara Desert in the middle of summer must be a lot of fun for the Marines, I guess. Once again, for the sake of tearing down a dictator, we gave weapons to rebels that we still don't know much about, except that most of them believe in fundamental jihad in Libya. Pure genius. Those weapons will probably come back to haunt us very soon, as they have every time we have armed a Middle Eastern faction. Although we spent hundreds of millions, or even billions, on cruise missiles and ground forces, and we went totally against what the Democrats are supposed to stand for on national security (anti-interventionist, don't intervene in Middle Eastern countries, don't break the Constitution, have Congress declare war, and don't support large corporations with American military power) the Benghazi scandal puts the icing on the proverbial cake.

The amount of bumbling you have to commit to not have security around the consulate the day after a major demonstration in Egypt, which just happened to be the day before September 11, would make Inspector Clouseau very jealous. Imagine for a quick second that you, yes you, are the president of The United States. You are faced, in the spring of 2011, with an emergent situation in Libya, where a tyrannical dictator is oppressing a faction of freedom fighters in the nation. Now imagine that you campaigned against George W. Bush's interventionist policies, and "meaningless" wars. Some in Congress are calling for a UN-enforced no-fly one over Libya, which would prevent Gaddafi from bombing his own population. Intelligence agencies are reporting that many of the members of the resistance are in support of strict Sharia law and belong to radical Muslim organizations. Would you go in on the ground and support the rebels? Of course not. But, if you did, you would at least pull out after 30 days, right, to preserve the constitutional authority of the War Powers Act, and stay true to your criticisms of George W.

Bush? I would too, because it is the right thing to do constitutionally. However, President Obama did not even do this; our troops were in Libya for over three months. At least if you committed ground forces, you would expect a hostile local population and keep security high around all the U.S. buildings in the region. With President Obama, no dice. What we did was to lean on the United Nations forces (which are mostly American anyway), violate the Constitution for absolutely nothing, then not have security around the consulate on 9/11. There are no words that can sum up the sheer stupidity that it takes to remove security forces from that consulate, and not respond to Ambassador Steven's repeated requests for increased security and feelings that he was in danger. I guess Pres. Obama thought that he was just so much more popular than President Bush that the Libyans would be grateful to be invaded by the United States with him as our president. Sadly, that was not the case.

When our embassies were attacked on related September 11, it was a military-style raid by a few people with high powered weapons, and many lower-level officials at the State Department testified that they were watching and hearing the entire thing play out, all while air support sat only a few hundred miles away across the Mediterranean. Air support could've been there within the first three hours of the eight hour fight, yet the people that did try to help Ambassador Stevens and his crew out were actually ordered not to help them by the United States. What's more is that a lower member of the State Department actually testified that the department was watching the whole thing unfold in real time, standing by as it happened. The man who went in had to disobey orders to try to save lives. Hillary Clinton recently said under oath that it didn't make a difference whether the attack on our consulate was an act of terror, and if the administration knew about it, and its motivations, before it informed the public. I happen to think that it is very important, and a little bit telling of the extent of the Washington elite culture, if the government knowingly lies to its people and thinks nothing of it. She also said under oath that the lack of a response from the State Department and a feeble understanding of the circumstances of the attack were spurred on by the State Department not getting the messages of Ambassador Stevens asking for more security around the consulate and the messages of attack on September 11. Assuming that the lower State Department official was lying about watching the incident in real-time for no apparent reason or gain, that statement is still a bunch of malarkey, to take a line from Joe Biden. Senator Rand Paul of Kentucky pointed out during the testimony of Hillary Clinton that the State Department responded to messages from consulates in India and Eastern Europe that were requesting funding for comedians and other entertainment. If the State Department was paying attention to those requests, there is no way in Holder (look at that; a pun) that it was not acutely aware of the Libyan consulate's requests for more security. In addition, I don't think that the lower-level State Department officials were lying about watching the whole thing unfold in real time. We let the murder of Ambassador Stevens happen, why, I don't know. Just like that scene *A Few Good Men*, now we'll never know, will we?

Due to our presence there, we are creating another hotbed of Islamic radicalism. All this under the administration of a president who ran his entire campaign, prior to the stock market crash in September of 2008, on a non-interventionist policy. I hope it was all worth it to get Muammar Gaddafi.

Since the earliest days of the Israeli state, perhaps its greatest and most immediate problem has been to its north and east. Today, Syria is considered a State Sponsor of Terror, and the Golan Heights area is once again divided between the two rival nations. Hezbollah has a significant influence in the Syrian government and the society as a whole. Bashar-Al-Assad has already slaughtered tens of thousands of his own people in an effort to quell the rebellion in his nation (largely made up of radical Islamists who believe in jihad). He really needs something to unite those people and distract them from the fact that they have a tyrannical government, in which they have no say whatsoever.

You can see where this is going. Just think of *Canadian Bacon* with John Candy. Remember the scene where the president's assistant suggests a war to distract the country from the tough economy and deteriorating morals? To the president's question about whether the thought of Canada preparing for war with the USA would distract the nation, the assistant says, "By the end of the week, we'll have the people burning maple leaves so fast they'll forget all about their dwindling savings accounts and pay cuts." That would be the perfect ploy for Bashar-Al-Assad to retain his power. If the Syrians went to war against the Israelis, it would not be just a nationalistic war, it would stir up religious divides, and the Syrians would probably be united against Israel.

The scary part is not that Syria is perpetrating such a horrific mass murder upon its own people (although that is horrifying), the scary part is that some of our politicians were suggesting arming the rebels, even in the face of our intelligence people reporting that the rebels were largely members of radical Muslim group. Yet, John McCain was on the Greta Van Susteren show in 2011 suggesting that America give the rebels weapons and military assistance in their fight. He seemed to have a romanticized vision of what the rebels represented. No matter how much we wish it to be so, almost none of the "freedom fighters" in the Middle East and North Africa will be fighting for a Western-style democracy. Unless thousands of years of history are prepared to just flip on a dime, all the foreign aid we're giving them is just a bribe, and probably won't work anyway, and war will eventually break out between Israel and its neighbors. In the meantime, we're just Rome. We're biding our time in the sun, trying to appease barbarians, building infrastructure in foreign lands on the taxpayers' dime, trying to outlast the expert out-lasters in their own territory, and hoping against hope that the radicals don't figure out that our way of life has become dependent on them and their actions.

As if the Middle East didn't want to make your head spin enough, we have our military policy in Europe, which is, put simply, to be the most popular kid on the block. We're the guy in the bar who just lets his friends rack up as big a tab as they want; because they know that we'll pick it up. In this case, the tab is in the billions of dollars.

Since the end of World War II, the United States has served as the defense department for every nation between the former "iron curtain" and the English Channel; supplying them with ample defense from the former Soviet Union and its allies. With this burden gone from their budgets, the nations of Continental Europe have built up a welfare system that has still somehow found a way to be financially insolvent. The trouble here is not that we are helping the Europeans, that continent is obviously very strategic; the trouble is the lack of participation from the native nations themselves, and our new policy in Eastern and Central Europe.

First of all, the Obama administration has adopted an entirely new policy in regards to Europe, which is one of non-support. In 2009, one of President Obama's first major decisions as commander-in-chief was to withdraw the missile defense system that we were installing from Poland, which the Poles asserted they needed to defend themselves from the Russians. When followed up by off-the-cuff remarks to a Russian dignitary that "This is my last election," and "I'll have more flexibility after the election," it is easy to see why the Eastern Europeans are a little bit jumpy right now. The Russians are not the same as they were in the 1980s relative to U.S. security, but they are still a main competitor on the world stage, and are gunning for Europe. The Russians hold nearly all of Europe's supply of natural gas, and most of Europe's non-Middle Eastern oil (two monopolies that could be broken by American energy development), and showed aggression toward their southern neighbor, Georgia, during August of 2008, when the Russians invaded a large portion of that country. Although it may not be in iron-curtain mode right now, do not falsely look upon the former Soviet Union as the benign bear in the room. The message that we are sending to our allies when we do something like that is that we are not a trustworthy partner, and that we are completely inconsistent.

In keeping with Thomas Jefferson's philosophy of non-permanent and binding alliances, I am not in favor of being completely bound to another nation, but some measure of consistency and loyalty would be in order. Thomas Jefferson's philosophy was not, "Turn on friends as fast as possible, even when it still makes strategic sense to support them." Eastern Europe is still a massively strategic position for American interests, bordering on entrances to the Indian Ocean Trade system via the Mediterranean, not to mention the Black Sea and its strategic position relative to the Middle East. While we need to coordinate with the nations of Europe and maintain it as a strategic position, those nations need to take some role in their own defense, and lighten our load just a bit.

The vortex that America cannot seem to get out of is the idea that there are only two schools of thought on how influential America should be in foreign affairs: the first saying that we need to be interventionist for the cause of democracy, be a greater force for good around the world, and protect everybody, and the second criticizing the first as wanting America to be the, "police of the world," arguing that we need to stay relatively isolated from the rest of the world, that we need to cut back our defense budget drastically, and that we shouldn't protect anybody or intervene anywhere. The fact is that there can be a happy medium between the two extremes of George Bush's expansionistic policy and Ron Paul's coveted isolation. That medium is one in which America respects the sovereignty of other nations, does not intervene for the sake of democracy unless everyone agrees, protects her strategic interests, cuts the pork out of the defense budget without cutting the combat or equipment budgets, negotiates more reasonably with contractors, or, better yet, cuts contractors and their influence completely out of the system, maintains stable and relatively constant allies that we are bound to by mutual friendship and cooperation rather than long-term commitments, negotiates for peace, but always has the option of making war and winning, and has peace through strength abroad without exploiting it. This has to start with Europe pitching in to its own defense and making some tough domestic choices, and the United States not supporting such a disproportionate share of the United Nation's funding.

Next are the Department of Defense appointments of Barack Obama. Chuck Hagel, who was appointed by Obama to be the new Secretary of Defense in the wake of Secretary Leon Panetta's retirement, is currently going through the Senate confirmation process. Through this, it has come to light that former Senator Hagel said that the Jewish lobby makes the Senate do stupid things, and that the American government is essentially an extension of the Israeli War Department. That comment takes the term ignoramus to new heights, not to mention the fact that Hagel was one of only four senators to vote against a measure to stand with Israel against Iranian nuclear ambitions a decade ago.

In his confirmation hearings, Hagel seemed to be somewhat blasé about the threat that Western society faces from Iran. That's not the infuriating part, however. When I flipped to the MSNBC channel between the segments of the Fox News programming, I saw Chris Matthews and a few other pundits talking about how the Republicans were simply grandstanding and trying to delay an inevitable confirmation, and that what the Senate was doing was disgusting. Does it occur to anyone these days that the Senate's job is to scrutinize presidential appointments to cabinet posts and make sure that jaded or unqualified people like Chuck Hagel don't become an integral part of the executive branch? Apparently not; apparently the job of the Senate is to blindly rubber-stamp the president's appointments and proposals without any deliberation. For those of you who are sarcastically impaired, that is not the Senate's job. James Madison set up a system in which making such a bad appointment is relatively difficult due to the deliberative process, and the legislature being completely independent of a presidential agenda.

In addition, the Obama administration appointed John Brennan to be the director of the CIA. Brennan is a man who has said that jihad is a legitimate tenant of Islam. Really; that guy is going to be the head honcho of the CIA? For those of you who might say that Muslims have the right to think what they want, and should not be persecuted for a Holy Book, let me just say that I hope nobody who approved of the Crusades ever advances past the rank of coffee-runner in the federal workforce. The Senate will probably confirm Hagel and Brennan.

This, combined with the sequester debacle that is going to take 50% of the cuts from 20% of government expenditures (yes, defense only accounts for around 19% of U.S. Government spending right now according to the CBO and other agencies), means that, within a few years, America will not have a Department of Defense, she will have a Department of Appeasement. While we're in the spirit, I think we should nominate Rick Santorum to be the head of Planned Parenthood, Ron Paul to be the director of the FBI, and Bernie Madoff to be the head honcho at the Securities and Exchange Commission (SEC). What could possibly go wrong?

The way to fix America's military future is rather complex. It is a mix of what Dwight Eisenhower warned us about, what Thomas Jefferson foresaw, and what Ronald Reagan implemented. First off, we cannot do what we're doing now. We cannot cut the defense department with a "hatchet," as President Obama would call it, to pay for the growing welfare state in this nation.

If we do, we will be forced to cut the Navy to fewer than 200 ships (that's where we're headed right now), not enough to even fully defend one of America's coasts. We used to have over 800 ships in the U.S. Navy, and are currently hovering around 300 vessels. What this means is that, if America were attacked in conventional fashion tomorrow, we would have adequate ships to defend one coast, plus a small part of the other one. Bottom line, we couldn't fight World War II again if we had to without an extreme military buildup. What the Obama administration is doing is simply rock-headed. Obama's administration set as a goal the reduction of America's nuclear arsenal to under 150 warheads. Although that sounds really good in theory, what adversarial nation are you really going to get to reduce its arsenal?

James Madison wrote that ambition must be made to counteract ambition. Similarly, force must be made to counteract force. You cannot fight gamma radiation with goodwill. Similarly, you can only fight ill will by instilling in it fear greater or equal to your own. Neither nation will want to be completely decimated, and few wars will ensue in this standoff situation. Think about this: in the 45 years between 1898 and 1943, three all-encompassing world wars ravaged the earth's Western nations. In this era, the idea of the atomic bomb did not exist. There was little disincentive for the rulers of Old Europe to attack each other, they would not lose their power, most of them were monarchs, and, if their respective nation lost, they would not be personally harmed. In the 68 years since the invention of the atomic weapon, not one such war had ensnared the world's people. Ronald Reagan said it best, "America has never gotten in a war because she was too strong." The world is a more peaceful place when America is acting as a powerful force for good around the globe, while still respecting other nations' sovereignty. We must maintain a strong military that no one wants to challenge to remain in this current era of relative world peace. If you want to see what happens when China has more warheads than the United States and America's navy cannot keep the emerging world powers from competing for the earth's dwindling resources, please don't take me with you.

However, we also cannot go back to the aggressive foreign policy of rendition for U.S. citizens and widespread intervention. Another empire has a lesson to teach us in this department: ironically, the Egyptians. During Egypt's transition from the Middle Kingdom to the New Kingdom, it became a much more expansionist civilization, advancing south into Nubia along the Nile River, in hopes of finding precious metals, and north into Syria and Palestine, fighting the Hyksos and the Canaanites. Egypt also attempted to expand west into Libya along the Mediterranean Sea coastline.

Their quest was driven by the need to fill Egypt's treasury and score short-term economic gains for the motherland, in addition to a feeling of moral superiority over the nomads of the Sahara and the agricultural residents to their south. The Egyptians did score short-term gains, but, in the long run, the cost of maintaining the frontier outposts and keeping up such a huge military force became unsustainable, and the Egyptians were spread too thinly across multiple theaters of action. The rebels that Egypt was fighting after the defeat of the enemy's conventional armies were zealots, motivated by a sense of survival, and a deep conviction in their own cultures and traditions.

This should all be sounding very, very familiar. It's the same thing that the radical Islamists are currently doing to us. Here's the terrifying twist: the Nubians eventually won the long, drawn out conflict. The Kushites eventually invaded Egypt when the Egyptians pulled out of Nubia and decolonized the area. The Egyptians were attempting to introduce their culture and system of government (in the Egyptian's case, synonymous with their religion) to the native people; as JFK would put it, a Pax-Egypt. The Nubians ruled Egypt for over 100 years, and were only pushed out by an emerging northern empire of Syrian origins, the Assyrian Empire. We are doing the same exact thing right now.

Think about it, we are going into a less-developed region of the world (the Middle East), and attempting to introduce them to a culture (Contemporary Western Culture) and governmental system (democracy) that we think will be beneficial for the Middle East. However, some short-term economic benefits accompany the whole operation. Whether that was intentional or incidental is irrelevant. For the New Kingdom Egyptians, the economic incentives were the gold and other precious metals, for us, it is the right to pull out Middle Eastern oil. To do this, we have to use about $150,000,000,000 (That's 150 billion dollars for those of you who are exponentially challenged) every year from the federal budget, a sum of money that looks ever-more ridiculous as the welfare state at home gets tougher to fund, and infrastructure in America crumbles. The option that America is currently choosing to take is to gradually pull out all of its influence from the Middle East, and stop attempting to impose our culture on them, much as Egypt eventually gave up on colonizing Nubia.

America is not just fighting in the Middle East right now; we have troops in Japan, South Korea, Western Europe, Cuba, and Eastern Europe. We are spread thin across the globe, with not a hope in the world (no pun intended) of defending the multiple strategic locations we hold at once. The Egyptians did the same thing, they had troops spread out in all directions, fighting in multiple theaters, and had to pay for upkeep on several outposts to hold all of their territories. The Egyptians also made many enemies to their north, as previously alluded to, notably the Assyrian Empire. If you create too many enemies, you will not be able to hold them all off, no matter how good your military is. As you can see, the strategy definitely cannot be to make enemies without care, and simply rely on the skill of our military as a backdrop in case of calamity, especially if you are going to be cutting its budget to pay for other things. The strategy has to include using your economic leverage, maintaining a strong military, and respecting other nation's sovereignty. While we must embrace peace through strength, we cannot afford to abuse that strength, we won't have it forever.

To that end, Thomas Jefferson and George Washington were crystal clear like Jack Nicholson in *A Few Good Men* about what to stay away from: permanent alliances. Thomas Jefferson's motto was simple. He said, "Free trade and liberal intercourse with all nations, permanent alliance with none." He favored diplomatic resolutions to conflicts, but recognized the need for war. What Jefferson feared was America becoming bound by treaties and agreements that would eventually force us into a war in which we had no interest or inclination.

By no means was Jefferson totally anti-alliance; he was for a loose friendship with France. What he was against was a formal alliance. There can be no better example of when Jefferson's words should have been heeded than the breakout of World War I. Although World War I had been brewing for years, the event that kicked off the war was the assassination of a single dignitary, which set in motion every army on the European continent through the alliance system.

Due to tight train schedules that took weeks to mobilize all the armies of Europe, once mobilization started, it could not be stopped, even in the event of a successful peace negotiation. The war started between France and Germany, who was allied with the Austro-Hungarian Empire. However, at the end of a week, due to Britain being allied with France, Britain had to jump into the war. Due to Russia's alliance with France and Britain, it was obligated to join the war in the East. Before you knew it, most of the planet was at war over one shot dignitary.

Thomas Jefferson feared that, one day, this type of thing would happen to America. Nations change, and friends don't remain friends forever, just ask any teenage female in America. A nation can safely maintain loose friendships with other nations that ally them temporarily, but any formal agreements are bound to cause trouble for future generations, who may not even fathom what they are fighting for. America is currently disobeying the words of Thomas Jefferson, as we are formally allied with Japan, South Korea, Israel, Britain, France, and most of Central Europe. Out of that list, I think only one nation deserves a formal alliance and an exception to the Jefferson rule, and that nation would be Israel.

Due to the formal alliance system, it would be possible for America to get tangled up in a war in South Korea or Southeast Asia for no apparent reason. Right now, that war would probably make sense. A war in South Korea today would probably mean that the communist North had invaded, or otherwise attacked, the capitalist South. That would be a perfectly sensible fight for America. But, notice the word *permanent* in Thomas Jefferson's quote. What if South Korea is not the benign capitalist republic that it is right now in 50 years, and it's attacked by the Chinese or the Japanese? What if we were forced into a war to help a trading competitor, and hurt our own trade and strategic positions in the process? It's entirely possible. I think about the world stage as a representation of Congress (no pun intended). Just like in America's legislative branch, the system is much more transparent and peaceful when no factions exist, and each member has complete independence. Although skirmishes will no doubt occur, and members should be well prepared for them, large fights on the House floor will be less common if everyone brings a unique perspective to the table, rather than having two opposing camps determined to destroy the other faction, with no regard for the integrity of the legislative body. The same applies for global conflicts. If two main groups exist, and are polarized heavily, with allies all around the globe, one little kerfuffle can become a world war very quickly. If everyone is independent and sovereign, with no outside interests other than trade, constantly in a defensive mood, the world would be much more peaceful. The conflict that became World War I might have just stayed a minor dispute between France and the Austrian-Hungarian Empire. Don't get me wrong, there will always be a rogue nation or two that is not in a defensive mood, and I am certainly not proposing that we all sit around a camp fire and sing "Kumbaya." Every nation, especially our nation, should be prepared for conflicts, and be very well armed, with loose friendships in case of an engulfing war. However, the world would be a much easier place to understand if we did not have a spider web of alliances, not to mention saving us a few hundred billion dollars, because Europe would have to defend itself again.

Speaking of diplomacy, maybe it's time to heed the words of arguably America's best diplomat: Benjamin Franklin. Ben Franklin once said, "Loan money to a friend, and you have lost him. Loan money to an enemy and you have gained him." First off, notice that he said *loan* money to an enemy; he did not say, "Give your opponent free money and military equipment blindly." The United States currently gives out tens of billions of dollars in foreign aid every year without any conditions. I think that that money would go a lot farther if we gave the foreign aid as a low-interest loan with strings attached. In today's interest rate climate, the U.S. could give out the 30 billion dollars in foreign aid as a loan at about 1.5% interest, bringing in about 450 million dollars of interest payments every year into the federal treasury. While that is a drop in the bucket in comparison to America's yearly budget deficit, why not rake in extra money if you can.

When the world economy temporarily turns around, and interest rates on bonds go back north of 5%, America would have massive leverage over poor rogue nations. After five years of borrowing, a nation would accrue interest payments yearly that would equal 7.5% of the amount of money that America sends them yearly. If those nations attack a friend of the West, or become a State Sponsor of Terror, we could threaten to raise the interest rates on their debts to the world market standard of 5% per loan. At that point, the borrowing nation would have to decide against an attack, because, otherwise, it would face a 25% interest rate per year, rising by 5% per year of lending. This would soon overwhelm a small nation's GDP and bond market. Instead, we hand out F-16s like proverbial candy, and give nations that hate us billions in foreign aid every year as they vow to destroy us and our allies in the region, while we reduce our own military capabilities. To be perfectly honest, this administration's foreign policy is positively dumbfounding.

As with any function that produces trillions of dollars, the military contracting business is a corruptive force on the American government. Dwight Eisenhower, a former five-star general, warned America about the influence of what he termed the "Military Industrial Complex," in his 1961 farewell speech, when John F. Kennedy took over at the helm of America's executive branch. Eisenhower was no slouch when it came to foreign policy, and wasn't exactly a waffling type of guy. If there was ever an American president that would be plainspoken and straightforward, it was Dwight D. Eisenhower. The slogan for the 1956 campaign, "I like Ike," must have faded away rather quickly, because America certainly did not heed President Eisenhower's advice.

In the post-1960 period, military contractors have been added faster than ever to the federal budget. We even hire private companies to provide the troops their water and food, in addition to laundry services. We hire corporations to make helicopters, airplanes, tanks, cyber-war viruses, infrastructure in the nation we are fighting in, and nearly anything else that makes its way to the front lines. While some see this as a projection of America's absolute faith in the free market system, I think it shows that our nation is currently hopelessly backwards. We are nationalizing motor companies and banks while privatizing schools and the military. Does anybody see something wrong with this picture?

The only place that a privatized military has a role is in a simple, agrarian society, in which no ulterior motives can possibly play a role in the private individual's contributions to the war effort. Such an event happened in the War of 1812. America, still in its early stages of economic development, was largely agricultural, and didn't have a federal navy to speak of. The defense of America's ports and waterways was carried out by private individuals with ships (usually the wealthiest citizens). These patriotic citizens were called privateers. Privateers sunk a large part of the British navy in Lake Erie after luring the British into the narrow Put-in-Bay of North Central

Ohio. They did not do this for profit, but for a love of country, and a need to keep the republic in our own hands and out of the Brits'. As much as I would like it to be, we are not living in 1813 anymore.

When KBR-Blackwater takes a massive job with the military, it doesn't do it for love of country; it does it because it can increase its stock prices if they keep producing weapons of war. I am an avid capitalist, an adamant individualist, and love the profit motive. But, if there is one time and place in which we should act more like a collective, and work toward a common goal without as much attention being paid to the bottom line of the individual, it would be in a time of war. The motive of sheer profit shows in the quality of goods and services that military contractors provided to the troops in America's most recent conflicts. The water was sometimes rancid; KBR-Blackwater sometimes cut safety corners to increase profits while shipping supplies through the front lines or dangerous areas. Horror stories abound from the troops about how the food was awful from some contractors, how contractors didn't care about the troop's lives, and how contractors didn't even provide the services they were supposed to in some cases. Just talk to any Iraq War veterans about the quality of service that they received from private contractors.

Set aside that the quality of service provided by the private sector was atrocious, and the worry of a corrupting influence on the government still persists. When an industry makes hundreds of billions of dollars during wartime, and hires thousands of lobbyists, it has the potential to lead America into some dumb decisions, pull the strings behind the scenes, and get whatever it wants. The only two ways that the "Military Industrial Complex" can make enough money to keep shareholders off its back about growth are to have the United States involved in a war, or to increase the amount of equipment that it makes in peacetime via the bloated Department of Defense budget.

One of these methods is complicit in keeping America's budget deficit sky-high; the other would keep America in a constant state of war if it were implemented. The fact is that defense contractors are major employers in so many congressmen's districts that actually cutting some contractors out of the budget will probably not happen until the Chinese decide to collect on their debt. Although most operations of contractors are necessary, we often subsidize over-production, thinking it will stimulate the economy. Congressmen lobbied by contractors would most likely re-authorize funding for obsolete weapons, rather than try to explain to his or her constituents why ads are running on their Television screens that their congressman wrote funding out of an appropriations bill that supported thousands of jobs in the district.

We are currently choosing to fund older airplane and tank models' production than update the military's aging 1990s-style equipment. Another once-great world power had trouble with obsolete weapons and military lobbying, believe it or not. In actuality, two did.

One was Rome (what a shocker), while the other was the Ottoman Empire. The Romans, as previously mentioned, had senators that only had one year to gain military glory (the main measure of a senator's greatness in Rome). Due to this, along with the need of the Senate to please its "clients," Rome was in a perpetual war. It drained the treasury, as the Romans had to spend money to maintain the territory, enlist more and more soldiers, and build infrastructure for the troops in the newly conquered territories. Rome kept gaining territory, but new politicians kept coming into power, so new territories had to be conquered (Isn't it funny how politicians seem to mess up nearly anything, even 2000 years ago?). I've already beat to death how Rome declined after that for multiple purposes, you get the point here, we're them, they're us, Finkle is Einhorn and Einhorn is Finkle.

The second empire that had the same problem that we do with military contractors lobbying the government is the Ottoman Empire. The Ottoman Empire was built upon the use of cavalry and the expert horsemen of the Turkish mainland. In the 14th century, with firearms spreading all across the Eastern Hemisphere, the old cavalry class of the Ottoman Empire looked like it was going to be rapidly displaced. However, since the vast majority of the society was overtly nationalistic and nostalgic, the changes were very hard for politicians to institute. In order to introduce firearms, the Ottomans had to give guns to slaves captured in war. These people were called, "Janissaries." Janissaries obviously weren't a very popular group of people in the Ottoman culture. However, by the 17th century, every empire in the Old World was using guns to enforce its will. The Janissaries found themselves executing larger and larger portions of the empire's military grunt work. The Janissaries began to demand a better life, with higher wages and living conditions. Although they were unpopular in the society as a whole, the sultans and consultants of the empire were all too aware of the important role that Janissaries had in keeping the empire alive, and often capitulated to the Janissaries' will in governance, and resistance to efforts to modernize the guns that the Janissaries were using.

Janissaries virtually controlled the government through ultimatums, or what we would call "lobbying" here in the USA. They used inordinate amounts of money to keep the military at full numbers at all times, causing the empire to go deep into debt. By the mid 17th century, the Ottoman Empire was known in Western Europe as, "The sick man of Europe," and Western nations began discussing "The Eastern Question," or, what to do about the power vacuum that would be produced when the Ottoman Empire inevitably collapsed. That did occur in time. In the Crimean War, the Ottoman Empire lost miserably, as it attempted cavalry charges against enemies armed with cannon and guns. The Janissaries were outmatched by better guns from the West. Although the Janissary ranks were already weakened by attempts to revolt against the Ottoman establishment, they would have undoubtedly lost either way. All of this happened because a politician (in this case, a sultan) didn't want to sacrifice a few jobs and a little nostalgia for the sake of modernizing his nation's defense.

To remain a superpower through the next century, we have to embrace Reagan's peace through strength, and maintain a strong military, while not letting the Department of Defense's budget stay this bloated. As President Obama put it, "We need a scalpel, not a hatchet." Mr. President, take your own advice. We need to repeal the sequester cuts (at least the Department of Defense part), which will devastate our military by cutting combat spending and production lines. However, there is plenty of room to cut billions in bureaucratic red tape out of the Department of Defense, and to cut non-combat defense spending, especially excessive production from military contractors. Otherwise, you end up having so many unneeded planes and tanks that you give out fighter jets and Abrams Tanks to your enemies. We have to believe that we are a force for good, on the whole, while respecting other nation's sovereignty and not entering into binding permanent alliances. It's a scary time for the world, but we can make it through it. We need more ships in the Navy, and more people fighting the cyber war. Above all, watch out for military contractors and their motives, and remember Benjamin Franklin's words: "There was never a good war, nor a bad peace."

CHAPTER 10

Forget the Stats, Give Me That Gun: The Second Amendment

With the recent Newtown and Aurora, Colorado shootings, the entire nation now seems to be polarized on gun control. This issue is not new by any means, but the sanctity of the Second Amendment has been generally respected throughout our history. This time, however, the left seems absolutely focused on taking guns, and making owning a firearm a thing to be ashamed of. Eric Holder actually said recently that gun owners should hide in shame. The argument seems to be that more gun controls will make us safer; that it will prevent such mass shootings as Newtown, Aurora, and Columbine. The liberals will say America has a murder rate much higher than any other Westernized nation, and that we suffer many more gun deaths per year than any other developed country. They'll most often say that hunting is obsolete, that Americans don't need guns anymore, and, most importantly, that the Second Amendment is a relic. Most liberals will also assert that if the Second Amendment is not a relic, its specific wording does not guarantee citizens the right to bear arms. The specific wording of the amendment only refers to the right to bear arms for "a militia." Though the liberals are technically right, they have their facts all mixed up, and clearly haven't read the Federalist number 46. Although today's liberals may despise the Second Amendment, it served liberal causes well in the past, because government is not something to trust; it won't always be on one side or the other. That would probably be an important anecdote to tell right now.

In Mingo County, West Virginia, in the 1890s, 1900s, 1910s, and 1920s, miners attempted to form unions, some of the first rural unions in American history. They tried to strike, tried to keep the "scabs" out, and were living in absolute squalor in the otherwise picturesque hills of Southern West Virginia. If you take a drive down U.S. 52, you can still see remnants of this today in towns like Delbarton, Williamson, Kermit, and on the outskirts of Bluefield, where the only homes are shacks with dilapidated sides and more vines that open space on the TV satellite. In the 1910s and 20s, as the conflict escalated between the mine owners and the coal miners, the mine owners hired "gun thugs." At the time, the policy of the government was to support business and crushing all union efforts, because the government believed it would stimulate business growth, and increase America's trade potential overseas. The government would never hinder, in this time period, a business trying to fight off the union struggle. In fact, the government would sometimes support it, like it did in the Pullman strike. The gun thugs threatened to kill anyone that didn't come to work. The only solution to the problem, it was becoming apparent, was to have an armed conflict.

The situation boiled over in the little town, immortalized forever in a film with James Earl Jones, called Matewan, West Virginia. The gun thugs had it out with the miners, who brought shotguns and rifles to the battle, and men on both sides died. After the mine owners saw that the miners were so desperate that they were willing to use force and stop the extraction of coal from the West Virginia hills, the owners capitulated on many fronts. Those liberals, at the time, were probably thanking God for the Second Amendment. If that amendment were not in the Constitution, the government would have taken their guns away, and supported the mine owners in the negotiations. The instrument that won the debate for the union supporters, and lifted the residents of Matewan out of the shantytowns, was the firearm. How ironic that only 90 years later, the same ideology would favor banning guns. If semiautomatic weapons were in the hands of the miners, the debacle would have ended much sooner, and in favor of the unions. The entire outcome of the Industrial Revolution would have been much different, and much less favorable to the worker, if the workers didn't have the Second Amendment couldn't have guns to defend themselves and their families from the very government that now, temporarily, wears the mask of benevolence.

Now to the argument that the Second Amendment only ensures the right to bear arms to the military and militia members. Not to take a cliché line from Joe Biden, but that's a bunch of stuff, and every liberal that keeps repeating that old hat knows it. There were not enough KGB agents in 1955 Eastern Europe to actually brainwash someone into believing that garbage. First off, militia had a very different meaning in 1791 than it does now. A militia in the 1700s was any group of people, no matter how small, defending themselves from something, namely tyranny. Second, James Madison specifically addressed this concern in the Federalist #46. As he and Alexander Hamilton tried to stir up popular support for constitutional ratification under pennames, the people kept voicing concerns. One was that the provision of the Constitution that allowed Congress to set up an army would create a standing army that would stage a coup and take over the newly formed country at some point. To address this concern, James Madison directly confronted the problem. He said that a military staging a coup in the United States would be impossible, because an army would only be able to field 15,000 or 20,000 troops. Why did that matter to Madison?

Because, he said, that army would be opposed by over half a million individual Americans with firearms of their own in the new nation, all fighting over small pieces of land. How do you think the author of the Constitution, James Madison interpreted the word militia? Exactly. The Founders meant any individual, family, small group, or town trying to defend itself. This is what the Founders meant by the word "militia." If anyone tries to tell you otherwise, give them the words of James Madison in the Federalist #46. If they don't listen, or are just too brainwashed to let the words enter their ear canals, pull out your handy copy of the Federalist #46, and ask them if they want to read it.

Also notice that Madison did not say that the citizens would use their guns for skeet shooting, but said that the armed citizenry would be used to keep the government in check. In the 1790s, the only types of guns available were long rifles and muskets. The citizens could easily obtain weapons equal to the grade of the weapons that the military was using in the 1790s. Today, that means that we have a slight bit of a dilemma, because citizens probably shouldn't have mutated Smallpox and Agent Orange just sitting around in their basements. But, you know the saying; if life gives you lemons, make lemonade. Conversely, if life gives you a dilemma, make dilemmanade. At the same time, we must make sure that the populace has adequate force to defend itself from the military or a foreign invasion. The solution is to let citizens have any gun that does not shoot an exploding projectile, essentially ending the definition of firearm at an automatic rifle, while an RPG, hand grenade, or Stinger Missile would not qualify. However, we cannot begin to qualify the Second Amendment on any type of gun. If we do, the government will take it as a signal that it can qualify the Second Amendment as much as it wants, because we will still technically have the right to bear arms. If we take that route, you'll wake up one day and realize that a BB gun is the only firearm that is still legal in America, and wonder what the Vlad Lenin just happened. When you call your legislator to ask why this is so, they will say that the Second Amendment still applies, it's just very qualified. Your hypothetical future representative will be technically be correct, but your right to defend yourself will have evaporated by then. Just for your information, the Japanese decided not to invade America after Pearl Harbor because they knew that Americans had guns in their possession, and would be able to stall the Japanese advance considerably, in addition to the fact that the Japanese were unable to locate their main targets at Pearl Harbor: the American aircraft carriers.

A liberal would say at this very moment, "Okay, the Founders didn't mean that just the military had the right to firearms, but that doesn't mean that it's not good public policy to restrict gun rights, it'll make us safer as a nation." Then, as I tried to respond, the liberal would most assuredly say, "Just look at our murder rate with guns versus those of other industrialized nations, like Great Britain. You've got to be crazy to oppose gun control." As Ronald Reagan said, the facts are stubborn things. If you look deeply into the stats and testimony, nearly all of them support the gun rights point of view. Do you know what nation in the EU had the lowest violent crime and murder rates on the continent last year (in addition to most years)? That would be Switzerland.

Ironically, Switzerland is the last nation in Europe to have gun freedom. The Swiss actually have a holiday in which every male in a certain age range competes in a target shooting contest. Even sixteen year olds are allowed to compete. Every male between twenty and forty-five years old in Switzerland is required to own a semi-automatic or fully automatic rifle (I'm not advocating that system, if you don't want a gun, that's your choice). According to American liberals, that nation should be in utter anarchy and have astronomical crime rates. Not so. Even the big city of Geneva has virtually no crime. In 2009, the entire nation of Switzerland suffered fewer than 100 murders, with or without guns, according to the Federal Department of Justice and Police in Switzerland. Why is this? Because, a criminal won't give up his or her gun because of a law, that's why we call them criminals! If more law-abiding citizens are armed, then fewer criminals will dare to commit a crime, because the threat of death is almost certain to be present. You'd have to be crazy to rob a convenient store in Switzerland, or you'd have to bring an army with you to get that all-important $100. Think of it this way: Madison said that ambition must be made to counteract ambition. Wouldn't that mean that force also has to be made to counteract force? You can't stop a murderer with goodwill, only force. If a war was transpiring, I would rather be on the deck of a navy cruiser than at home hugging a Bible. By the same token, if a robber breaks into my house, I would rather be holding a shotgun than a Bible. God gave Remington the idea to invent the pump-action shotgun.

This system relies on the majority of the society being sane, reasonable, and responsible. Aristotle said 3000 years ago that government's primary job had to be cultivating virtue within its people. John Locke and Thomas Jefferson disagreed with Aristotle, saying that, in order to cultivate virtue among its people, the government would have to be incredibly strong, and that, if the majority of the people were not virtuous already, that government was just a reflection of the collective, and that it would be just as hasty, greedy, irresponsible, and despicable as the people themselves. Therefore, if you do not trust your average citizens with guns, you know that your nation is in trouble with a capital T. If you don't trust more citizens than not to be responsible with lethal force, no government program can save you, because, as the liberals frequently remind us, government is just a reflection of the society as a whole. The only way to minimize crime rates in a country is to let everyone bear arms. Now imagine what the crime rate would be if criminals knew that the entire society was unarmed. I'm sure that system would work really well. Although my voice does not come through here, I hope you can catch the sarcasm there, because, like David Spade in Tommy Boy, I'm laying it on pretty heavily. I'll get to the statistics of that argument later, but I'd like to get an analogy out there.

If we signed an arms treaty with the Russians that said that both the United States and Russia would eliminate all of their nuclear and biological warheads, and we got rid of every one of our warheads first, would we make the world any safer? Of course we wouldn't. The Russians would be laughing hysterically and throwing a Vodka party as we eliminated our nukes. When we eliminated all our warheads, the Russians would be the only ones with force; the piece of paper would then mean nothing. Russia would launch all of its warheads at America and simply take us over. It's idiotic to think that if you only take weapons away from people responsible enough to use them, that you'll become safer. Although it does seem somewhat counter-intuitive to have a safer society with more guns, it has been widely experimented with. People thought for thousands of years that heavier things fell faster until Galileo proved that everything fell at the same rate by dropping a bowling ball and a golf ball off of the Leaning Tower of Pisa. Socratic circles don't get anything done, they are theoretical. Talking about something in terms of what might happen is not the same as making a judgment call based on what has been tried in other areas of the globe or the country. As George Washington so eloquently put it, "If we cannot find wisdom from experience, it is hard to say where it may be found." If you're still not convinced, let's look at some other examples form around the world, and some from inside America.

The most obvious example I can think of is the nation to our immediate south, Mexico. Mexico is a nation that has had over 55,000 gun-related homicides since 2008. According to the United Nations Office on Drugs and Crime, Mexico had 10 gun homicides per 100,000 citizens, while the United States only suffers 3 gun homicides per 100,000 citizens, on average, in 2010 and 2011. You may be led to believe from these numbers alone that Mexico is an unsafe nation because it is too loose with its gun control measures . . . . and you'd be wrong. In Mexico, it is illegal for any citizens to own a firearm!! So, how could 55,000 people die in that nation from gun violence, you might ask? It's simple: when you ban guns, it is like signing an arms reduction treaty with the Russians. You take the only force on the side of rationality off the table in exchange for a promise. Then, surprise, surprise, the other side fails to follow through. The bad guys are the only ones with the force, and that fancy piece of paper isn't worth one share of Lehman Brothers in September of 2008. Who cares about the piece of paper if that person is the only one with a gun, and the other side can't enforce the agreement with force? The Mexican people have learned the lesson of gun control the hard way.

Police officers in Mexico are unable to protect the nation's towns from crime, and citizens are unable to defend themselves from drug cartels and roving criminals with high-powered weapons, many of whom have bribed the centralized government, because only a few levers of power exist, unlike Madison's federal system. Mexico's politicians proposed ever-stricter gun control regulations as a seemingly fool-proof (with politicians, nothing is fool-proof) plan to stop the growing crime of the nation, and the populace bought it hook, line, and sinker. The next example is a nation that is frequently cited by the left as being a hallmark of the success of multiculturalism, liberalism, European socialism, and gun control measures: Great Britain.

In a debate about gun control, liberals will always come back to that trite and true blue statistic: Great Britain suffers fewer than 100 gun murders per year. Sure, that's right. But, here's what the mainstream media isn't telling you: according to statistics from the police of England and Wales, England had a lower homicide rate before the passage of its handgun bans and strict regulations on ownership. England and Wales often suffered fewer than 10 homicides per year per million citizens before those nations passed their handgun and firearm bans. Some of you may think that those stats are fueled by the violence occurring in Northern Ireland and Scotland in that period, and you'd be wrong. Those stats include only England and Wales. Violent crimes are actually up over 300% in England recently, and after England passed its handgun ban, deaths related to handgun violence skyrocketed by 650% according to its own Ministries. Why don't you hear about this?

Because, bringing up stats from other nations that have used gun control, and saying that the more guns you have, the less crime you get, is considered outside the mainstream. It seems completely counter-intuitive to think that, and the minute you do, people will think that you're a complete wing-nut if you don't have a very strong case to back it up. The fact of the matter is that Great Britain is less safe now then it was before all the gun control measures were put in place. Petitions are circulating in England to repeal some of the gun legislation, although British politicians are proposing even more gun laws (aka a shotgun or rifle would be banned) to "fix" the problem.

An article written in 2003, as gun crime leapt by 35% in one year in England according to its own Ministries, appeared as an editorial in the BBC that stated "Britain needs more guns." Since then, Britain's crime rates have continued to steadily increase, and gun regulations have gotten even stricter. This isn't a debate, as President Obama would so eloquently say it; it's math.

In addition to Britain and Mexico, India is having its own problems with ineffective gun control policies. India has some of the strictest gun control policies in South Asia, yet it suffers from some of the highest crime rates. According to UN-compiled statistics and the provincial police of Delhi province, the province with the strictest gun control measures, Delhi, is one of the most dangerous cities on the face of the earth, and the province suffers from more crime than any other province in India (per capita for those quick-witted liberals currently dismissing it due to the province's massive population). Just for your information, the UN is not exactly the premier recruiting venue for the National Rifle Association. The rape, manslaughter, and murder rates in India have gone up at a rapid pace since the government began instituting more gun controls. As a result of the inability of the police to respond to crimes quickly enough (boy, that sounds familiar), the women of India are signing petitions in large numbers (millions) to repeal gun control measures, and allow themselves to own firearms. The people of India (especially the women) are essentially telling the government that they can defend themselves if given the power, rather than having to rely on under-staffed police to show up to the scene quickly.

In 1982, the Department of Justice (DOJ) did a survey of America's prisoners, in which it asked inmates about the effect of citizen firearms on the prisoners' nefarious activities. The DOJ found that exactly 40% of male felons in the survey had been deterred from committing a crime because they thought that the would-be victim had a gun on their person. Almost 70% of prisoners said that they personally knew a criminal that had been scared off, shot at, wounded, captured, or killed by a victim with a firearm. Finally, almost 35% of the inmates in the survey had been shot at, scared off, or wounded by a citizen with a gun. According to the DOJ, once again, over 40% of all Americans will be the victims of attempted violent crimes (rape, murder, assault, and robbery) within their lifetimes. Here's a hard fact: Americans use guns for personal defense about 990,000 times per year according to a 2000 study (the number is probably much larger now) by the *Journal of Quantitative Criminology*. To think that fewer than 20,000 gun deaths occur in the United States each year is substantially encouraging for the proponents of home defense through firearms. How many more deaths would occur if the only one with a gun in the equation was the rapist, home invader, thief, or murderer? I would be willing to bet that we would have many more gun deaths in America if guns were illegal. Your logic may be telling you once again, what did that just say? That's ridiculous, the guns are illegal; no one will have them. Well, let me ask you this: did Prohibition keep drunkards from their booze? No, it did not, just in case you didn't know that. What makes you think that a law on a piece of paper is going to stop a serial killer from having a gun? He already shirks the law, that's his nature. Just in case you're not convinced, let me introduce you to a policy called right-to-carry.

Right-to-carry is a law in many of the union's states, and entails giving every citizen with a relatively clean criminal record the right to carry a concealed weapon nearly everywhere in public. We all remember the Newtown shooting tragedy, which, for those of you who don't know, happened in Connecticut, which has some of the strictest gun laws in the United States. Aurora, the "Movie Theater" massacre, also happened to take place in a state with very strict gun control laws. Colorado is not what you would call a bastion of gun rights. Many shootings are stopped before they even start in right-to-carry states when a citizen with a gun is nearby.

In the 2012 Texas A and M shooting, a civilian bystander was shooting at the suspect along with the police, and the crazed gunman was only able to kill three people before being hit. Police don't always get to the scene of a crime immediately. In fact, police almost never get to the scene of the crime within five minutes. In five minutes with an automatic rifle, a lot can happen. The only way to reduce crime is to make guns more accessible to those citizens who are responsible enough to have them. For those of you still saying that I'm crazy, you're still on Aristotle's side of the issue.

Stats from the Department of Justice and the states themselves show that the rate of violent crime and murder goes down after the implementation of right-to-carry legislation. I was born in Kingsville, Texas. A few years later, Texas became one of the first states in the union to implement right-to-carry legislation, and its murder rates dropped sharply, falling well below the national average. Analysts at the time were predicting that letting citizens carry guns would increase the murder rates even more in Texas. Texas is one of the safest states in the union today. Explain that one, liberalism.

Another good example is Florida. Florida had a murder rate of about 16 per 100,000 in the 1980s and early 1990s. After Florida passed right-to-carry laws, its murder rates dropped to nearly seven per 100,000, representing a drop of over 50%. The murder rate has stayed around that mark, rising periodically to nine or ten per 100,000 ever since. Michigan, my current home state, passed some of the elements of right-to-carry in the early 2000s before the governorship of Jennifer Granholm. Michigan's violent crime and murder rates have dropped from their mid-2000s highs, despite a recession that crippled our economy, and continues to drearily roll on. Some of you might be saying, "I'm sure that you could get the same result by passing gun controls so strict that not even the criminals would be able to get their hands on a gun." You'd be on Aristotle's side once again.

Chicago had the same thought for a few decades. Prior to the 2010 Supreme Court ruling, Chicago had a *complete ban* on gun ownership. Let me say that again: Chicago had a complete ban on any citizens owning firearms. You'd expect Chicago to be an extremely safe city to visit, right. No, Chicago actually had one of the three highest murder and violent crime rates of any major American city for the vast majority of that time. Chicago has consistently been one of the most dangerous cities in America, despite all of those gun controls. Other cities that have fewer gun regulations, like Dallas, Houston, or New Orleans have murder and violent crime rates that are infinitesimal compared to Chicago. If the liberals are right, this scenario should be impossible; every criminal and hooligan should have given up their guns before the mighty and all-righteous power of the State, lest they break the law.

In 2010, the Supreme Court ruled by a 5-4 decision that Chicago's gun ban violated the Supremacy Clause of the U.S. Constitution, which is roughly interpreted to mean that the states cannot overpower the federal government on any matters laid out within the Constitution, or abridge citizens' rights that are given to them under the Constitution. It is this clause which caused the Supreme Court to rule against Jan Brewer's SB 1070 immigration law in Arizona, as the court saw it as the state government trying to override the will of the national government on immigration (I would say that the state government of Arizona was attempting to enforce the laws that the Obama administration refuses to enforce, but that's beside the point). The court's overturning of the Chicago gun ban was a landmark case for conservatives and libertarians, as it opened the door to countless other lawsuits about the same type of close-to-home tyranny. As you can imagine, liberals were very upset with the decision, and were saying that murder rates in Chicago were going to go through the roof. In the past few summers, since the gun ban has lifted, crime has marvelously dropped according to the city of Chicago. This is obviously occurring because gang members are not the only people on the South side of Chicago with guns now. Everyone has the right to defend themselves, and committing a crime becomes a risky venture for any criminal.

In the irony of all ironies, Washington, D.C., the nation's capitol, and home of the nation's politicians when Congress is in session, has the most dramatic example of failed gun control. D.C. now has the strictest gun control laws of any state or district in the United States, and one of the highest murder rates. The nation's capitol used to trail only Chicago. Washington, D.C.'s troubles began with the 1970s passage of a trigger-lock law and handgun ban, when the city's murder rates were in the 20s per 100,000 (manslaughter included). For those of you who don't have a point of reference here, 20 per 100,000 is a rather high number, the national average in the 70s was about 10 per 100,000. After passing gun control, Washington's murder and manslaughter rate shot up dramatically, hitting a peak of almost 85 per 100,000in the early 1990s. Inevitably, the murder rate started coming down from that inflated level, and the trigger-lock mandate and handgun ban was struck down during a re-increase in 2007, while the murder/manslaughter rate was an incredible 31 per 100,000 in a boom economy. Since then, the murder rate in Washington has continued to drop. Part of the reason that Washington, D.C. repealed some of its gun control laws was that multiple murders happened between the 1990s and the 2000s in which the victims called 911, but the police got there too late to save them. Now that we've beat a dead horse relentlessly, let's move on to assault weapons.

First of all, the president is proposing an, "assault weapons ban." That sounds peachy, until you delve further into the issue. America has actually had an assault weapons ban before. It was in the 1990s, under the Presidency of Bill Clinton. For those of us who don't remember or care to recall that decade, a big shooting was executed with an assault weapon right in the middle of that ban. That was the Columbine shooting. Some of you might be having that "Eureka" moment right about now. "Son of a gun, you cry, sixty doesn't equal forty," as Lewis Black would put it. That's right, just because you ban those big, scary, intimidating looking weapons doesn't necessarily mean that a crazed gunman won't get his or her hands on one anyway. For those of you saying, "Columbine was just an anomaly, it is good policy to ban assault weapons designed for military use," how do you explain that Bill Clinton's own Department of Justice said that the assault weapons ban of the 1990s didn't have an effect on the overall crime rate America? It's inexplicable. An assault weapons ban is supposed to be the be-all, end-all that will end all crime. You can't stop crazy with a piece of paper.

Second of all, how do you define an "assault weapon?" I hear many people that are unfamiliar with guns talking about the dangers of semi-automatic weapons. At first, that name sounds really terrifying; it conjures up an image of a spray of bullets coming out of the gun in question. From the way they are demonized, semi-automatic weapons are treated almost like murderers themselves. What is a semi-automatic weapon? Simple, if you pull the trigger, you get one bullet. If you pull the trigger again, you get another bullet. If you hold down on the trigger, you get nada, zip, zero, zilch, nothing. Only fully automatic weapons can shoot rapid-fire via the carrier holding down on the trigger. Semi-automatics are what you neighbors probably duck hunt with, what you might defend your house with, or what a retired cop uses at the shooting range. So, while an assault weapons ban could be passed with the best of intentions (with our government, I'm not so sure that would be the case), it would probably end up banning a good portion of the guns owned by everyday Americans.

You can probably think of some other examples of awful things done with really good intentions. Why should we pass a law, under the guise of protecting children from assault weapons, just to discover that it doesn't protect a soul, and that we have obliterated any vestiges of God-given rights that we still have? We shouldn't; that was a rhetorical question. In addition, if you look at the stats themselves, the vast, vast majority of gun homicides are committed with shotguns and handguns, not automatic rifles. An assault weapons ban didn't work in the 1990s, so what makes the administration think that it's going to work now? If liberals really thought that banning a certain type of weapon reduced the violence that was committed with that type of weapon, shotguns and handguns, not semi-automatic rifles, would be the subject of their fury.

The government won't come after your shotguns for now, because it's a political loser right now. It won't be forever, you watch. In the first half of the 19th century, most high schools had a shooting range, and owning a fully automatic rifle was not frowned upon at all. In fifty years, people may very well look back upon this time period as different because so many people had home defense weapons if we don't stop gun control in its tracks. The second proposal that many people are talking about is a ban on magazines that hold more than a set number of bullets.

The state of New York recently adopted such a measure, infamously accompanied by Governor Andrew Cuomo's tirade against Second Amendment rights, in which he famously said, "It's simple, no one hunts with an assault rifle; you don't need seven bullets to kill a deer." Well, you might need a few shots rather quickly to protect your home from a burglar or robber. You might need a few shots rather quickly if the USA is ever invaded and a militia is needed. No one wants a flint-lock musket to defend their house, and you can extrapolate the reason without me taking up more space in this book with it. Would that measure really make us safer? No, it wouldn't. The New York law says that any shot clips containing greater than seven shots are illegal (well, technically you can have up to a ten shot clip, but if it has greater than seven shots loaded into it, it becomes a misdemeanor charge). A story told widely among conservatives in the midst of the law's passing is one of a Georgia mother who had to empty six rounds into a home invader with a semi-automatic weapon to kill him and protect her children.

If she had used one more bullet in New York, she would be a felon. She had multiple children. Chalk up a few lives saved by guns on that one. A magazine ban won't stop anybody from committing a major crime. People are so eager to use Newtown as a tool to enact strict gun controls that they forget how the crime even happened. The murderer, whose name I will not mention, because that breeds copy-cats, stole the legally purchased guns from his mother's home, and would have bought them on the black market if he couldn't get them from a legal owner.

Even most Democrats admit that most of these measures wouldn't have stopped the Newtown or Aurora tragedies, yet they press on with such vigor. In addition, bans on assault weapons, even if only on fully automatic weapons, would hinder the efforts of historic gun collectors. I know one of them; he sits next to me in a class. He goes to nearly every gun show that has guns from World War II and prior between the Ohio River and Lake Superior, collecting all sorts of guns, including weapons that once functioned as fully automatic, and assault weapons that have huge shot magazines. Are we to abridge his Second Amendment rights for political expediency? According to the left, absolutely. NYC mayor Michael Bloomberg also voiced his support for gun control by saying that 19 year-olds weren't fit to handle assault weapons. Mr. Bloomberg must have forgotten who defends his freedoms. Because, the last time I checked, 19 year-olds are allowed to enlist in the military, where they can get their hands on weapons much more powerful than the guns he's talking about banning. The sooner we come to terms with the fact that over one hundred million Americans own over three hundred million guns, the sooner we can have a serious discussion about gun safety and gun freedom. We can't take away the guns of the majority for the sake of preventing calamity, all the while knowing that calamites will still occur regardless of what is written on a piece of paper in the Department of Health and Human Service's or the ATF's rules and still maintain a sense of intellectual honesty with ourselves. Gun control isn't about guns, it's about control. I'm sure that most Democratic lawmakers know that gun control measures won't really make us safer; they can't possibly be that dumb. In addition to the fact that gun control measures will make us less safe, and increase crime rates across the board, it would erode the rule of law, directly violate the Constitution, and remove one of the last lines of defense against tyranny.

The Founders never mentioned recreational or home defense purposes for guns; they only mentioned firearms as a tool to be wielded against a tyrannical government. The Second Amendment speaks of militias (no matter the size of the militia), which would presumably be defending themselves from an oppressive government. When you're fresh off of throwing a monarchy off of your back, you're bound to clearly outline how to defend individual rights, and make sure that no king would ever hold power over the body public again. The Founding Fathers did just that with the drafting of the U.S. Constitution. Thomas Jefferson once said, "When the people fear the government, it is tyranny. When the government fears the people, it is liberty." That statement embodied the spirit of the time.

Perhaps the biggest fear among citizens about the new constitutional government was its power to create and maintain a standing military. The purpose of the Second Amendment is not to ensure duck hunters the right to shoot waterfowl every fall, or ensure that deer hunting remains legal, it is there to make sure that the people always have a strong defense against a tyrannical government that seeks to drastically expand its powers, whether through expanding the powers of government through the "Elastic clause" of the Constitution (which isn't really elastic unless you're looking for a way for it to be elastic), or through usurping the Constitution directly. In response to Shay's Rebellion, an uprising of Revolutionary War veterans from Western Massachusetts against the state government due to the power of the banking sector over the state legislature (not to mention the foreclosure notices on their farms), Thomas Jefferson famously remarked from France, "I hold that a little rebellion, from time to time, is a good thing." The Founders wanted the people to be just as well-armed as the government itself, as James Madison implied in *Federalist #46*.

Once you start peeling away the layers of the onion, there's no precedent that will keep the government from continuing to peel. If you can ban an automatic weapon, you can ban a semi-automatic rifle. If you can ban a semi-automatic rifle, you can ban a semi-automatic shotgun. If you can ban a semi-automatic shotgun, you can ban all shotguns. If you can ban all shotguns, you can ban all handguns. If you can ban all handguns, you can ban all rifles. It's like the scene in *Inherit the Wind* in which Jack Lemmon goes through what you can ban if you can ban teaching evolution. "If you can do one, you can do the other." The fundamental argument underlying an assault weapon ban's constitutionality is that the people would still have access to weapons, just not certain kinds of weapons, and that politicians are trustworthy enough to decide what kinds of weapons are permissible. The Founders didn't want our freedoms to hinge on the majority vote of politicians, that's why they passed amendments in the first place! The Founding Fathers didn't even want popular opinion to have any sway over those rights; James Madison was terrified of tyrannical majorities running the government, just read a few of the Federalist papers that he wrote sometime. Those rights are supposed to be entirely untouchable. What if, at some juncture, Congress decided that only BB guns were safe weapons? If we had an assault weapons ban in place, the constitutional safeguard against that sort of madness would be gone. The law would technically be completely constitutional. You'd still have access to arms, just not most arms. The Second Amendment would be circumvented entirely.

Although a tyrannical government on the scale of mass genocide is not an imminent threat, it may be at some point in the future. As Thomas Jefferson once so eloquently put it, "The beauty of the Second Amendment is that we won't need it until they try to take it." The people's judgment is not always perfect, just look at Andrew Jackson's widely supported removal of the Cherokee Native Americans from Georgia and the rest of Southern Appalachia. Our constitutional system was set up by James Madison and the other Founding Fathers to safeguard the nation against swift changes spurred on by the whim and fancy of a tyrannical majority that oppresses other's rights. Many people make a mistake when they speak of America as a democracy. She is not a democracy; she is a republic with democratic principles.

The majority cannot violate the rights of the minority that are protected in the written text of the Constitution. Many governments throughout recent history have taken away their citizen's guns before denying them any rights whatsoever, or much worse. Here are a few examples: China in the 1940s, Russia in the 1910s, and Germany before World War II. Every tyrant knows exactly where their power emanates from, and it's not goodwill. Tyrants' power comes from their ability to use force.

From the earliest days of man, the power of force has been a driving factor in how civilizations are ruled and carried out. The most effective way to wield force to get your will to become reality is to make sure that you're the only one that has it. Mao Zedong once said, "Political power flows out of the barrel of a gun." That is

SIC SEMPER RES PUBLICA | 139

never truer than when you're the only one with a gun. Mao Zedong defeated the nationalist Chinese leader Chiang Kai-shek in his long march with the Guomindang party, crushing all political opposition to his Communist agenda. As part of Zedong's "Great Leap Forward" for the Chinese people, the government confiscated the firearms of all of its citizens, rendering them defenseless. The "Great Leap Forward" was Mao's social platform for the new communist republic, carried out by his form of Orwell's "secret police," the Red Guard. Once the populace of China was completely unarmed, Mao was free to carry out his agenda at gunpoint, marching the Chinese people onto communes under the threat of death, and forcing them to labor for "the common good," as he defined it. Over 50,000,000 Chinese were murdered by Chairman Mao's Red Guard according to some estimates. Other lower estimates put that number in the twenty to forty million range.

That makes Hitler look like a Red Cross volunteer; he killed about six million Jews, and ten to twelve million people in total. Imagine how much differently that situation would have played out if the people of China were armed the whole time. The same thing transpired in Russia during the Bolshevik Revolution in the 1910s. During the Bolshevik revolution, which was caused by a combination of nationalism and jealousy toward the inherited wealth of the tsar, the Communist Party brought a large part of everyday Russians into their camp by using class warfare and promising benefits if the Communists took over the nation (where have I heard that one before?).

The other side of the equation was made up of the class of more affluent farmers, traders, and middle to upper class landowners that saw their success as earned, and respected private property. The Kulak class, the Russian version of our upper-middle class, got most of its property stolen in the two waves of the Russian revolution that occurred in 1905 and 1917. Among the most important things taken from the Kulaks and put into the collective pot were the guns that they possessed. The property was taken into the hands of the new Communist state under the guise of "re-distributing," or equalizing the resources of Russia among its people (déjà vu?). Once the guns and farm equipment of the Kulak class were taken (the Kulaks owned most of Russia's farmland), the only work to be had was to come from the new government.

Thus, with only the Communist State holding the power of the firearm, the people were forced to be completely subservient to the government. The Soviet Union's first two premiers, Joseph Stalin and Vladimir Lenin, killed over twenty million people between them, committing mass genocide on a scale about twice the size of Adolf Hitler's operation. The people of Russia were forced to work on the government's communes growing wheat that they would never be allowed to eat, in the mother land's factories making weapons of war, building the Trans-Siberian railway in the freezing cold, and extracting natural resources under the most dangerous conditions conceivable from the Russian North. All of this was compulsory work. When you have an AK-47 pointed at your back, your freedoms don't matter; you're going to do whatever Big Brother tells you to do. Using this method, Joseph Stalin withheld grains and oats from the people the breadbasket of Europe, Ukraine, partly due to its resistance to Communism, as his government raked in profits from selling the cash crops in wartime.

So, now that we have established beyond a shadow of a doubt what the wrong way to go about gun control is, and what the Founders thought about guns in the hands of citizens, the big question is: what is the right way to go about it? Obviously you don't want a civilian to own an Apache helicopter or M1A1 Abrams Main Battle Tank. It is plainly obvious that the Second Amendment must be interpreted literally, or its integrity is gone, and you start sliding down that slippery slope. The big question that we conservative-libertarians have to iron out is how to define the word "arms" (sounds like it belongs in Bill Clinton's testimony).

If the word arms were defined as a weapon that shoots a solid, non-exploding projectile, then most military weapons are excluded, while all civilian-style guns would be permitted. A dirty trick might be in order to make sure that no one takes advantage of that loose definition to buy a World War II artillery piece. The government could make the process of buying a fully automatic, high-caliber rifle, or anything that gets around the definition of arms so cumbersome and laden with paperwork that no one in their right mind would go all the way through with it, and nearly all criminals wouldn't have the patience to purchase the weapon legally. Am I saying that this would stop criminals from getting automatic rifles? Not in a trillion parsecs at a snail's pace. The criminals would still find a way to get an automatic rifle or a military-style weapon on the black market if they really want one, but if faced with a highly armed populace with semi-automatic shotguns and handguns aplenty, law-breakers would have to be certifiably suicidal, and wouldn't be able to do much damage anyway. We need to keep our freedom to own a weapon intact, and not lose sight of why the Second Amendment is there in the first place. If nothing else, we have to be intellectually honest with one another, learn from the rest of the world, and take a lesson or two from history. An assault weapons ban isn't going to work any miracles, and the more guns you have in society, the more peaceful the society becomes, just like nuclear weapons and world wars. For now, we still have our Second Amendment, but for how long? Will there come a day when the government comes looking for every gun? I don't know, but the only way to make sure that situation never plays out in government's favor is to be prepared.

CHAPTER 11

Going, Gone: The Erosion of the Rule of Law and the Constitution

E ver since the times of the twelve tables in the early Roman Republic, the rule of law has been the unshakable foundation of Western civilization. It is a means of ensuring that common vengeance and familial or political dispute does not decide the fate of an accused or accuser's life, and carries on the traditions and governments of generations past to the new ones without a hectic battle for power, in addition to providing fair and equal treatment for all (legally, not economically, for you conceptually-challenged liberals). The rule of law was a novel concept in the Roman Republic, and, looking for a way to describe the new system, the Romans named their first law codes, written on the twelve tables, mos maiorum, literally meaning the custom or way of the ancestors. The Roman Emperor Justinian finally codified most of Rome's laws, which remarkably survived the Middle Ages period in Southern and Western Europe, presumably being passed down from generation to generation among those who knew what the laws were, providing Western scholars today with most of our understanding of the Roman justice and governmental system. As some of you may have already gathered, the reason we have the word justice in our language is because it was derived from the previously mentioned Roman emperor's name. As Rome lost its republic status and became an empire, it abandoned its Rule of Law, allowing the emperor to subvert the traditional powers of the Roman Senate, the elected body of Roman politics. What caused the Romans to make this change?

Although we don't have a concrete answer to that question, the events near the time of the switch can lead us to draw conclusions about what likely happened. At the time of the transition, the Roman economy was in a time of great uncertainty, largely caused by the volatile prices of foreign necessity imports (ring a bell?), and the emperor gained an unprecedented power: the power to set the prices of goods and services. As previously mentioned, this is the exact power that Richard Nixon gained in the 1970s when the Republican Party was a national security-based party. What's more is that the Romans transitioned to a more centralized, executive-centered system of government as the Roman economy went though a transformation from an agrarian economy to a complex trading economy, and the military allowed the nation's territory to expand.

As misguided as it may be, there is a logical reason to change your government to an empire under the circumstances. The reason is that your elected legislature is too slow and too deliberative to handle the issues associated with a large empire or nation that is constantly engaged in battle, must manage a complex economy, and has to relieve its problems quickly. That should all be sounding rather familiar.

Presidents have been taking an ever-more important role in the governance of America since the early 1900s "Progressive Era" of Theodore Roosevelt and Woodrow Wilson. Faced with global terrorism and the management of a complex economy (we conservatives would prefer that last part omitted if possible), we turn to the president and his large executive branch bureaucracy to do nearly all of the government's grunt work. Most bureaucracies under the power of the executive branch can issue their own regulations and rules for the nation completely independent of America's elected legislature, which has been declining in influence, moreover, since the peak of its power in the latter part of the 19th century.

The executive branch, as outlined in the expressed powers in Article II of the Constitution, is only allowed to enforce the laws that Congress passes, and "take care that the laws be faithfully executed." That phrase is the cause of much debate in American political circles, and has been since the beginning of our federalist republic. In the beginning sessions of Congress, the existence of a Department of State to assist the president in dealing with foreign affairs sparked days of debate in Congress, as the power was not explicitly listed in the U.S. Constitution. The vote was decided by a vice-presidential tie-breaker in the U.S. Senate, and the State Department was established. However, its purpose was only to carry out expressed presidential duties with the direct consent of the president.

Until the 1930s, no bureaucratic agency had the power to make the laws, in effect, by writing regulations and rules for itself. This power was held by the Supreme Court to be strictly in the hands of the legislative branch until that decade. The new power to legislate from the desk, so to speak, has been expanded exponentially since then, making Congress essentially the tool for shaping generally which direction policy will go, and the institution that delegates power to make rules, empowering the executive branch to exert greater control over the nation.

On the national security front, just as the Roman Senate relinquished power over the direction of Rome's military forces and declarations of war, our president, due to the Patriot Act and the War Powers Resolution, can send troops anywhere he pleases without so much as telling Congress for thirty days, can command covert operations in foreign lands without Congress, can wiretap the telephone of a U.S. citizen without a warrant from a Constitutional Court, in violation of the Fourth Amendment, and can declare a "conflict" with the help of Congress, and engage the United States in a war without declaring one. Just as the Rule of Law in Rome collapsed with the increasing sophistication and centralization of Roman society, our statutes are eroding before our very eyes on multiple flanks.

The United Nations seeks to force treaties on America that violate our sovereignty, the Tenth Amendment is widely ignored as a relic of Anti-federalism, the National Supremacy Clause is used as a political weapon and enforced sporadically, we find ourselves with freedom from religion instead of freedom of religion, the First Amendment is under attack on all sides, the Second Amendment couldn't catch a break with a telescopic net, every Evangelist I know seems to hold the misconception that America's Constitution is based closely on the Bible and that religious law is as applicable as statute law, Sharia law is seeping its way into American courtrooms, liberal judges all over apply the lightest possible punishment to offenders, eroding the people's faith in the rule of law, the Interstate Commerce Clause is being abused by the national government to control every single transaction that takes place, the president has nearly unlimited powers in his executive orders and singing statements, which blatantly alter the intentions of the laws that Congress passes, and the right to due process for Americans being spied on with domestic drone aircraft is fading fast while Aldous Huxley and George Orwell look more and more like Nostradamus every day.

As I have previously stated, the United States is not a democracy, but a federalist republic. The rule of law is as important to the maintenance of a free society as the concept of liberty itself. If we did not have this safeguard for liberty, the nation would be subject to rapid changes brought about by rapidly moving events and a panic, or other misguided public cries for action. Our system is designed to move more slowly than a Western European democracy or other form of government. In our system, the national government can only do what is absolutely necessary in crisis, or what is widely agreed upon. In accordance with the Tenth Amendment, the more controversial domestic decisions are intended to be left to the states. The system is specifically designed to carry on precedents and preserve the sanctity of human rights, not expedite the work of over-reaching government. Right now, our politicians are circumventing our laws to re-structure the republic to do the latter. We need to start any serious discussion of government's role with that simple fact that Americans have lost sight of.

The first threat to the Rule of Law comes in the form of treaties from the United Nations, including an international firearm agreement and the renewed Law of the Sea Treaty. The Law of the Sea Treaty was one of the first documents passed through the United Nations upon its establishment in 1945. The treaty was designed to regulate disputes in international waters, and give each nation what oceanographers call an EEZ, or exclusive economic zone, which extends for two hundred miles off of any nation's coast, in which that nation alone has the right to extract resources, try crimes committed there, and regulate the trade conducted there. If you study any history, you can figure out why the United Nations was so eager to pass the treaty and lay the issue to rest.

From the days of impressments of U.S. sailors onto British naval vessels before the War of 1812 to the disputes between the powers of Europe in the trading days of the 16th, 17th, and 18th centuries, the sea, and the ability of a nation to capitalize on its resources, has long been a source of conflict on this planet. The old treaty is not the trouble at all; it does not violate any U.S. laws, and provides an unbiased way to try international sea crimes. However, the treaty is up for renewal every so often, which means that amendments to the treaty are up for consideration in the UN.

This time, the United States agreed to a Law of the Sea treaty renewal that gives the world community the right to regulate and profit off of resource extraction that takes place within America's EEZ. The treaty calls for a royalty (a fancy way to say international tax) on all seafloor extraction of natural resources and mining from the ocean floor (we're talking in our EEZ). Those taxes would go to the United Nations, and be re-distributed to nations without as much wealth as the United States or China, an effective system of global wealth transfer. In addition to being just a flat bad idea, the treaty, in essence, gives the UN the power to be the world's tax collector, directly violating the text of Article I of the U.S. Constitution, which explicitly states that Congress alone shall have the power to, "lay and collect taxes." Once again, the legislative branch is becoming a more obsolete institution everyday. The United States Senate would not pass most elements of the treaty, as the Constitution mandates that it does for the treaty to take effect. Did that stop today's government from taking us closer to the *Brave New World*? Of course not, if the Senate doesn't approve the treaty, the president can always just executive order the treaty into effect from the Oval Office. The president is not supposed to be able to do that, but who's paying attention anyway?

What President Obama did last year by executive ordering a foreign treaty was completely unprecedented, and will be used as precedent when future presidents don't get what they want from the legislature. Even the liberal Woodrow Wilson, arguably the most progressive president in American history, did not have the audacity to do that. Woodrow Wilson wanted the U.S. to join a group that he lobbied for in the aftermath of World War I and the Treaty of Versailles: the League of Nations. This body was the precursor to the United Nations of today, serving as an international committee to regulate disputes, and see to it that international governmental transactions were fulfilled (in those days, the reparations payments of Germany to France and the United Kingdom).

The Senate saw this day coming all the way back in 1919, as it argued that the new body would eventually cut the power of national sovereignty right out from underneath us, and that the legislature and separated system of government that America has would be subverted by the new body, even if it was not its intention. The

Senate ended up rejecting the League of Nations, leaving the nation that devised the idea not to be a part of it, and leaving Woodrow Wilson's "Fourteen points" out to dry. Despite the fact that Wilson had spent the better part of a few years fighting for the League on the world stage, he accepted the decision of the Senate as that of our government at work, albeit with much chagrin.

The ability of a president to executive order a function of government specifically delegated to the legislative branch signals a dramatic shift toward a more centralized, executive-controlled system of government much like that of the Romans in the period between the republic and the empire. The second United Nations treaty that is very questionable is the United Nations Small Arms Treaty, which would regulate the international sale of firearms, and require signing members to have databases that track who owns a firearm in their respective countries, what the make and model is, and how long the gun has been in that entity's ownership. Although not yet at the stage of international strict gun control, this treaty would require the United Nations to play a role in regulating the sale and possession of firearms wholly within the nation, setting up the legal groundwork for stricter future regulations coming out of the UN to completely abolish the Second Amendment at a global level. The mere presence of the United Nations in regulating American firearms in any facet would effectively nullify the Second Amendment and the sovereignty of the United States to set its own regulations and laws. Although I detest the conspiracy theorists on both sides of the political spectrum, things like that can draw you toward the "New World Order" theorists in a hurry.

Add to these proposals the repeated proposals for a global standard education system that portrays the West as the oppressors, which is now being pushed in colleges throughout America, and the world starts to look very Orwellian. The nations of the world can create much more prosperity separate from each other than as a collective, and government farther away will not be any more responsive to the needs of the people, but less so. A world government is a gross violation of one of Thomas Jefferson's most commonsense statements about the ideal government: "Government closest governs best." The statement embodies the anti-federalist (today conservative) idea that an official at city hall will respond to what his constituents want more directly than a president or Prime Minister can, as the latter has to deal with a much broader array of interests and contending factions. As previously stated in the education chapter, you can think of how much money the bureaucracy takes as a system of Direct Current (DC) electricity. The further the money has to travel, the more of it is lost to friction (bureaucracy and transport). The faction that wants one world government is relatively small compared to those of us who would like to maintain control over our own lawmaking process. The only effective weapon that faction has is stealth; we have numbers and enthusiasm. This is one threat that the Romans never had to face; we'll have to find our own way. I can only pray that we don't choose globalization.

Secondly, America's Rule of Law is under attack from religious law. Christians, Muslims, and other religions alike try to utilize America's First Amendment to allow them to be judged by the tenants of their religion in courts of law. We'll start with the misguided notion that America's Founders wanted our legal system and government to be closely based on Christianity. Although a few of them might have agreed with that statement, the most prominent Founders would not have. Thomas Jefferson, frequently cited as the author of the letter to the Danbury Baptist Church regarding the separation of church and state, said something much more profound. He said, "It does me no harm if my neighbor says that there are twenty gods or no God; it neither picks my pocket, nor breaks my leg." Thomas Jefferson's letter to the Danbury Baptists is consistently misinterpreted by secular people and atheists as meaning that the government can have nothing to do with anything religious, and that religion in public places could be considered religion sponsored by the government, which is outlawed by the First Amendment, which states that the government shall not establish a State religion.

In fact, Thomas Jefferson only said that it would not be appropriate for the U.S. Government to fund the operations of a ministry, which it wouldn't be (I don't think I would want to go to that church anyhow; it would buy $3,000 candles and communion plates). Thomas Jefferson never said that religious acts on public land would be inappropriate, only that the funding of a religious institution would be. The First Amendment says that we have the Freedom *of* Religion, not Freedom from Religion. The application of Jefferson's correspondence has been used countless times to order towns to take down nativity scenes or Christmas trees, and misguidedly so. The Founders would want any religious group to be able to put up a display around a holiday. Although some of the lesser well-known Founding Fathers were hardcore Evangelists who wouldn't even want Catholics and Jews let into the country, perhaps the three most important figures of the time, Benjamin Franklin, George Washington, and certainly Thomas Jefferson were on board with complete religious freedom. Thomas Jefferson's quote about his neighbors is quite obvious in interpretation, think what you want, we'll see who's right eventually, but we don't have to squabble over it in this life.

Franklin was an extremely tolerant person, allegedly patronizing Jewish synagogues in Philadelphia and giving his time to Protestants and Catholics alike. George Washington, although deeply rooted in Christian faith in his personal life, was one of the foremost proponents of the Rule of Law independent of religion and the First Amendment. Washington, however, did want society as a whole to be a Christian-based nation with faith in a creator. The Founders didn't want us to have a Christian-based law system, but a precedent-based law system. Although the laws of the United States were created in the image of Judeo-Christian values, they were not intended to favor one religion over another or institute an official theology.

The fact that we have laws based on Judeo-Christian values is just a product of the majority group that founded America and the sentiment of God-given rights that pervaded the culture at the time. As for Evangelists who ask you to explain the fact that most criminal laws are based on the Ten Commandments, there is a simple answer. Because, murder is frowned upon in every one of the world's cultures, rape is generally considered wrong, and stealing angers the property owner. As for the more Christian-specific commandments (Sabbath, graven images, coveting neighbor's property), we don't have any laws on the books! The Founders were shooting for a tolerable republic in which all religions could live together, and all display and advertise. America's First Amendment is the epitome of our assertion of being a free marketplace of ideas. By the same token, Christians should be free to put up nativity scenes at Christmas if they want to as they aren't taking federal funds to do it. In fact, there is no law on the books that says the states cannot set up their own religious laws. Here in Michigan, until recently, we still had what are commonly referred to as the "blue laws," or laws that prohibited drinking on Sundays. In some conservative areas in the Northwest part of Michigan, you could get a ticket for mowing your lawn on a Sunday as late as the 1990s. The First Amendment, however, is backed by the Supremacy Clause, and, thus, no locality or state is allowed to legally abridge it, causing the repeal of our blue laws recently. Since we have freedom of religion, the system is supposed to go like this: Muslims can put up a statue of Mohammed if they want for Ramadan, the Hindus can put up a tribute to Shiva and Vishnu if they want, and the Christians can put up a nativity scene. The Scientologists can erect a volcano, and the atheists can have a Darwin awareness week. Everyone is happy because no one is oppressing the other religions, and the best religion will attract more followers. No one's rights are being infringed upon, and if you get offended, that's your problem. I'm quite certain that the right to not be offended does not appear in the Constitution, but the right to practice religion freely does.

However, our rule of law is being eroded on another front when it comes to religion: the application of Sharia and other religious law to court cases. In a 2010 marital rape case in New Jersey, a confessed marital rapist and member of Islam was found innocent of raping his wife, and was not given a restraining order by the court on account of his religion. In the fundamental tenants of Sharia law, (the Muslim holy laws) taken from the Koran, a wife is obligated to have intercourse with her husband whenever he wishes as a duty of marriage. Thus, the district court found that a restraining order was not in order (no pun intended) for the woman's ex-husband, as he was "acting in his religious beliefs." In a nutshell, what that judge decided was that Sharia law trumped the written law of the state of New Jersey, the laws that had been enacted by a majority of the dually elected legislature.

The New Jersey Appellate Court later overturned the ruling, saying that the man's religious beliefs were completely separate from his compliance with the laws of the land. The Appellate Court finally issued the restraining order. The idea here is not to criticize the Muslim religion; crazy defenses have been used by my fellow Christian believers as well. The concept is that we are letting religious law begin to pervade over our courtrooms, trumping the consensus that the majority has reached about what is acceptable and what is not in society. No religion should have the right to use its tenants and theology as a defense against criminal charges. Here's a quick news flash: if you're deciding criminal cases based on religious law, you have broken the First Amendment and established a State religion! We have freedom of religion, but if the law and religious beliefs collide, the Rule of Law has to win out for the sake of a somewhat orderly society.

Outside attacks on the Rule of Law are not the only ones that we have to worry about; our government knowingly defies the written words of the U.S. Constitution in countless ways. Among them is the grotesque abuse of the Interstate Commerce Clause of the Constitution. The Clause simply says, "The Congress shall have the power to regulate commerce with foreign nations, and among the several States, and with the Indian tribes." From that statement, an unimaginable growth of government regulatory power has sprung forth. From this clause is drawn the root of government's claim to have the power to set a minimum wage, establish the EPA, enforce the Americans with Disabilities Act, monitor anything it wants, set healthcare standards, enforce benefit rules, regulate 401 (k)s and 403 (b)s, fund public schools and mandate standards, support trade unions with the National Labor Relations Board (NLRB), and perform countless other tasks.

The constitutional kerfuffle here is commonly overlooked by even the most contemplative politico. The clause is called the *Inter*-state Commerce Clause, not the *Intra*-state Commerce Clause!! This simple fact hit me as I was sitting in an Advanced Biology class, and the notes got to the topic of inter and intra-specific competition for resources and shelter in the natural world. If the commerce takes place entirely within one state, how can it be considered inter-state commerce? The Supreme Court, in its Progressive Era, set a precedent that any activity that will eventually lead to an exchange of goods or services between states can be regulated. In other words, if you are the nighttime janitor at a Ford factory in Michigan that sends its cars to be sold in Virginia, even if you have never left the state of Michigan, and your employment is wholly within the state, the federal government claims the right to regulate your work conditions, hours (if necessary), and healthcare. This would have been considered a direct violation of the Interstate Commerce Clause at any point before the 1890s in American history.

Another thing about that Clause is that the words "among the States" are most often interpreted to mean that the government has the right to regulate commerce that takes place entirely within the borders of one state. That interpretation, taken together with the interpretation of the Necessary and Proper Clause and Supremacy Clause, to be discussed later, represents a major threat to individual freedoms and free enterprise in this republic. It is this set of clauses that enables the government to live up to how Ronald Reagan described its attitude: "If it moves, tax it. If it keeps moving, regulate it. If it stops moving, subsidize it." Once again, Mr. Reagan, you're right on point.

The Supremacy Clause, which says that the national government reigns supreme on all matters enumerated in the Constitution, has been used since the late 1800s to say that the national government reigned supreme on anything and everything, essentially erasing the idea of state's rights for almost a century until Ronald Reagan and the 1994 Republican Stampede revived the idea. In addition, the Supremacy Clause today is not used as a legitimate component of the Constitution, but as a political weapon to be used on one side or the other of a debate. For instance, as Eric Holder's Department of Justice prosecuted Arizona for having immigration laws (mentioned specifically in Constitution), it failed to confront Chicago on gun control, and turned a blind eye to the sanctuary cities of California, which were in direct conflict with federal statutes, while Arizona's laws were mostly in concurrence with national laws.

In addition, if the Obama administration really believes that the Necessary and Proper and the Interstate Commerce Clauses give the federal government the power to make any law, it should have gone after Colorado the minute that state legalized marijuana in violation of federal drug bans, and it should have taken Vermont and Massachusetts to the woodshed when those states approved gay marriage, in contradiction with DOMA (Defense of Marriage Act). With the power of the Interstate Commerce Clause, the national government mismanages the economy (to be discussed in the economic philosophy chapter), much like the final days of the Roman Republic. Just for the record, the Supreme Court's change in interpretation of the Interstate Commerce Clause took place in the turn of the century period, as the government was looking to cash in on America's transition from a simple, agrarian economy to an industrialized powerhouse greater than the likes of Great Britain. The Romans let government begin to control more of their economy under nearly identical circumstances, except that instead of industrialization and trade, Rome's small-scale agriculture turned to corporate agriculture and trade.

Another part of our modern day mos maiorum that is slipping away from us is the Fourth Amendment of the U.S. Constitution. This is the amendment that guarantees that the government will not partake in any, "illegal search and seizure," or searches without warrants. The Patriot Act combined with the increased domestic use of drone aircraft and surveillance cameras by the nation's law enforcement agencies have all but incinerated that section of the Constitution. The Patriot Act was passed in 2002 following the 9/11 attacks (which were carried out by Islamic radicals for you 9/11 truthers, read the Purdue University report), and created the newest Department in the president's cabinet: the Department of Homeland Security. The DHS was given sweeping new powers, to be carried out with a behemoth budget. Among these powers was the power to wiretap the communications devices of American citizens on U.S. soil with a FISA Court warrant that can be more non-descript than a traditional warrant, not to mention the power to detain American citizens without a warrant, a charge, or a writ of habeas corpus.

The reason for the abridgement of the Fourth Amendment in this case is at least somewhat understandable and halfway logical, but the passage of such an intrusive law in the first place reflects a concession of defeat. If your enemy's stated goal is to change the way you live and alter your society in subtle ways, don't change your way of life. The Romans fell victim to the same mentality 2000 years ago, levying heavy taxes on their citizens and lowering the standard of living of their own citizens to fight the Spanish, North

African, Germanic, and Middle Eastern rebels. America is a nation known for her freedom. If we concede our freedoms for the sake of defeating the enemy, and change our style of government, the radicals have already defeated us one thousand times over, as they have sentenced us to an inevitable, slow, tyrannical end! As for the passage of the bill itself, the bill was hardly deliberated upon, but rushed through the legislature at lightning speed at the urging of an all-empowered executive branch.

This process, in itself, directly contradicts Madison's vision for Separation of Powers. Madison foresaw three branches that barely communicated with each other on legislation, voting on each other's proposals blind, without coercion or collusion. That system was dead gone less than ten years after Madison left office with the "Corrupt Bargain" of 1824. Madison didn't want the executive branch to play any role in guiding or assisting the lawmaking of the legislative branch. There goes that constitutional idea. That aside, the Patriot Act tramples right (no pun intended) over the Fourth Amendment with its wiretaps without warrants provision. It would be one thing if that provision was not applicable to American citizens, but it is. This is where I differ with the extreme libertarians out there. If you are not a U.S. citizen, how does the Constitution apply to your situation? Madison, Jefferson, and Washington never said that the Constitution applied to the citizens of Great Britain! Those citizens were at war with the United States. Today, radical Islamists are at war with the United States!

Even though the Constitution was not passed and ratified until 1787, I'm quite sure that if it was around in 1777, General Gates would not be reading constitutional rights to the Redcoats he captured at the Battle of Saratoga. As for water-boarding being against the Eighth Amendment of the Constitution, which mandates that no cruel and unusual punishment be dealt, if you agreed with that assertion, you missed the point again. An enemy combatant is at war; they don't have any constitutional rights! Many liberals will correctly point out that the Constitution does not give "citizens" rights, but gives "people" rights. Although this assertion is technically correct, the reason for this is that if we didn't put the phrase "people" into the Bill of Rights, only white, property-owning adult males 35 years of age and older would have had any rights for the first 40 years of our existence. Thomas Jefferson was quite the isolationist; I'm pretty sure he wasn't implying that an armed opponent in Tripoli or Munich has constitutional protections!

If you hit a liberal with that line of logic, they will say that the Geneva Conventions of 1949 prohibit torture. Well, not if you are a terrorist. In order to qualify for Geneva Conventions, according to the actual text of the Geneva Conventions, combatants must be under an identifiable flag (terrorists aren't), have a recognizable leader (terrorism doesn't), and conduct their hostilities according to the laws and customs of war (terrorists don't). Check mate on that one. Anyway, back to the Constitution.

When we carry it too far is when we say that we can violate the rights of American citizens who are suspected of terrorism or other crimes. At that point, we have nullified the entire document. If American citizens can be denied their rights, anybody can be denied their rights. What just ticks me off, other than Lyme's disease, is when we make a distinction between American citizens on U.S. soil and American citizens currently in other countries, and say that the latter don't have any rights. That's reassuring. So, what we're saying is that the moment I leave American airspace or the American EEZ, I have relinquished all rights under the Constitution? Good Heavens, with that interpretation of having to be on, "American soil" to have rights, future politicians might deny anyone their God-given rights. Those politicians could say that none of us are on American soil, as our electrons repel the electrons in the ground and keep us from ever getting closer than 10^{-3} millimeters from that soil.

Even without that absurd claim, the president, and by default, his massive cabinet bureaucracy, have the power to listen in on anyone it wants to, or take anyone prisoner that it fears, whether for the public good or not. As if the Patriot Act just wasn't bad enough, the American government is now making heavy use of surveillance drones, and the Obama administration recently issued a memo that suggested that killing American citizens on U.S. soil without due process is perfectly constitutional. The memo was answered by Rand Paul's (R-KY) now infamous 13-hour filibuster of CIA director John Brennan's confirmation (you remember him), in which Paul spent hours lambasting the constitutional basis for any domestic drone program, lethal or nonlethal. The memo was nothing short of the executive branch out and out defying the Constitution.

The use of a drone is a means of quickly killing somebody without giving them a chance to even utter their side of the story. In war, that's acceptable because it can be safely presumed that the person in question is hostile to the United States. However, the power of a president to use this method on anyone could result in the executive branch declaring any ideology too far from its own, "a threat to America," and killing its members without due process. We would have constant power struggles and vacuums, not to mention a near monarchy.

For those of you who think this could never happen in America, look back to the Cherokee, the Japanese internment camps, and the patronage system of the 1800s in which a political party's only concern was repeatedly winning, enlisting new immigrants, coercing, and threatening to get it done. Now look at the 2009 memo by Janet Napolitano's Department of Homeland Security that categorized America's conservatives and libertarians as "domestic terrorists," while classifying Islamic radicals as "man-made disasters," and the Iraq and Afghanistan wars as "overseas contingency operations." This president might not abuse his new-found power to play God with citizens of a formerly free republic, but do we want any president to even have that option? Those of you who answered yes to that question need to seriously evaluate what your priorities are.

Any American citizen, on U.S. soil or otherwise, has the constitutional right to a trial by jury for any accusation owing to the Sixth Amendment, and the right to due process of law by the Fifth Amendment. For the last decade, we have ignored the integrity of these two amendments, choosing instead the false sense of security provided by a strong chief executive. The use of drones in surveillance by domestic law enforcement agencies also violates the Fourth Amendment, much like the Patriot Act. The drones give the police the ability to search private property and land from above without a warrant, collect data, and patrol subdivisions. With the infrared cameras available today, law enforcement agencies could also monitor people inside of dwellings and their activities without a warrant. What's more is that DHS and the Department of Defense have already received over thirty thousand applications for the possession of drones by local and state law enforcement agencies, and the two departments expect all of these drones to be in use by 2020. Combine that with the new rules as part of Obamacare that require your doctor to turn over medical records or private information about a patient if asked to, the proposals that would require your physician to ask you if a gun is in the home as part of a "check-up" (effectively a search without a warrant), the proposals in Cap and Trade that narrowly failed in the Senate in 2009, including the government keeping track of how much energy and carbon everyone consumes and the status of our homes, and the cameras now mounted on every street corners in urban and suburban areas, and it is safe to say that the Gestapo is back in style.

As if that wasn't bad enough, the NSA (National Security Agency) thinks that it is perfectly constitutional, under the Fourth Amendment, to collect staggering amounts of "metadata" in the form of e-mails and phone records. First, what's the logical argument for this program? National security advocates say that monitoring cell phone call patterns leads to catching terrorists more easily, and that, if we monitor e-mails and phone calls, we can foil terrorist plots without much trouble. Then, in a complete contradiction, those same people will tell you that the PRISM program, as it is called, is not a threat to privacy or individual liberty because the information being collected is just, "A bunch of ones and zeroes." Which one is it?

If we are just collecting trillions of ones and zeroes, we would never be able to catch a terrorist, and the program would be useless. On the other hand, if the program has already foiled terrorist plots, that means someone is deciphering all of those numbers. If someone is deciphering those ones and zeroes, they can decipher the ones and zeroes from your computer or, say, the computer of a challenger for political office. In addition, after collecting this treasure trove of information, the government would have to get one specific person's records if it suspected terrorism at a later date, which could just as easily be done to that one person with a conventional warrant without demolishing the entire Constitution.

The only purpose of this program is to collect information on citizens and punish political enemies. Given how the current administration used the IRS to punish political enemies (I'm not saying that Obama was directly involved, but it seems very peculiar that Tea Party groups would be targeted for extra audits and paperwork in a critical election year, only to have the early reports of a "few isolated incidents in Cincinnati" and "a few rogue employees" refuted by those that take the Fifth and employees that say they were taking orders from higher up), do you really want a government with that kind of power? Lest I remind the reader that some of the worst things in history have been done with the best intentions, and this program probably doesn't even have those.

The PRISM program was carried out with what have been called "blanket warrants," warrants that cover sweeping things to be searched. For example, some warrants could cover hundreds of millions of phone calls from a certain major phone company. This is one of the specific objections that the Founding Fathers had to British power in the New World. When a colonial judge would issue a warrant, it would be for sometimes an entire town, and the British soldiers could go from house to house with the same warrant without a probable cause to suspect any one of the individual citizens that they were searching. Due to this violation of individual rights, the Founders wanted to make sure that this type of thing would never happen in our nation, and authored the Fourth Amendment so as to make all warrants issued without probable cause and a specific description of what was to be searched specifically null and void. The warrants that the FISA Court issued to the phone companies to execute PRISM were plainly unconstitutional, as they didn't contain a probable cause to search anyone, and weren't specific as to what was to be searched.

While watching Fox News recently, I realized what is really wrong with our nation—we don't understand our liberties. Greg Gutfeld, a co-host on the show *The Five*, said that the government had probable cause the minute that a terrorist attack was possible. Holy mackerel, I said to myself, that's always; can the government search anything anytime it wants in the name of national security? Then, another co-host, Juan Williams, said that the PRISM program was constitutional because it was authorized by Congress!

As the reader should know, or at least figured out by now, Congress can't pass a law contrary to the Constitution and have it be legal. That's the whole point of a constitution! Many people say that because Snowden leaked the existence of this program, we will be in horrible danger. Really, that's the best comeback the statists have? Do you honestly think that terrorists didn't know that we monitored the internet and cell phones? It is a free population that scares the government; a thinking and liberated populace that causes them to wake in a cold sweat. This tactic is as old as tyranny itself.

The point is to make people more terrified of liberty than of tyranny. Frederick Douglass describes how slave owners in Maryland put this theory into practice in his autobiography. Every Christmas, the slave-holders would let their slaves have a break until the day after New

Year's Day; the slaves' only experience with relative freedom. This was the time at which many separated slave families temporarily re-visited. However, to keep slaves in line, the masters would devise clever means of manipulating them. One of the most popular was for the masters to bet on which slaves could drink the most without getting drunk, encouraging every slave on the plantation to get drunk and make bad decisions. This way, after the seven days of sinful revelry, the slaves would think that freedom was a wretched thing that they could not be trusted with; some new instrument of St. Lucifer. Thus, on the Second of January, the slaves would happily march back into the depths of serfdom. The U.S. Government is perpetrating the same technique on its own citizens today.

If you thought that we ignored the Fourth, Fifth, and Sixth Amendments, you're going to be blown away by how we treat the Tenth Amendment. People often say that the National Supremacy Clause and the Tenth Amendment are in contradiction, and I say that's nonsense.

The Tenth Amendment states that all powers not enumerated in the Constitution are delegated to the states or the people themselves, while the National Supremacy Clause states that on matters that are enumerated in the Constitution, the national government's power has to win out over that of the states'. What's the contradiction there?

The only way you can get those two provisions to be in disagreement is if you dramatically expand upon the powers enumerated to the national government in the Constitution, cutting states out of the process. The National Supremacy Clause was passed within the context of the 1780s, when state governments were coining their own money and levying their own taxes. If the National Supremacy Clause was left out of the document, states in the 1790s would still claim a power greater than that of the federal government to tax and regulate, effectively nullifying the purpose of the new national government.

The Tenth Amendment, a history teacher would tell you, pretty much became an artifact after the civil war, which turned out to be the death knell of states' rights for almost 150 years. After the "War Between the States," as a southerner would refer to it, nobody wanted to hear about or respect states' rights, and understandably so. However, the Civil War was not fought between people who respected the Constitution and people who did not, it was fought by two sides of a great philosophical divide, two groups that had different understandings of what their constitutional obligations to the union were, not two groups that disagreed as to the validity of its amendments.

The fact that we completely ignore the Tenth Amendment is telling as to the direction of our republic. It illustrates plainly that we are headed toward a more centralized and hierarchal society without the distinct local cultures and enterprises that Alexis de Tocqueville said made the United States a truly remarkable nation. Look around you out on the highways and listen to the radio while you do it. You will hear the National Association of Realtors advertise its message that "Home ownership builds strong communities" with the help of the U.S. Ad Council. Why do we have an Ad Council? It beats me; maybe it's to trick the middle class into buying huge houses on credit and fueling a boon for the financial service sector, all the while knowing that prices are inflated.

It doesn't say anywhere in the Constitution that the government has the power to advertise or fund it. The radio station you're listening to might operate entirely within your state, but the FCC has to issue it a license regardless of the fact that the commerce it carries out does not cross state lines, and that the Constitution does not give the government the right to regulate communications. Look to your right, and you will see a car. That car has had efficiency standards imposed upon it by the Environmental Protection Agency, without constitutional authority.

Look above you, and a jet soars above, directed by the FAA, even though the national government does not have the enumerated power to control transportation. The government regulates the protection of the environment on the grounds of regulating Interstate Commerce despite the fact that no commerce is taking place in most of the EPA's actions (or it's being eliminated). The elected tyrants in Washington pass healthcare legislation that "creates commerce in order to regulate it" and taxes negative actions to avoid the Tenth Amendment of the Constitution.

The Tenth Amendment clearly states (no pun intended) that the government doesn't have any powers except those granted to it in the written text of the Constitution. In accordance with this rule, every cabinet department, executive agency, and independent agency is currently unconstitutional. To make them constitutional would be rather simple: we just have to make amendments to provide room for each approved bureaucratic agency in the Constitution. For those of you who are currently saying to yourselves, "That's crazy, not every department would make it through that process," you're very sharp, because that's the whole point. The Founder's idea for the new republic was that we would need fifty percent of the politicians to get most business done, but that it would require seventy-five percent of the votes in Congress to do anything outside the established framework of State (the capital S there indicates the national government) power. The idea was that, within the constitutional powers of the government, we could pass agreed upon pieces of legislation, and move quickly with business as usual.

However, very controversial measures that went outside the framework of the Constitution, or controversial measures in general, would be hard to pass through the national government. Those measures would be passed at the state or local level, where the government was more responsive to the needs of its citizens. Therefore, only the consensus of the nation was to be represented nationally. In accordance with that, we should put every agency through a constitutional amendment process. If the FAA loses, that means that we have morons in Congress that need to be replaced ASAP, because that is one function that is much better left to the national government than the state government. This way, the national government would retain the functions we widely agree upon, and would shed those that are highly controversial. These measures would go to the state level or local level. If the state or local government didn't want to do these things, it would begin telling people to elect congressmen that would put that function back up to the national level. For those liberals who are saying, "We'd lose the EPA," we probably would. But, the states won't just sit on their hands if pollution like that seen in the 1960s started right up again. My guess is that someone would be pretty unhappy about the presence of dangerous chemicals in their yard or a local stream, and would probably contact their state legislators in more than just a bit of a huff. In this system, we are in adherence with our Constitution, and the will of the people will be better represented. For all the misgivings we have about Congress, at least we have the power to elect them. I would rather trust them than an unelected bureaucratic agency any day of the week and thrice on Sunday. Right now, however, we use the Tenth Amendment as an area rug for the proverbial feet of the national government. In other words, although this amendment was a key part of Madison's plan for a decentralized republic, it might as well not even be there today.

Another threat to the rule of law in America is the occurrence of selective enforcement, when the executive (governor or president) decides to enforce the laws he likes, but not the others. President Obama has chosen not to enforce much of our immigration law, even issuing driver's licenses and work permits to known illegal aliens via executive order. The president also chose not to enforce the federal bans on marijuana and other drugs that states have tried to legalize. His Department of Justice under Eric Holder famously ignored the 2008 case of the Philadelphia Black Panthers intimidating voters at a Southeast Pennsylvania polling place. The president refuses to enforce DOMA at any level, and doesn't enforce the Second Amendment, instead relying on citizens to take the fight all the way to the Supreme Court themselves. But selective enforcement is not a partisan problem by any means.

George W. Bush refused to enforce the Fourth Amendment and some of the executive orders on the environment that Bill Clinton signed in his last year as president (understandably so; Bush probably felt that the orders were unconstitutional). Republican and Democratic governors alike across the United States refuse to execute the laws implemented by their predecessors from the other side of the aisle. However, that is not the executive's job! Executive officers are supposed to enforce the laws regardless of what they think of them. Sure, those executives can suggest legislation in their "State of the union" or "State of the state" addresses, and they can raise public support for an issue, but they cannot make the law, or choose what of it to enforce. Those past laws represent what the public widely agreed upon. If the laws don't represent the will of the people, that's the fault of the people for not electing members of Congress to repeal those pieces of legislation. This is why I hold immense respect for former Governor Sarah Palin (R-AK). Sure, her voice may be slightly abrasive, and she might have made a couple of gaffes on the 2008 campaign trail, but at least she understands what the job of the executive is. In her book *Going Rogue*, she discusses her experience as the governor of Alaska, including an episode in which she had an extremely difficult choice to make. Her predecessors had passed a bill that allowed late-term abortion, to which Palin is firmly opposed. She did not have enough votes in the state legislature to repeal the measure, so she decided to just enforce the law. She says in her book that it was one of the toughest decisions she'd ever made, but that she thinks she did the right thing. She's right. The voice of the people comes through the legislative branch, not the executive branch. Unfortunately, she is in a pretty slim minority in her realm. Most governors and presidents in the past century have seen themselves, and have been looked upon by the public, as the head honchos of their respected governments. So, the next time your governor decides not to enforce a law, call his office, and ask why the governor won't just do his job, and let the legislature do theirs.

No one of our constitutional amendments is safe from the onslaught on the Rule of Law that has been steadily accelerating for the past century. The First Amendment is no exception to this attack; the only odd thing about it is that the conservative side of the spectrum supports part of the amendment, while liberals champion the other side. The Founders felt that the Freedom of Religion and the Freedom of the Press were the two most sacred rights that we had. Thomas Jefferson weighed in on this one as usual, saying, "As long as the press is free, and every man able to read, liberty is safe." As far as the regulation of the media goes, I'd like to deregulate the industry as much as humanly possible. Some of the conservatives reading this book may be getting pretty perturbed with me right about now, but we'll get to my reasoning after this philosophical explanation.

All of our political questions break us down into two camps that have existed since ancient China: the people who trust human nature, and the people that think human nature is evil and must be constrained. In ancient China, the people who trusted human nature at its core were called Confucians (following the words of Confucius). Confucians wanted government to be smaller, less restrictive, and modeled after the family unit. Although they had distinct societal ideals, the Confucian camp felt that human nature would lead us there without heavy government intrusion.

The Legalists, on the other hand, didn't trust human nature as far as they could throw it, which was nowhere. The members of this ideology wanted the government to expand and regulate human behavior with strict punishments and excessive laws. They saw people as things to be made subservient to the State, which was, in this case, a regional kingdom or dynasty. Legalists also felt that government had to set strict rules to keep private individuals from accumulating too much power, and wanted the government to reap nearly all the benefits of the productivity of the individual. Legalists in ancient China were the original inventors of the cornerstone of modern liberalism: the thought that we work better as a collective society; and that we are more destructive as individuals.

The Confucians had the idea that we all work better when we have an incentive to benefit from the fruits of our productivity, and that we have a personal responsibility for our decisions. They had this conviction due to their belief in freedom and their faith in the individual conscience.

Every person will come to this revelation at one point in their life, and they will come down solidly on one side of the argument or the other. I am solidly on the Confucian side of the debate, and it is imperative that we conservatives be consistent with our constitutional ideology here. If we don't trust individuals to have the right to write and publish as granted in the Constitution, why should liberals respect the right of Republican gun owners to have firearms? If we don't trust individual Americans to write the news, why should we trust them to independently manage the greatest Industrial economy in the history of the earth? If the liberal media is surviving and thriving, whose fault is it? It's our own fault.

When markets are free, the realities therein reflect what the consumer wants; otherwise companies would not make money, and would readily go broke. In a climate of deregulation, the only people that enable obscenity, slander, or nonsense are the citizens themselves. Either you trust human nature and capitalism to get the nonsense out of the media or you don't. If you don't, that says a lot about human nature. At that point, you have to make a difficult decision philosophically.

Would you rather let people freely commit their own mistakes, and not restrict the rights of the others, or would you rather have a government futilely attempt to control human behavior, when government itself is just a reflection of society? Obviously you can tell what side of this issue I am on. The FCC exemplifies the other side of the argument. In the 1940s, 1950s, 1960s, and 1970s before the Reagan-era deregulation, any television or radio station had to submit evidence that it was doing "community service" to renew their five-year television or seven-year radio licenses. Although regulations on the industry have recently declined, the government still wields its power to coerce the media and threaten the integrity of the First Amendment.

In 2009, the FCC was in battle with Rupert Murdock's Fox News Channel, and Newscorp in general, threatening to revoke the licenses of Fox, and Rush Limbaugh's parent network, EIB, for no apparent reason other than political disagreements with those networks. That same year, the White House made a move to exclude the Fox News Channel from the White House Press Corps, but most of the rest of the media came to Fox News's defense, seeing the plain threat to the First Amendment. What the White House was trying to do was nothing short of undermining the viewership of an unfavorable institution by taking away its access to breaking White House stories. This isn't the first time that the president has tried to coerce and silence the media; it has been commonplace for most presidents since Theodore Roosevelt.

Upon seeing that the press was growing exponentially in size and influence around the turn of the century, the White House started to court reporters, treating favorable reporters nicely. Reporters that were favorable to the president were given stories before other news agencies and were allowed to stay in the West Wing of the White House. This tradition has lived on in the West Wing, and serves as an effective form of government control over the media.

Recently, however, allegations have come about against the Obama administration that assert that the White House has been verbally hostile to unfavorable stories, and is selling access to the president. Bob Woodward, the noted columnist who took part in exposing the Watergate controversy, wrote a column recently in which he gave blame to both the president and Congress for the sequester debacle, saying that the president originally proposed the sequester cuts in the first place. Woodward came under heavy fire from the White House; one senior advisor even told Woodward that he would "regret" his column, although he has since revised his comments, saying he didn't mean it to be a threat.

This harkens back to the days of Woodrow Wilson, when, during World War I, President Wilson even claimed the power to censor newspapers and imprison reporters that spoke out publicly against the American war effort, leading to a complete silencing of the American press until the end of the war.

The likes of this type of government power had not been seen since the Alien and Sedition acts of John Adams, and that almost started the civil war sixty-five years early. The party that passed the Acts quickly declined in popularity, losing two straight elections to the Democratic-Republicans' Thomas Jefferson, and collapsing after the infamous Hartford convention. Woodrow Wilson's Democratic Party declined slightly due to the perception of tyranny, but re-emerged with the stock market crash of 1929. The precedent that was set here is a dangerous one: that the executive branch has the right to temporarily cancel the First Amendment during a time of war. In accordance with that precedent, the government now has the power to censor newspapers that are going to print articles that critically endanger national security, and can pressure reporters to give up their confidential sources. President Nixon nearly got away with not releasing the Watergate tapes to the court on account of, "national security concerns." That's utterly stupid. The court is still a part of the United States government, and it decides whether the information is too secret to be presented in a court. It's not as if the judge is going to announce to the world whatever he saw in the files while reviewing their relevance to the case.

Furthermore, we have the First Amendment for a reason. The reason is to ensure that the government cannot censor what is put in a newspaper that is harmful or helpful to the government's reputation or agenda. If we asked the Founding Fathers when the First Amendment would be the most critical, I would be willing to bet that they would say that it was most important during a war. Think on it; during a war, the government has some of the most profound powers over the republic, and the dissemination of information not previously restrained by the government is absolutely necessary to keep the public from being hoodwinked by a government growing too forceful. If there was ever a time when the Founders would probably expect a military coup to occur, it would be in the aftermath of a war; the time in which the government is the best funded, when the public is on the government's side and getting accustomed to a life without as many liberties. So, can you restrict the First Amendment and still have a truly free society? No, you can't!

So, how do you deal with national security secrets getting out? You trust that the newspaper that published the revealing article goes out of business because no one reads the paper anymore. If your society is relatively smart and patriotic, then its citizens will not take kindly to a publication revealing sensitive information like it's nothing. Pretty soon, the entire readership of said publication will have switched papers. With this example, every other publication that wants to stay alive will not dare print secret national security information, and leaks from the government would quickly decrease. If the publication that prints the sensitive information stays alive, either the public does not like what the government was doing, or the public is not patriotic enough to keep a free-market economy controlled by the consumer. If the former is true, then the leak should have occurred anyway. If the latter is true, economic conservatism is debunked anyway, and the chances of keeping that inept of a society running for long are, well, slim.

In addition to all of that, the president has been using executive orders and signing statements for a while now, with no constitutional provision except the one that states that the president should, "Take care that the laws be faithfully executed." This is the executive branch's form of the elastic clause. On this small and general provision is based the entire authority of the federal bureaucracy, and the ability of the president to issue signing statements and executive orders.

Signing statements are opinions which the president writes when he signs the bill of how he thinks the law should be enacted. Many of these opinions are directly meant to change the entire meaning of a piece of legislation. How that is making sure that the laws are faithfully executed is frankly beyond me. Although many presidents have used signing statements to alter the direction of government, George Bush (the younger) used more of them than any other president, issuing over 800. Rather than blaming Bush blindly, however, we have to look at the underlying trend. Signing statements have been steadily growing in recent decades, and the massive amount of signing statements that came out of the Bush White House was largely a product of a Democratic near-supermajority in both houses of Congress between the 2006 midterms and when President Bush left office.

Normally, a president would just veto the bills coming out of Congress that he didn't like, which is solidly within the confines of the Constitution. However, due to the large numbers of Democrats in both houses that could override any veto that President Bush issued, his best bet was to succumb to the legislation's passage, and use the power of the executive branch to carry out the law in a way that favored the views of the executive. This runs completely contrary to what is laid out in Articles One and Two of the U.S. Constitution, and what the Founder's ideals for the new republic were. The executive's job is simply to carry out the policies that

Congress enacts as the legislative branch enacts them. But, no, we've got a better idea. The executive can just blur the lines of his job and the Rule of Law, and disobey a full house of people directly elected by the people to legislate. So, when the Founders said that the executive should, "Take care that the laws be faithfully executed," they meant that if Congress passed a law that the president didn't agree with, he had to enforce it anyhow. That's why the Constitution instructs the president to faithfully execute the laws in the first place! A singing statement does the exact opposite; it takes care that the law passed by the dually elected legislature will never be faithfully executed. James Madison would be rolling in his grave if he knew how that provision was being twisted to take power away from the "first branch" of government.

The other action that the executive branch is using to seize power at an alarming pace is the "executive order," which allows the president to set forth a policy or mandate, especially within his vast bureaucracy, without the help of Congress. The immense transfer of power that has transpired in the last century or so to the president has culminated in the president's free use of this power. In the 1990s, President Bill Clinton signed executive orders that protected coral reefs from any development or drilling without any congressional approval, preventing oil production in those areas. It's not that I would like to drill in pristine coral reefs; it's that I don't want a president that has the power to protect or destroy them without the consent of the people's house.

Currently, the president has the power to order the death of an American citizen overseas via a drone from his desk, he can send troops anywhere he wants for ninety days, and doesn't have to tell anyone for thirty days. In thirty days with today's military capabilities, the entire world could be gone. For those of you currently saying, "Isn't that a contradiction, I thought you said earlier that nukes made us safer as a deterrent?" good question. If the entire Congress had to make the decision to launch those nukes, you would be right.

However, now imagine that you have put the fate of the world in one man's hands. What if you misjudged that man? What if he's a crazy man at heart? I would much rather have 535 people in the room trying to decide the course of action than one man, because cooler heads should prevail. This was the entire idea behind the Constitutional Convention in Philadelphia.

The judgment of the people is not perfect, as was said before, and you cannot trust one man elected by the people with the entire world. The Constitution was specifically set up to make sure that this kind of thing never happened. So, my answer is that with five hundred people considering the consequences of eviscerating the entire world, and sending it into nuclear winter, both sides should decide to settle the disagreement peacefully due to the deterrent provided by nuclear weapons. If every nation had one person at the head of its government that could decide to launch, a few of them would be off their rockers, and World War III would quickly ensue. That is why you don't want a dictator to have a bomb, you would much rather have a nation like France or Britain with a parliament have the bomb. The whole point of Article One's asserting that only the legislature has the power to declare war is that the Founders wanted to have deliberation aplenty on any issue so important. That's another place where the president is circumventing the Constitution: he does not have to get a declaration of war to engage America in a conflict.

Many Americans have already forgotten that the Korean War, the Vietnam War, Desert Storm, the War in Afghanistan, and the War in Iraq were all fought without the consent of Congress via a declaration of war. Although President Bush is the eternal scapegoat on this issue, he actually consulted Congress before invading Iraq and Afghanistan. Congress willingly gave its power to President Bush in a vote of the full House and Senate. However, President Johnson simply ordered hundreds of thousands of Americans into Southeast Asia without Congress, and President Nixon decided to carpet bomb Hanoi and to invade Cambodia without congressional approval. How do we really think that that's constitutional? We can't be that ignorant. The answer is that people love to turn a blind eye to things that are going wrong if things are going well overall at that point in time.

If you're still the largest economy on earth, the largest military on earth, and have the best standard of living on the planet, what do you care if your government is obeying the rules or not? Much like the emperors of Rome, the president is gaining power ever-faster, especially in relation to foreign policy. We're not a dictatorship yet, but we're getting pretty close. We already have tyranny, because the president has been violating Articles One and Two of the Constitution for multiple decades now. All I'm trying to get across is that we need to tell our executives to do their jobs, let the legislatures do theirs, and watch out for Augustus.

CHAPTER 12

Chip, Chip, Chip: The Disappearing American Culture

E verybody has heard that common expression regarding American culture that describes it as a "melting pot," whether you heard it at home, in a discussion about immigration, in a history class, or in a civics book. The term generally refers to an attitude that most Americans had toward immigration throughout the 20th century. The idea connotes that the immigrants assimilate into existing American culture, becoming somewhat like everyone else, but also contributing their customs and traditions to the society as a whole, enriching our overall national culture. This idea was taught widely to immigrants and others in the late 1800s and early 1900s in public schools, along with a sense of strong patriotism and duty to country. The goal here was to get a nation of very diverse immigrants to have some common culture and background that would keep tensions at bay.

Nations with more homogenous populations generally have much lower rates of violent crime and clashes, because there's not very much to disagree about. Along with a sense of commonality and shared history come a sense of civic duty, obligation to your fellow citizen, and a sense of community. It's pretty much an embodiment of the Jeffersonian ideal, which argues that more public governance closer to home will be more effective and cohesive than a government constituted of more diverse interests. In contrast to James Madison, who wanted the national government to govern from afar, but to not get very much done, or provide many services, Jefferson envisioned a Tocqueville-like society that had a distinct culture and government between regions and states, largely based on how the residents make a living, that was very productive at the local level, while James Madison wanted a large republic with so many interests that none could possibly take over governance, often referred to as the pluralist view of government. America took the Jeffersonian approach toward immigration, trying to make everyone as conformed as possible, to an extent. While we wanted to assimilate them, we did not want to entirely stamp out native culture, but embrace it as part of the new common culture. This approach worked rather well, with high political participation throughout the early part of the 20th century.

In the last half-century, most Westernized nations have adopted a policy called "multiculturalism," which calls for non-assimilation, a higher value on diversity than cohesiveness, and a complete lack of common culture. Multiculturalism has been in wide use across mainland Europe for some time now, and the results are something less than enviable. Ethnic clashes have broken out in Germany, France, and, to a lesser extent, Great Britain, in the past decade. The new policy of the United States is pretty much to emulate what the Europeans have been doing with immigration. Right now, the USA is transitioning from a melting pot mentality to more of a multicultural one. We are not assimilating anybody into our national culture, which is rapidly becoming non-existent itself. The American culture is one that used to be based on traditional family values, financial independence, freedom, the right to carry a firearm, responsibility, respect for the land, enlightenment, self-sufficiency, and an industrious attitude. How much of that do we really adhere to today? Not much. The other element of American culture that was, and still is, to an extent, unique, is our diversity in tradition from place to place, our different outlooks on life and politics based on where we live, and our occupations.

This is what a French visitor and onlooker into American politics that I have referenced twice already, Alexis de Tocqueville, said made our nation so different from any other nation on the face of the earth. Tocqueville noticed that America's homogeneous communities had vast private charities that were obligated to the common well-being without being intrusive, that we had a strong faith in God and each other, and that our sense of freedom and liberty was unmatched, and reflected in the town-hall meetings and local pure democracies that governed this nation. We are losing that culture for a few different reasons.

First of all, the national government has become much stronger in relation to state governments over the past two centuries, with the small exception of the period between 1995 and 2010.

Secondly, large corporations have crowded out smaller businesses all across America for the past half-century, although this is a natural trend. This trend naturally occurs when a business gets so big that it can buy in bulk and offer much lower prices. However, government intervention in the last bubble kept large corporations alive that would have gone under in a purely free-market system. This system obliterates local customs and habits, as the company sells the same thing all across the United States, even the globe, and takes in the majority of young people into its payrolls, which is not a bad thing, unless the government is funding it.

Thirdly, the national government's policies in the last twenty years have been extraordinarily favorable to global enterprises, and extremely disadvantageous for local businesses. One example is the infamous, "Wall Street Reform Bill," or Dodd-Frank.

It's sort of humorous that two congressmen who admitted getting sweetheart deals on their mortgages from Wall Street "reformed" it, for starters. Anyway, the bill was sold in the summer of 2010 to the American people as the end of the equally infamous "Too Big to

Fail" doctrine of the latter years in the Bush administration and the beginning of the Obama administration. In fact, the bill was thousands of pages long and regulated every bank in the U.S. A bank would have to hire so many lawyers just to interpret the legislation that most local banks could not survive. Since the passage of the Wall Street Reform bill, droves of local bank branches have closed because they cannot afford to be in compliance with the law's regulations. So what, you may say; too big to fail is over. Wrong again. Dodd-Frank practically institutionalizes the Too Big to Fail doctrine, ensuring every bank the ability to continue what Gordon Gecko would call, "Moral Hazard."

Moral Hazard is the practice of making risky bets that have the potential to either pay huge dividends, or to sink the entire figurative ship, with other people's money. Banks made trillions of dollars in the early 2000s mortgage bubble before they lost it. Why not make those bets again and try to get out before the music stops? That's exactly what the banks are doing now. Mortgage-backed securities are becoming widely available on the market, and toxic debt is still being traded between the financial houses. The government is once again forcing big banks to make risky loans to borrowers. Democrats will tell you that the Wall Street Reform bill has no provision that codifies Too Big to Fail, and those Democrats would technically be correct. The Wall Street Reform Bill's advocates were able to successfully sell the bill to the American people as the end of the bailout age because that is one of the bill's stated goals. However, what the bill does is to substitute the bailout process with a new process that would allow the government to take full control of a private bank that has failed, "fix" the problems with the bank, and return the bank to the private sector after it has once again become solvent under government leadership. What the heck does that mean? It means that if a bank like Citigroup overextends itself for the ten thousandth time, the government will be authorized by Dodd-Frank to take full control of the bank. At that point, the government would have to pump federal money into running the bank and paying off its debts to keep it afloat. After we had spent a few hundred billion dollars to get the bank out of hot water and double-crossed any investors that had stock in the company, we would turn the bank back over to its former owners in the private sector with no worries. Call me a free thinker, but doesn't that sound an awful lot like a bank bailout in disguise? That's exactly what it is. Now back to what that means for our culture.

As different communities and regions have the same exact places to shop in, and are developed in the same style by the same financial houses, as the housing of every region looks the same, each place loses its own character and tradition. Before you know it, while driving from Michigan to Florida down I-75, with the exception of the accent and the temperature, you can't tell Cherokee County, Georgia from Macomb County, Michigan.

The American culture of respect for the outdoors, competition, and sportsmanship is slowly disappearing with time. Part of this is due to government intervention, but part of it is due to our own tendencies as consumers in recent times. This comes back to the debate in the literary/political world of George Orwell vs. Aldous Huxley, which I have alluded to several times.

Aldous Huxley was a student of the great George Orwell, who thought that, in time, the government would push upon the people a message of collectivism that would resonate, and that we would be entirely controlled by a Big Brother-type government. Orwell thought that the government would have an easy job controlling and observing society because of new technologies. Huxley, although he agreed with Orwell's premise, thought that we would take ourselves into a Big-Brother society dominated by the government and the largest corporations alike through new technologies. The recurring theme of Aldous Huxley's writing, especially in his smash hit novel *Brave New World*, was that humans are essentially slaves to their own pleasures and wants. The internet and wireless technologies are proving Huxley right today. How do you explain a group of people like us Americans with such a rich history to learn from, such a diverse culture to take in, such a great land to love, and such a sacred system of governance to uphold, with access to all the world's information at the tips of our fingers in seconds, being completely clueless and ignorant?

Look around you sometime when you are sitting in a public place or walking down the street. You will see hoards of people sitting on their brand new phones, bought on credit, talking to their friends through a screen about completely useless information, not even spelling things correctly, while North Korea sits ready to start World War III. If you want to see how truly ignorant and aloof our society has become in recent times, take your own personal poll in a public place. Go around asking people relatively common sense questions like: "What decade did the American Civil War occur in?" or "How many people inhabit the United States?" or, better yet, "What president was in office in 1955?" or "Which political party freed the slaves?" You will be both shocked and appalled at some of the ludicrous answers you find yourself on the receiving end of, as I was when I took a poll to see if anyone knew what FDR did about a month before the Japanese attacked Pearl Harbor, which as the main catalyst in the attack. The answer, of course, is that FDR cut Japan's oil imports after it continued to expand through Southeast Asia.

We have a disappearing culture because we have very little reverence for our elders and their stories; the most important job in most cultures. In the 1950s, we had shooting ranges at high schools all across the United States, people went hunting on the weekends for fun, and people knew their natural environment very well. People in this time period, for the most part, respected the land, and reacted harshly in the 1960s when it was discovered that the pesticides that farmers were using were actually poisons. Today, a declining number of people hunt, and we talk about gun control as if it will solve any gun problem. The only reason I know all of this is from talking to my grandfather and my great-grandfather, who I referred to as Bopa. He used to tell me stories about how the depression started, why World War I and II happened, how people lived through the depression, how hard times showed people's true character, and his most frightening predictions.

In 2006, a few years before he died, I will never forget when he uttered, in his frail voice, that America would see another depression soon. All the signs were there, he said. The risky lending was back, the sky-high prices of everything were returning, and the firms that ran America had grown to monstrous proportions once again. I get much of my economic philosophy from him, as he saw it all, from the roaring twenties to the depression, the baby boom, the lost decade of America, and the return of prosperity. He said that the economy was recycled every now and again when companies get too big, get too greedy, lose touch with reality, and take too big of bets, and that smaller and more consumer-oriented companies would spring forth from the ashes and start to grow.

He equated it to the Jack Pine forests of Northern Michigan, which have to have a wildfire for the adult Jack Pines to drop their seeds. If this does not happen, the forest will be taken over by faster-growing trees. The system he described to me in his dying years was one that no longer exists today; we are more like Western European democracies than our old self today. The government will not let that cycle occur, and, thus, the forest cannot replenish itself. Today, our people, especially our young people, do not understand what bound Americans together in times past and what our rich traditions are. We have lost sight of that "Shining City on a Hill" mentality in the last few decades, and the culture that goes with it. How many Americans truly feel safe in a nation with unhindered Second Amendment rights? How many people know the true statistics about any issue? Not very many; the vast majority just get the tidbits that the mass media force feed us. You may say, "A disappearing culture or lack of common culture has never brought a nation down."

If one takes a close look at France in the years before World War II (mid and late 30s), it was experimenting with its first round of multiculturalism. In addition, France was teaching its own history to its young people in a way that degraded France's position in world affairs (teaching the Treaty of Versailles and World War I from a neutral perspective, for example). When the Germans invaded France in 1940, most military experts thought that the French would stop the German offensive dead in its tracks, and quite possibly take it all the way back to Berlin. However, with a weak common culture, an absence of nationalism, and an anemic sense of duty to country, the Germans rolled over the French like a bulldozer in just a few weeks. The French would not be a free people again for another four and a half years after 1940. That takes me to my next point about our culture: our de-emphasis on history.

For as long as civilization has existed, learning and re-telling the history of your people has been maybe the most important thing for young people to be able to do. In early agricultural societies, and still today in third-world societies, the most important job in the village is "storyteller." Learning our history is important because, as the old quip goes, "History repeats itself." That is probably the most prophetic quote ever spoken. People have known this simple truth ever since the time of the ancient Greeks, and have treated the past with some measure of reverence over the millennia. Currently, we are putting less and less emphasis on students learning the basic history of the United States in our schools, and de-emphasizing the need to learn about our system of governance. Governance and history are usually wrapped up with social science and geography in "Social Studies" classes.

If you ask the average 18 year-old, or maybe even the average, American what system of government the United States has, they will invariably, and much to my chagrin, say "Democracy, of course." Of course, we all know that America is truly a republic governed democratically, not a democracy. Our educational system as it pertains to history has not always been this way. In the late 1800s and early 1900s, as part of the nationalist and assimilationist policies in the school system (which was run entirely by the states and localities at the time) and the country as a whole, there was a special emphasis put upon American history in schooling, especially parts of our history that defined what road our nation went down. Today, that time is long gone, as we put more and more emphasis on computer classes and technology in our schools. Not to get off point here, but anyone on earth can get into a basic accounting or computer-based job with probably under one year of training. Even worse, many people, especially those in the educational system, dismiss our Founding Fathers and our heritage, saying that we were founded by a bunch of "rich, old white men." We also seem to hold the belief that the Constitution is a dusty old document that is completely irrelevant in today's society, and that America is an institution that has been the oppressor of the third world and minorities; a force for entrenched, moneyed interests. This, combined with putting an emphasis on the darker moments in American history when we do teach it (Cherokee march, Japanese internment camps, and segregation in the South) creates a feeling among the younger generations that being an American is nothing exceptional at all. This is not to say that our nation has never made a mistake or mistreated anyone, it certainly has.

However, I am inclined to think that the United States has been a force for order and goodness overall. The examples of America's compassion are visible all over: fighting AIDS with billions of dollars that we don't have in Africa, intervening to help Muslim Bosnia ward off Orthodox Christian Croatia in the 1990s, donating immense sums of money to our own poor despite a tax system that is supposed to take care of those people for us, and our private citizens going all over the world as humanitarian workers with organizations such as the Red Cross. Overall, America is a very righteous nation that consistently fights for democratic government around the world, and protects the oppressed. Moreover, the effect of what we are currently doing with the new generation is to destroy any national pride that we have left in the coming decades. In short, we're following in France's footsteps.

Another problem that America is having with our current culture is that we are currently experiencing a downturn in civic participation, community attachment, church attendance, and voting levels. In the late 1800s and early 1900s, when political parties were very strong institutions, we regularly had voter turnouts in presidential elections that were above 70% of the VAP (Voting-Aged Population). Not to completely mutilate a dead horse, but I think that this occurrence was due more to the common culture that America shared at that time and the immense sense of duty to our traditions and customs that we felt, not the strength of political parties. However, Boss Tweed's notorious coercion and brutal tactics probably didn't hurt voter turnout levels either. If you talk to any political scientist, especially the more statist ones, they will tell you that the abysmal 40% and 50% voter turnout levels that we are seeing are due to a spirit of individualism that has emerged since the first election of Ronald Reagan and the modern conservative movement. These politicos assert that a feeling of individualism and an unwillingness to share your wealth or time with other people will invariably lead to a non-existent sense of community and civic duty.

With all due respect, Ronald Reagan and the conservative movement did more to re-establish a sense of community and civic obligation than anything post-1970. So, what is civic obligation and community connection? The way I would define it is being rooted in a community, knowing and respecting your fellow man, and being involved in a spiritual organization of some kind. In short, it's being social. Isn't that what the entire "Moral Majority" and "Christian Right" movements were all about? The entire conservative movement of the 1980s was about being more connected to the poor through personal charity instead of taxes, more involved in your church or synagogue than to your television, and being more friendly to your neighbors while maintaining a sense of what's yours and what's not, which was a larger share of your paycheck, and a smaller share for government.

If you're still not convinced that individualism is not the reason for America's poor political participation levels as compared to other Westernized democracies, consider some of the presidents elected when voter participation was at its height in the early 1900s. One of those presidents was Calvin Coolidge, perhaps the most individualistic president in American history, who was elected in 1924 by a whopping margin by a humungous electorate that included newly enfranchised women. Just how individualistic was Calvin Coolidge? Well, he was quoted as saying, "If the federal government were to go out of existence, the common run of people would not detect the difference." Now there's a real conservative. Also to be elected from this time of great political participation were Presidents Grover Cleveland, who vetoed a bill to help Texas farmers cope with a historic drought, and Herbert Hoover, who was so confident in the free-market system that he let the markets keep going without government assistance for many months after the great stock market crash of 1929, and decided to implement only a tariff in 1930 (the Hawley-Smoot Tariff), not a financial aid bill, nearly a full year after the New York Stock Exchange had taken a nose-dive. So I say to those who would have us believe that our apathy for politics and our cynicism is caused by the bliss of the American free market system and the politics of self-sufficiency, our apathy is caused by a lack of reverence for our own heritage, an avalanche of instant-gratification technology, the blunders and mishaps of the federal government and public sector that warrant actual cynicism, a decline in the importance of social gatherings, and ultra-liberal ideology itself, which argues that religion and faith are not important components of our life at all, and that a common social fabric is not necessary in society. If you actually think that low church attendance is caused by Ronald Reagan's conservative movement, not the secular progressive movement that has taken religion out of every holiday possible, I would suggest the nearest psychiatric ward.

I would also contend that the low voter turnouts that we have been seeing during recent decades have been caused by an abundance of cynicism for the political process and politicians in general. This is not to say that these feelings are unfounded, they are as well-founded as a secret underground military base. The people have plenty of reasons to be pessimistic toward their political leadership when every large bank in America gets a federal bailout, the job creation situation is utterly stagnant, we are due for hyperinflation as a result of Federal Reserve policies, hypocrisy runs abound in the government, the Republican Party can't hold to principles, the Democratic Party can't figure out where the heck it is, and we spend billions of taxpayer dollars on a literal bridge to nowhere. If Congress were a lawn mower company, it would have a really tough time selling its new model, because the advertisement would be: "Buy the Congress 2014; it stalls all the time, it gets little accomplished, it requires repair, and it can't decide which direction it wants to go."

As I discussed in the chapter regarding the 2012 presidential elections, Americans have plenty of good reason to be very cynical of the intentions of both parties. What would politicos and optimists have us do? Would we jump for joy as the U.S. Congress disobeys the will of the American people on any one of a multitude of issues, spend trillions of dollars on a healthcare system that nearly everyone agrees will fail, burns the Constitution for political expedience, or gives all of its constitutional authority to the executive branch? As an extremely politically informed would-be voter, I can honestly say that, if I was eighteen in time to vote in the 2012 presidential elections, I might have just stayed home out of depression, although I definitely preferred one candidate over the other. Why should we have dazzling turnout levels if we are forced to choose between a quasi-oligarchy and socialism? The low turnout in American politics is not a symptom of a fault within the American people, but a sign that the money flooding our political system is stymieing the voice of the party bases in favor of a moderate who will keep the status quo.

As far as a lack of civic obligation goes, what obligation can you feel to a government that functions aloofly more than 1000 miles away? The "good-old-days" America of the 1950s and 1960s that politicos long for existed as a decentralized republic in which everyone realized that their actions and political actions had immediate and local consequences that had the potential to better their respective communities. In short, it was the last gasp of Alexis de Tocqueville's America. That country is dead and gone, I hate to say.

Why would you waste your time showing up at a community school board meeting that discusses teacher pay and contracts if the state government is just going to file a lawsuit if it thinks that the community is wrong? You wouldn't. Neither would I. By the same token, what schmucks are going to raise money for private or church-based charity if they think that their taxes are completely taking care of that issue? This is the fundamental problem, I believe, underlying our lack of civic responsibility and involvement. Once again, if you talk to an elitist political scientist, they will say that the "rights culture" that developed during the mid-1960s along with the civil rights movement turned the focus of Americans from getting government to work more efficiently to getting the government to not work at all.

Frankly, that's a bunch of stuff; the focus of the individualistic movement in America was, and still is, to get the *federal* government off the backs of the people; no one said anything about local and state government. Thomas Jefferson outlined this idea pretty clearly in his writings, constantly emphasizing his "government closest governs best" mentality. The concept of Jeffersonian Conservatism is that the individual has supreme power over their own life, that the local government has more control over people than the state government, and that the state government has more power than the federal government, which provides the services that only a large, united society can provide to its people, which are outlined specifically and strictly in the federal Constitution, which serves as the most legitimate and holy agreement between the government and its people. The local and state governments are supposed to be able to do anything to maintain order and run their domains, as long as it does not infringe on its citizens' fundamental constitutional rights. If a citizen does not like the way his government is running things, he can move.

If I live in Vermont and oppose gay marriage, I can always "vote with my feet" like the people of other nations do. However, if political power is highly centralized at the national level, I can't move away from the problem without exiting society. The rule of thumb that most Founders would agree with would be that the national government cannot do anything unless the Constitution specifically says that it *can* do it. At the state and local government levels, the government can do anything that is not specifically prohibited by the national Constitution or established state constitutions. Why did the Founders set up such a discrepancy in governmental powers? If the government at city hall decides to ignore the peoples' will, or has a disagreement with the ultimate source of governmental authority as James Madison saw it: the people, it doesn't have a standing army to enforce its will. The federal government does, and, thus, the Founders reasoned, it had to be constrained in as many ways as possible. To understand the Founders, you have to be as paranoid as a KGB agent, but the enemy is tyranny, especially by way of force or factions. To get back to the point, we have long since abandoned the Jeffersonian model of self-governance in favor of an all-intrusive national government, causing people to be disinterested in the operation of a government eerily similar to Inspector Clouseau on a case: utterly lost, overtly confident, unbelievably arrogant, and constantly bungling any situation at hand. The solution to our political participation does not lie within the hands of a more powerful and dictatorial government, but of a closer government that works for the people more effectively.

Our sister republic in time, the Roman Republic, also had some problems with a lack of civic duty, and an absence of common morals. As Rome's economy modernized as previously discussed, the number of men that held the minimum amount of land required to be able to serve in the Roman armed forces pulled a Lehman Brothers move. Since not only serving in the armed forces, but also voting, in the Roman Republic, required owning some sort of property (much like the early days of the American Republic), political participation in Rome became more and more concentrated as time went by, making nearly all decisions highly centralized and insurmountable, as all the wealth and power was held by just a few in Roman society. What citizen was going to worry about the economic implications of what the government was doing if they were too busy worrying about where their next meal was going to come from?

The next problem that America has been developing over the last few decades with its culture is the disconnect that we now have with reality, each other, and serious political discussion. In large part, this problem can be attributed to the burgeoning of communications technology in the past score (Think four score and seven years ago). People don't get their news from evening TV broadcasts anymore, and they generally don't read the newspapers. What people do now to attain their daily fix of news coverage is to go on the internet to news websites and blogs, which tend to have dominant leanings one way or the other. This would not necessarily be a bad thing if people did not personalize their news, something that most people are able to do now. Don't misunderstand me; I don't want the federal government to intervene, and I don't think that I have any business telling someone else how to get their information fix, but if everyone is hearing only their side of the argument, they tend to demonize the other side of the point, and not understand their fellow Americans very well.

This phenomenon can be plainly seen on every single news program on television now. Just watch one and you'll realize something rather chilling: Americans can't even agree on what reality is anymore because everyone is trying to score political points. It's not that this is a new technique by any means, muck-racking, mud-slinging, and slander have been going on as long as people have walked the earth, but we always could find something to agree on before. A good example of what I mean can be found in the coverage of the recent Benghazi conundrum. If you talked to Democrats that only watched MSNBC or listened to Howard Stern and other liberal talk programs, they would call the Benghazi hearings a "witch-hunt" regardless of the fact that someone changed the CIA talking points a dozen times to edit out the real story, a presidential election was in full swing, and the Accountability Review Board did a horrendous job interviewing everyone that needed to be interviewed.

Even though it is plainly obvious that no one showed up for a spontaneous protest with Rocket-Propelled Grenades and was dead silent, and that the CIA knew what happened and chose to disseminate a lie instead at someone's request, liberals and conservatives have two completely different viewpoints on an issue that should be no more complicated that ascertaining what reality is. On some issues, conservatives would be just as out of touch. My point is that as our society gets more and more technologically complicated and isolated from each other personally, we find ourselves in a world that looks increasingly like the creation of Ray Bradbury in *Fahrenheit 451.*

Try to have a really profound conversation about politics and the direction of our country with just an average Joe when you get the time, and just see what happens. Nine times out of nine-point-one you'll lose him when you start talking about what actually drove the recession, what the Federal Reserve actually does, or the Founding. Something else you might observe when conducting this experiment is that at least one-third of the people that you converse with will text at some point during the discussion, and it will be a text about something rather meaningless and mundane. The big question here is this: How can you solve all of your problems with a populace that is more interested in the latest episodes of a TV series and what happens in the imaginary social world than what the price of oil is going to be in twenty years?

Our culture is disappearing in another disturbing way—the traditional family unit is losing reverence—even being undermined-by government and society at large alike. When I discussed my birth in Texas in the illegal immigration chapter, I said that my parents had to foot a bill of over $10,000, and that illegal immigrants didn't have to foot anything. A few months before my birth, a nurse made another cost-cutting suggestion that infuriated my parents. She said that the government paid for the births of children that are born into separated marriages, and that, if payment was a problem, my mother and father should have just gotten a separation, let the government pay for my birth, and then gotten back together. This is the nature of many welfare programs today. The programs discourage American families from having two parents or a limited number of children by providing adults financial incentives to have many children without getting together, in addition to refundable child tax credits. This is one of the major reasons why American divorce rates are at all-time highs and over 50% of the children born in America are born out of wedlock. What we are doing is incentivizing bad behavior and sending out a message that nearly any behavior is acceptable socially. Most young people see marriage and the traditional family as out-of-date institutions that are obsolete in the modern world. This trend is not going to abate any time soon given the general direction that our culture is heading. For many people, it is much more profitable and frugal to be a single parent or to not work than to have a two-parent household.

Whether or not we like it, the most effective way to teach a new generation and bring them up is to have two-parent families. Just ask any teacher what child is going to do better, one who has been in day care for the first five years of their life with no instruction, or a child that has had a parent teaching and nurturing them for those first five years. The teacher will tell you that the child with parental guidance is going to be more socially aware, generally more knowledgeable, and more amiable overall than the one that has spent five years in day care. The most critical years of learning take place before we are ever in a classroom setting, in terms of raw knowledge volume. I am a direct product of this. Because of my mother sacrificing income to spend time with her children, my earliest memories are of learning all 50 states by shape at two years old, taking hikes to identify trees, and my sighting of a Garter Snake on a walk at three years leading to my learning every Midwestern reptile and amphibian within a short few years.

Sadly, this type of situation is growing rarer and rarer in America today, as inflationary policies of the Federal Reserve and stagnant wages force both parents into the workforce. There are those who will attack this short paragraph for being anti-feminist or anti-women in the workplace, when it is neither. I firmly believe that women and men alike should be completely free to choose how to live their lives and whether or not to work. I am simply saying that children who receive more quality time with their parents and less time sitting in front of a TV or a game system usually turn out much better than the latter, and that this tradition is being abandoned in an America increasingly based on materialism rather than morals. Moreover, when both parents are working to provide for their children, and when they provide PS3s, I-Phones, and the like, we create less reverent children that inherit a culture of pretentiousness and materialism through osmosis. Why do you think that we have seen children become less and less disciplined and more disrespectful as we have gone through the years?

Anytime a discussion of American families and social issues arises, the issue of gay marriage always comes up, and I will not disappoint. Honestly, gay marriage should be a state issue; it's as simple as that. As I have previously mentioned, the republic was set up to have experimentation within the states that did not apply to the union as a whole. If what one state does works, other states will adopt similar measures. If Vermont wants to be the gay marriage state, I'll oppose it in that state, and I might campaign against it, but I'm not going to use the federal government to try to stop them; it's the prerogative of the state's people, not the nation as a whole. If I don't like that my state government have enacted those laws, I don't have to live there! This is the beautiful thing about state and local control. Why should gay marriage be a state issue? Because we have a Tenth Amendment, that's why! When liberals pass sweeping health care reforms or welfare programs that we think are unconstitutional, we aren't going to have much credibility when we say so if we violate the Constitution's Tenth Amendment for our own interests. If you don't want to live in the midst of legally recognized gay unions, like I don't, live in Texas. In twenty years, let's see what states have the highest crime rates, the lower GDP growth rates, the higher unemployment rates, and the higher welfare recipient percentages. I'd be willing to bet that the states with gay marriage would have all of those things. However, if those states didn't, it wouldn't be a big deal, because we didn't take the entire country in one direction or another. Only a few states would be affected.

It seems to me that the main beef conservatives and religious Americans have with gay couples is that they just don't want that relationship to be called "marriage." Maybe a compromise could be reached by allowing same-gender relationships to get all the tax benefits of normal marriages (or, better yet, eliminate everyone's tax exemptions and adopt a flat tax) as long as those relationships are not called marriages, reserving that title for traditional couples.

The most compelling argument for national gay marriage is the one based on the Fourteenth Amendment's Equal Protection Clause, which states that all citizens get equal judgment before the law. Since the federal government gives tax credits to normal marriages that it does not give to gay marriages from the states that have them, same-gender advocates say that their Fourteenth Amendment rights are being violated. The Equal Protection Clause of the Fourteenth Amendment is what allowed the decision in *Brown v. Board*. Here's my humble take on the Equal Protection Clause: the clause only applies if the trait that is differentiated upon is something that you can't help. For example, the amount of work that you put into your education has a heavy bearing upon how smart you are, which has a direct influence on how much you get paid. The Supreme Court cannot step in and say that smart people being paid more is unconstitutional because it violates the Equal Protections Clause, in my view, because intelligence is a largely alterable characteristic that is determined by oneself every bit as much as genes. In contrast, when African-Americans and Caucasians have to go to separate schools, it is unconstitutional because no one can help their own ethnicity. This, I believe, applies only to race, gender, etc (physical characteristics). Since it is widely up for debate whether or not people choose their orientation, it does not apply to the Equal Protection Clause. Therefore, the issue of marriage can be left entirely to the states' discretion.

Since I mentioned the Equal Protection Clause, why not get into affirmative action for the heck of it? As the Supreme Court hinted at with the recent decisions in the *Bakke* and *Gratz* cases, affirmative action is a form of discrimination itself. The only reason that we have affirmative action programs is to give minority groups preference over everyone else for past injustices, I guess. That's not what equality is supposed to be. To be blunt, the fact that equal is the root word of equality is not a coincidence. Affirmative Action programs directly violate the Equal Protection Clause of the Fourteenth Amendment by differentiating based upon an uncontrollable characteristic. Instead of deciding who gets to go to college or get a public-sector job based on race, why don't we decide that question *entirely* based upon merits without regard to what race of people the employees or applicants are? This would be a truly equal system. The system we have right now doesn't make us color-blind, or even encourage color-blindness; it amplifies our divisions.

The only way to judge someone is to look at the content of their character and their merits; anybody who judges another person based upon someone's appearance or ethnicity is an idiot. There's no way to be nice about this. A nation or civilization that stratifies itself based on uncontrollable characteristics has no right to call itself a bastion of liberty. For those of you who are for affirmative action, I would have you consider whether it is possible to discriminate against a majority. If it is possible for a minority group being given advantages based upon its minority status to be called discrimination, then what we are doing now is definitely discrimination. This is not the vision of the 1960s civil rights movement. Martin Luther King was for equal opportunities and a level playing field for citizens; a tolerant nation that was color-blind, not a nation in constant pursuit of a social justice that will never be had through means of bigger government. If, on the other hand, you answered that a majority is the only group that can discriminate, first check the dictionary, then consider this: Caucasians will be fewer in number than those of Hispanic heritage in this country by the turn of the next century. At that point, the tables will turn, and Caucasians will be the ones benefitting from affirmative action programs. Why does anyone have to benefit from affirmative action programs? The most effective way of running a society is to let the free market determine employment and college entrance based on merit. Some might say, "That's a bit of a rosy outlook, don't you think, Mr. Author?" No, I don't think that's a rosy outlook at all.

In the capitalist economy, the businesses and colleges that succeed will be the ones that hire people with the most merit. If a business chooses to be racist and hire people without merit because they are a certain color, it has relegated itself to defeat when in competition with a company that hires solely based on merit. It shouldn't make a difference if the CEO of GE is orange, green, or checkered as long as he can keep a balance sheet. Many people see opposition to affirmative action as racist. I would say that just the opposite is true. Opposition to affirmative action is an endorsement of everyone's ability to compete without advantages, and support for true equality. I don't want my firemen to be employed because they are white and the station was low on Caucasians, I want them there because they can fight fires better than anyone else for heaven's sake! The disturbing bit about this whole thing is that the situation that I just cited actually happened recently in Connecticut. Now-Supreme Court Justice Sota Sotamayor presided over the case, and found that Caucasian firemen that scored higher on their tests than their minority counterparts didn't have a case because their unemployment was caused by perfectly legal affirmative action programs. Sotamayor's decision was later overturned by the Supreme Court.

The way I see it, call me naïve, is that every citizen is not a Caucasian-American or a Hispanic-American, but is just an American, and many people would appreciate it if our legal system started acting like it. That leads me into one of the most ridiculous notions I have ever been displeasured to acquaint myself with-the hate crime. If you're not familiar with the notion of a hate crime, it's a charge applied when your crime was motivated by malice for a particular ethnicity, gender, or race. So, essentially, if someone killed a Jew because that person was anti-Semitic, the charge would be a hate crime plus murder. You know, maybe it's just me, but I think that just the murder charge should probably be enough to nail the son-of-a-gun. Are we really at the point where charging someone with murder or manslaughter is not enough? It seems utterly inexplicable why we have to qualify crimes based on whom the crimes were directed toward. Assault of a white man is a charge that should have disappeared along with Jim Crow if you ask me. A murder is a murder, that's all there is to it. We don't need to qualify crime based on uncontrollable characteristics; we just need an equal justice system. As I have previously stated, multiculturalism never works, and it only increases tension. Affirmative action is a symbol of America not being a place of equality, not the other way around. The best equalizer on earth is the free market.

CHAPTER 13

Laissez-Faire: Keynes vs. Adam Smith and Milton Friedman

E ssentially, two views on the economic liberty front collide in this nation: the first being that the government spending money and printing it stimulates the demand side of the supply-and-demand equation, and that the government should serve as the rescuer of any business that falls, lest it lay off workers. The second view argues that the free market, not government intervention, will always be the best course of action for the average person in society and that voluntary trade improves society through Adam Smith's theory of an "invisible hand," of free markets. These two factions have been battling in America since the late 1800s; going back and forth multiple times. The supporters of Adam Smith (free-market side) would favor dismantling the entire federal welfare system, ending most government bureaucracies, the end of the Federal Reserve System, deregulation of every industry, and the discontinuation of the bailout system. The supporters of John Maynard Keynes (government intervention side) would support even more quantitative easing by the federal government, embrace the "Too Big to Fail" doctrine, want higher taxes on all classes, and support the government providing more services and borrowing more money.

The first subject of contention between the free-market supporters and the Keynesian economists is the issue of welfare. Those who support a strong welfare system maintain that it is nearly impossible to rise from poverty in America, that the poor are victims of society, that welfare is the way out, that it is our obligation, and that only government can efficiently help those people in need. First of all, American society is the most socially mobile society on planet earth; with nearly no barriers to people based on ethnicity or previous class, but based on merit and appeal to the consumer. My family experienced this societal reality first-hand. My grandfather is part Native American, and grew up poor in Fort Wayne, Indiana. How poor is poor?

Well, try no indoor plumbing. My grandfather grew up in a family of five (a father, mother, two boys, and a girl) in an 800 sq. ft home with no interior doors—just curtains. My grandfather's family had food often, but not always, and when they did, it was the product of extensive hunting, fishing, gathering of dandelion greens, asparagus, walnuts, mulberries, apples, peaches and more, and various vegetables from a huge garden that was plowed, which was tilled and weeded using only rudimentary implements and muscle. They took monthly trips to the "dump" for both essentials and extras. My great grandfather often rode his bicycle several miles and arrived at about sunrise at a wooded area known to abound with squirrels, where he waited for hours until he had the opportunity to bag two squirrels with but a single reloaded shotgun shell (the product of his ingenious use of a file, scrap metal, etc.), squeezed one of the two triggers of the 1800s double-barreled shotgun that could have easily blown up in his face, and hoped for the best. Thankfully, his hopes were realized, and he brought home 10 to 12 squirrels. He and my grandfather caught numerous turtles from the St. Joseph, St. Mary and Maumee rivers. My grandfather would wade through the muddy bed of the long, unused Wabash-Erie Canal, which was operational from 1832 until 1871, feeling around for the burrows of large Blanding's Turtles.

He would return to the same canal bed late at night to gig frogs. In addition, the entire family would go the "dump" (an old-fashioned one, not a refuse-filled receptacle like today's typical landfill) where the well, somewhat well, and a bit well-to-do citizens would bring or send unwanted items to be covered with soil at a later date. Here, the family would search for, often find, and take home useable and repairable items such as washboards, small motors, furniture, clothing, toys, building materials, and more. In short, my grandfather and his family members were struggling to stay alive. Despite the family's poverty, my grandfather was able to get into Hillsdale College because of his hard work and merit, where he was introduced, for the first time, to the savory condiment-butter, became an All-American defensive lineman, and graduated as the valedictorian of his class. All the while, he was playing the spoons in local bars after his school days in exchange for hamburgers. It's a darn good thing that a helpful government worker never approached my ancestors and told them that Uncle Sam would take care of their every need and that they did not need to strive to get out of their situation, or I wouldn't be writing this book.

This brings me to a very important point that is lost on most of America's liberals—the American poor live better than kings did in Europe a few centuries ago, and certainly better than the poor of a few decades ago in this country. The poor are able to get cheap food and obtain low-income jobs relatively easily. By world standards, the lower classes of America are at least middle-to-upper class. What other nation's poorest classes have enough money to have cell-phones? Are there completely flat broke people in this country that have absolutely nothing? Of course there are, but there are not many of those people compared to the masses that we consider "poor."

Someone working minimum wage now has so much more purchasing power than a minimum-wage worker in the 1940s or 1950s that it is astonishing. By looking back at historical minimum wages and prices, I calculated that someone working minimum wage in the 1940s over a summer only had enough money to buy a select few small items like a black-and-white TV set and a camera without factoring in any other living costs. Today, that same worker could buy an HD TV for $1,000, a used car for $2,000, a zip drive, ten albums, an electric guitar, and other miscellaneous goods without factoring in living costs.

The only times in which the conditions of living for the poorest among us and the average people have improved are those times in which the government got out of the way and let private ingenuity take the lead. Take this example: in the 1940s, the American poverty rate was over 20%. In the 1950s and early 1960s, the private sector made many advances, and investment in the post-war economy and baby boom era abounded. By 1968, the American poverty rate, according to the U.S. Census Bureau and the Department of Labor (DOL), had dropped to 13%.

That year, President Lyndon Baines Johnson declared his infamous "War on Poverty" that created many of today's government-funded welfare benefits. Welfare payouts have increased by about 1000% between then and now, and the lowest the American poverty rate got during that time was 10%, with an average right around the 13% mark. Today, according to the Census Bureau and DOL, the poverty rate is 16%. President Obama has a clever word for this—he calls it recovery!

What's more is that the poverty rate would be nearly 100% around the late 1800s if we measured it the same way back then! What do you think lifts up the boats of the poor, a rising tide for all fueled by private-sector innovation, or government inefficiencies and programs? The truth is that we could have a much more efficient system of taking care of America's poor fueled by private donations and community organizations.

Earlier, I alluded to the fact that President Grover Cleveland vetoed a measure to relieve Texas farmers from a severe drought. He told the farmers, upon vetoing the bill, to wait for private charities to respond to the disaster, and count on everyday Americans giving money out of the goodness of their hearts. When the stories of drought hit the national papers, people from all over America were sending money to Texas communities, and the farmers received ten times more in private donations than they were seeking through the federal government. This is one glaring example of a contrast between the efficiencies of community-based charity and private generosity and the deficiencies of government bureaucracy. Another glaring example happened just recently, when a man from Texas (God bless Texans), fed up (no pun intended) with the governmental response to "Super-storm" Sandy, drove his pickup truck from Texas to Connecticut with a few generators for $1,000 in fuel, besting FEMA, an agency that managed to get a whopping one generator operating in the state of Connecticut two weeks after the storm with hundreds of millions of dollars in government funding. That's one expensive generator. There can be no greater example than this of Milton Friedman's economic principles.

As to the claim that welfare is a moral obligation and an effective way out of poverty for the poor, consider this: the African-American teenage unemployment rate immediately following the Second World War was 9%. Today, that number stands at nearly 40% according to the U.S. Department of Labor. What changed during that period of time more than anything else? America's attitude toward the obligation to work and welfare changed big-time, that's what happened. Also, reconsider the statistic cited at the outset of this chapter about Lyndon Johnson's "Great Society" plan. Welfare is not the way to get a struggling people out of the dumps, free-market capitalism is. Free trade can enable businesses to grow to the point that they have more jobs available than people to fill them, at which point the laws of supply and demand that Keynesian economists do not believe in take over, and wages rise dramatically, even faster than inflation or the standard of living. This is the way that Western Europe went from a mercantilist economy of agrarians and archaic farming practices to an Industrial powerhouse in just a few centuries.

To be perfectly honest, the biggest thing that keeps the poor in poverty (although many do become better off) is the minimum wage set by the federal government. That may seem counter-intuitive, I know. First off, before I get into the nitty-gritty, let's see how many of you know why we have a minimum wage. In the late 1800s and early 1900s, according to stats taken by the U.S. Census Bureau, the African-American unemployment rate in this nation was actually lower than the Caucasian unemployment rate.

Construction companies from the South were hiring African-Americans for low prices compared to highly unionized Northern building companies, and African-Americans were gaining financial independence as their respective companies grew by underbidding the northern construction firms for summer jobs. Congress decided that it had to do something to eliminate African-Americans working in small firms with not much capital from the market. So, what did Congress do?

It passed a bill called the Davis-Bacon Act, better known today as the minimum wage. It said that construction firms had to pay their employees "prevailing wages." Many of the start-up construction companies that were getting southern African-Americans away from sharecropping with higher wages, but lower wages than the Northern unions and much less capital, couldn't afford to pay their employees "prevailing wages," and went out of business, sending the people who worked for them back to sharecropping in the rural South. Not only were politicians looking out for unions, but they supported a bill that had a direct racial correlation. William Greene, the leader of the American Federation of Labor-Congress of Industrial Organizations (AFL-CIO) in 1931, testified before the Senate in favor of the minimum wage law, saying that "colored labor is being brought in to demoralize wage rates." Wow.

It's a good thing that those politicians were looking out for the less fortunate. Since then, highly unionized firms have had the advantage in crowding out less unionized competition with more low-paid workers. This trend holds every time the minimum wage increases. When the minimum wage goes up, businesses can't afford to hire as many people without established skills, because those businesses aren't going to take a risk by paying an unknown quantity $10 an hour starting out. What ends up happening is that the labor market shrinks and the average wages in America remain relatively constant. So, the idea behind the "living wage" becomes more of a "dying will." So, you may be asking yourself, "How the heck are we going to get along without a minimum wage; I'm not going to work for twenty-five cents an hour!?" I'd say, "Exactly!" We'd enter a bit of a "Who's on First" routine, and I'd finally explain that wages wouldn't come down to anything near $0.25 an hour precisely because you won't work for it.

Employers may be greedy, to an extent, and that's exactly what will keep your wages about where they are now. If everyone in the business quits because wages are $4 an hour and the boss is going to rake in 75% of the profit, the boss doesn't have a business anymore, and he will re-negotiate until he reaches a level acceptable to both parties that preserves both your wages and the boss's ability to make a profit (Adam Smith's principles at work; both sides must benefit in a trade). Any profit is better than zero. Unless people are willing to work for $1 an hour, it is never going to happen. If the people are willing to work for that wage, let them get what they deserve. In the end, we might complain about our labor, but we're the ones that ultimately control the price of labor in a free market. The problem with that system arises when a rural Kentucky mine owner hires gunmen and forces you to work for a certain wage. At this point, a union is probably preferable to a minimum wage anyhow.

By the way, the Davis-Bacon Act (minimum wage) was passed in 1931. Anybody have a guess as to what decade saw African-American labor participation rates fell below Caucasian rates, to never come back? The 1930s did. What a remarkable coincidence.

Not one supporter of the minimum wage or Keynesian economics has ever been able to explain to me why the standard of living in America rose so dramatically under a completely free market system in the late 1800s and early 1900s, and why all the minimum wage laws that we have fail to improve the average wages of U.S. workers. The answer is relatively simple. If we impose a mandate on businesses requiring them to pay people $20 an hour, that will not mean that everyone will start magically making $20 an hour, but that's what the government assumes it would mean. What would happen, as it should be plainly obvious to anyone, is that the business would have to lay off workers to maintain some sort of profit margin, meaning that those who are left with a job would make much more, but that a business would not be able to afford to keep all of its employees, and if the number of employees it can retain is not enough to keep it productive, the business will shut its doors, and Uncle Sam will find himself paying those workers unemployment benefits rather than seeing them make $20 an hour. Once again, this just goes to show the pure economic genius of the federal government. The end result of this minimum wage increase will be that larger businesses can afford to keep more people on board at the new rates and stay alive, while many small businesses have to close up shop. From this, about the same amount of capital overall would be going into hiring employees, and the average wage, including those not working, would remain relatively constant. That sounds kind of like what's been going on for the past three decades in America-stagnant wages and increasing prices.

Perhaps the most pronounced and important divide between the right and left with regard to the appropriate role of the federal government is that the left believes that political equality has to translate into economic equality in order to have a "fair" or "equal" society, while the right believes that keeping a small federal government is the best insurance policy against a government seeking to take away political freedoms, and that economic opportunity is superior to dependence. Milton Friedman would have put it more succinctly than I just did and say, "A society that aims for equality before liberty will achieve neither; a society that aims for liberty before equality will achieve a great measure of both." The simple truth is that freedom is not freedom if the government is telling you how much of your labor you can keep and how to help your fellow man who has fallen off the tracks. This battle can be exemplified by multiple mini-struggles throughout the issue spectrum, but can be easily represented by two issues on which most liberals think they are on sound footing when they are in fact standing on an unstable ledge: Equal Pay for Equal Work laws and the morality of helping people out of poverty and inequality through government.

Equal Pay for Equal Work Laws were originally passed in the late 1970s and early 1980s on the basis of helping working women achieve full equality with working men in terms of income. At first glance, one's inkling is to say that these laws are entirely justified and righteous; that it is entirely a benefit to women and a stride toward equality to adopt such provisions. However, let's quickly look at the economic merits of the issue. The general accusation here is that women are paid less, and obviously on the basis of sexism, as any legitimate reason for a differential in pay would not merit legislative action. So, imagine I'm an employer that has 100 positions to fill, and I'm a sexist (I'm really not, I assure you). The government tells me that if I hire a woman, I have to hire her at the same price as a man. The first thing that I am going to do is to just hire all men in my business, because I prefer them, and they are the same price as women.

Under these alleged conditions, the only bargaining chip that women have is a lower wage. If each woman offered to work for $4,000 less per year, it would cost me $400,000 a year to exercise my bigotry. That's a pretty hefty price to pay just so I can stay in an all-male environment. If you pass an Equal Pay for Equal Work law, you price women right straight out of the marketplace (if employers truly are bigots). In this scenario, the best thing for women would be to let the market work freely, unless you want to have about 10% of the workforce be female-comprised.

We did pass a set of these laws in the 1970s and 1980s, and woman employment in the workforce has only grown, which shows that employers were not bigoted in the first place, and that some of the empirical data from the 1970s showing that women with the same educational experience and job experience as men were actually making more than men was probably correct. The more factors are evened up in studies, the more the gap closes. Let's think about the implication of that startling piece of information for a moment. If women were making more money than men in equal situations, then Equal Pay for Equal Work laws increased their participation in the workforce because it decreased their wages in relation to those of men. Women consistently make less than men, you say? Technically, you're right. But, what you would be referencing are studies that compare the "average" or "median" American female and male, not females and males with the same amount of job and educational experience. The average American female statistics take into account stay-at-home mothers that don't earn a living, and don't account for women taking leaves or breaks from the labor force to have children. When you actually look at women and men side-by-side with the same educational and job experience, study after study shows that women make more money than men. That means that the "Equal Pay" laws probably benefitted men more than women. In either situation, these laws didn't help women one bit. The only logical plan of action would be to compete on the free market with your wages or to stage a boycott against a discriminatory business, unless, that is, you want the government spending even more money and creating new departments to figure out whom of what race and gender should be employed where regardless of anything else. Until that day when the underworld has to put a weatherman on its payroll, let's let the free market work based on merit, can we please?

Everybody knows the tired old expression, "Don't give a man a fish; teach him to fish for himself." Trite as it may be, that antique quip has plenty of merit. Giving people government assistance when in hard times to remove them from the hard times has never, ever worked, because it takes away a person's incentive to get themselves out of that situation with their own talents. Keeping the poor in the squalor and destitution they are in with tangible gifts is immoral at its core. Anytime the government tries to institute an "anti-poverty" program, the poverty rate stays the same or increases because the giveaways incentivize that style of living. The government could put a black and yellow cover around its anti-poverty policies and sell it as "How to keep people in serfdom for dummies." I don't think it would be much of a smash hit, and the government would probably lose money because it'd take years to even print it. I refer to serfdom plenty; so, what is serfdom?

In old Europe, almost everyone served (serfed if you prefer) a feudal lord, someone who owned the land. The reason that the feudal lord owned the land is not that he went to Medieval University and got a PhD in agriculture, it was that someone in his bloodline had been granted land by the king, prince, or what have you, at some point in the past. Serfs were unpaid workers; slaves of a sort. Serfs were required to work for the feudal lord, to which they were bound, and could not leave without his consent. Some serfs of higher status (villains) could spend some of their time farming their own fields for profit. However, most serfs had all their needs provided for and were protected in exchange for their labor on roads and in the fields. In theory, these people were free and were only obligated to their feudal lord because of their ancestors' follies; temporarily working the land without pay or rights.

However, because the all-mighty feudal lords were the only ones that could protect enough land to provide food for the serfs and ensure a place to stay, the concept of freedom was just that: a concept. Few if any serfs ever changed social status, and society was completely hereditary. What was the reason that this system developed? Very simply put, when a continent is as crowded and heavily developed as Europe was in the Middle Ages, the people that already have the highly valuable land really don't feel like competing to keep it, and intertwine their economic power with the political power and military might of the State (the capital S in State stands for collective society, not the kind that elects a governor), in this case, a king or queen. The society, the people at the top of the societal scale probably reason, has gotten plenty rich and free, because they themselves are both. In essence, the feudal lords were getting rich because they enslaved generations by providing for their needs, driving serfs into a cycle of dependency on them, during which the common people forgot how to provide for themselves. In short, the lords were handing out fish. Morality does not compel me to lock people into their current socioeconomic status, it compels me to enable them to get up on their own, and to teach them. The greatest way to help people out of poverty and let them climb the economic ladder is to let free markets pervade, wherein the economic interest of an employer to educate and hire a recruit that can aid his profit-making ability outweighs the government's incentive to keep that person on welfare to secure his vote for he who promises the most goodies in the next election.

The next point of contention that Keynesian and Adam Smith economists have is whether or not government spending stimulates the economy by propping up demand. Keynes would argue that when the government spends its money on economic stimulus, it can increase the amount of money in general circulation, thus increasing demand and the health of the economy. Most conservative economists that abide by the rules of laissez-faire would disagree, saying that the government had to get that money from somewhere, and that only the people by themselves can decide what is the right level of demand. Frankly, the idea of stimulus, and Keynesian economics in general, should be disproved by two events: the Great Recession we are experiencing and FDR's Great Depression stimulus programs.

During the Great Depression, FDR put forward a massive stimulus plan as part of his "New Deal" that included the building of the Blue Ridge Parkway, the construction of dams and other infrastructure, and many of America's first welfare programs. At the outset of FDR's presidency in early 1933, the American unemployment rate was about 19%. After FDR increased federal spending exponentially, unemployment in America soared to nearly 22%, and it was still a dumbfounding 17% in 1939 when the tide of war saved FDR's economic plan and his political clout by bringing huge amounts of money into the USA from wartime production and arms dealing (DOL stats). So, did stimulus spending really help us out of the depression? The answer is a resounding no! FDR's government overreach was more of a feel-good measure to make the people feel like the government was doing something for them than it was a real economic plan. In other words, we had a virus, the doctor prescribed an anti-biotic, and the doctor got all the credit after the virus finally ran its two-week course and subsided.

In addition to FDR's spending programs not helping the nation recover from the depression in any meaningful sense, the Great Depression was originally produced not by a downfall of the private enterprise system, but by the flaws and mismanagement of the Federal Reserve System. As early as 1925, soon-to-be president and scapegoat-in-chief Herbert Hoover warned then-President Coolidge that the Federal Reserve was charging much too low an interest rate on speculative loans to banks, which you should understand thoroughly by now.

The interest rates were so attractive that people were willing to bet on anything, because they had no fear of not being able to pay back the loan. So, the policies of the Federal Reserve propagated an "easy money" crisis that would start the depression when the bubble finally burst, only to be followed up by policies that did not let the economy recover from its deflationary spiral after 1929. The Fed viewed the decrease of the M2 supply (money in general circulation plus the money deposited in bank accounts) of fully one-third between 1929 and 1933 as deflation and panic speculation selling set in as a natural cycle that did not have to be stopped. To an extent, I agree with the Federal Reserve; the amount of consumer indebtedness that we had prior to the stock market crash was unsustainable and bound to cause a bubble. However, if the Federal Reserve did not exist like it did not exist between the 1830s and the 1910s; banks would have independently doled out more cash from their reserves upon seeing the price of goods falling as investments were taken off the market. When those banks did this, the amount of money in the system going up would have combated the stifling deflationary effect that we were facing in the early years of the depression. Would every bank have made this move and survived? No, some banks would have held onto their assets and went under when deflation continued.

But, overall, central government decision-making and stupidity in not aiding the money supply crash turned what was going to be a one or two-year recession into a decade-long depression. The notion that the federal government helped us out of a horrible depression that would have been worse had it not been for good old Uncle Sam is simply not the case, but that's the way we'll always remember it for a simple reason: as my favorite history teacher says, "History is written by the winners," and, in this case, protectionism and government intervention simply beat the argument for free trade. Herbert Hoover, the president in office when the stock market crashed in 1929, had no political power after the economic downturn, and left one message for future generations in his writings: that the Federal Reserve was a completely inadequate system for handling the U.S. monetary system competently.

The second event that should totally lay Keynesian economics to rest forever is the crisis that we are currently in. What caused the crash of 2008? I've already gone over a large part of it, which was the risky-lending bubble created primarily by government mandates and the use of Fannie Mae and Freddie Mac, and we have already traced the roots of speculation and extreme market volatility back to Europe and the Tokugawas. However, what really drove that risky lending, what does our economic outlook look like today, and where are the markets headed based on the Keynesian Economics that Washington D.C. has been implementing for half a decade now?

Well, just like in 1925 when Herbert Hoover knew that speculation was too easy, speculation was made much too easy by the monetary policies of the Fed in the lead-up to the Great Recession. Why the Federal Reserve pursues such risky policies is beyond me, but the cynical thought that maybe because former heads of big banks sit on the Federal Reserve Board, those former heads propagate policies that aid the moral hazard of large financial institutions, has occurred to me. At any rate (no pun intended), the Fed made speculation so easy that nearly everyone was heavily leveraged in the market, everyone was making huge amounts of theoretical profits on the derivatives of profits to be made maybe sometime in the distant future, and everything looked like peaches and cream to the politicians and economic policy-makers in Washington. Then, one day the inevitable happened, and the financial markets built on air collapsed. To save the floundering U.S. economy, the reasoning of the later George Bush and Obama administrations went, we had to abandon capitalism and transform ourselves into an economy where no large corporation failed and the government pumped huge amounts of money into the system to save the financial sector. Setting aside all of the past examples of inflation we talked about earlier, notably the Ming Chinese dynasty, that policy is still nothing short of stupefying. If you bail out the biggest banks and tell them that Uncle Sam is on the way with QE, what bank president would stop making the biggest risks that he can imagine? None would, because those banks are not gambling with their own money; they are gambling on the leveraged Forex commodity market with your money.

What has been the stock market result of the Federal Reserve's genius policies? Another bubble, that's what! As I write this book, the Dow Jones Industrial Average has crossed the 15,400 point mark, the highest mark it has ever passed. However, the rally is not driven by consumer confidence, because consumer confidence has been slipping in the first half of 2013. It's certainly not powered by glowing numbers from an increasingly rosy-looking job market, and if the investors are paying any attention to the manufacturing and export orders that continue to slip amongst this feeble "recovery," investors would keep their dividends out of the leveraged long-bond market and stop borrowing from their portfolios. Jobs reports this year are consistently showing a job market that is struggling to keep up with population growth, featuring six digits worth of people leaving the labor force (and, thus, the unemployment statistics) every month.

Corporate earnings, while being the strongest ever in the last quarter of 2012, are forecasted to be weaker in the second and third quarter of 2013, meaning that investors looking for a big dividend or margin gain around earnings report time will be sorely disappointed. So, what's behind all the bullish sentiment on the street? The answer is equity prices, cheap interest, stocks moving ahead, and the continuing easy money policies of the Federal Reserve. When an investor borrows on margin, he or she uses it to buy more stock in a bet that the stock will continue to rise, which is just another form of speculation. Investor margin borrowing hitting an all-time high usually means that the market has hit a peak, or will in the very near future. Investor borrowing hit a peak in the year 2007, amid the start of the Great Recession, in 2000 before the "9/11 recession," and in the 1920s and late 1980s before major market pullbacks. Where is the needle for investor margin borrowing right now? It is at its highest level ever, even topping the insane amounts of margin borrowing that were occurring in the 2007 Bull Run. These indicators, coupled with the growth of speculation in the post-recession market spurred on by the low interest rates the Federal Reserve is maintaining, all point to a major market pullback and possible crash by the beginning of 2014, which may well have already happened by the time this is published. So, on that side of the coin, Keynesian economics is producing yet another bubble based on the intervention of the federal government and the securities purchasing of the Fed Reserve. On the other hand, how has Keynesian economics helped the overall economy since the stock market crash in 2008?

The honest answer is that it has not helped us at all at this point in time. The effect of a government stimulus is to take productive money out of private sector hands during a time when investment is low and use it as capital in the market in hopes of creating demand. In this sense, the government is very temporarily successful. Government intervention keeps the economy from hitting the bottom, but it also precludes investment, hinders economic growth, and creates more bubbles in the long run.

A good example of this is the once-roaring powerhouse of Japan, which recently experienced and is just now emerging from a lost decade and three-fourths. At the start of Japan's recession, the Japanese government offered up a round of stimulus spending to help the economy get back on its feet; and taxed a massive amount of private capital to get this accomplished. When that failed to get the economy back to a state of exuberance, the government decided that another round of stimulus was necessary, and then another, and then another. Can you predict what happened next? That's right, another round of stimulus spending. At the end of ten years, the Japanese economy had managed to keep from completely imploding, but growth was non-existent, and the job market had long since dried up. Moreover, the effect of government spending is to keep things in a state of equilibrium in which no market is allowed to hit its true bottom and recover with the investment of private capital, where a dreary economy persists but is sold to the voting electorate as the only option for averting the abyss that lies below if the nation were to revert back to free enterprise. The same thing is happening to the United States right now.

The economy of the USA has had GDP growth numbers anywhere from—0.1% to about 3% growth, with an average somewhere around 1.25% GDP growth, historically (DOL, CBO, and BEA). Just for some perspective, that number is dismal. China grows at 5-6% annually, India, in 2009 and 2010, grew at over 8% year over year, and the United States has had many periods of economic growth of above 5%. But, the people seem to reason, it is worth it to resign your nation to mediocrity and business as usual, no matter how bleak it is, if the alternative is an unknown. Every month, the jobs reports are just enough to keep the unemployment rate stagnant or push it down 0.1%. We create around 150,000 jobs per month, only enough to keep up with population growth; and we sometimes fail to even hit that number. The way we calculate unemployment in America today is extremely dishonest. What we do is to count the number of people "in the labor force" that do not have jobs. What that means is that if you are not actively seeking a job, and have decided to drop out of the market or give up, you don't count. If you went from being a six-figure professional to serving hamburgers, you don't count.

What's more is that the job market for young people has almost completely dried up, with very, very little hiring of teenagers by companies. If we calculated unemployment rates the same way the FDR administration did, we would have an unemployment rate of well over 10%. This figure would much more accurately portray how little Stimulus spending has really helped the American economy. If you're still not convinced, take the example of how well the economy has been doing compared to how well the Obama administration predicted it would do in its selling of the Stimulus Package to the American people. The Obama administration predicted that unemployment would never top 8% if the Stimulus bill was passed. What actually happened? We topped 8% unemployment by the start of Obama's first summer as president, and we did not come down below that benchmark until just very recently. In fact, the president's economic team of Keynesians estimated that unemployment rates in America would be about 5% by this point in time, when we are actually above 7% with persistent threats of a "double-dip" recession looming. The president's economic team certainly did not predict that the manufacturing sector would still be contracting every month at this point, which it has been. What all this suggests is what any Founding Father could have told us in the 1780s, what the Great Depression temporarily proved to those who paid attention, and what the revival of the 1980s economy proved: that tax and spend is the real "voodoo economics."

Another major point of contention between Keynesian economists and free-market economists is that free-market economists, while distrustful of both large corporations and a big government, would prefer that large corporations were more influential in society, as the lesser of two very evil options. Keynesian and liberal economists, on the other hand, have virtually no qualms about putting more power in the hands of a big government, and view corporations as things that go bump in the night. The reason that I prefer big corporations to big government is that a corporation doesn't have any power to take a dollar out of my pocket without me voluntarily handing it over; the government does. That means that private businesses have to conform to my needs to stay alive, not the other way around.

In addition, corporations don't have the force of law behind their decisions. If the government tells me to pay my taxes at once, it doesn't matter if I agree that my taxes are being put to good use or not, I have to hand it over. That's the trouble with government. If you don't have any incentive to make sure that money is well spent, why on earth would you make sure that it is well spent? Like most of the people in Washington who build salamander tunnels (and I love salamanders), bridges to nowhere, host Star Trek video conferences, and gripe about the going out of the Northern Nevada Cowboy

Poetry Festival, you wouldn't. Some of you may be wondering who a corporation has to answer to if it spends its money on stupid stuff like that or treats its workers unfairly with record profit margins. The answer is simple: shareholders and customers.

For those of you currently envisioning shareholders as a bunch of rich guys having a conference in the Hamptons, think again, because about half of the investing done in this country is done by middle and upper-middle class people in an effort to better their lives or save up for retirement. If everyday investors didn't like the behavior of a company like, say, Wal-Mart, those shareholders could sell off all of their shares of the company, flood the market, and drive the value of that company through the floor in a heartbeat (quite literally). The beautiful thing about the free-market system is that the way in which workers are paid and wealth is created is a direct reflection of our own morality. If you don't like people being employed without a single shred of healthcare, don't lobby the government to make the commodity more expensive, lobby everyone you know with a retirement account to sell off all their Dow Jones stocks and roll them over into bonds or something. On the other end, if you don't have enough money to influence a corporation with your retirement account or investments, vote with your feet.

No one is making you shop at a multinational grocery store at gunpoint, and there isn't a sentry standing post to make sure that no one buys their school supplies from a "mom-and-pop shop." Are you going to pay a higher price if you exercise this right? You probably are. However, if you keep choosing to buy cheaply, you will have no one to blame but yourself when you hear on the news that 10,000 more American jobs are being shipped to China, or that Wal-Mart employees are living in poverty. I guess the whole point of this rambling paragraph of an English teacher's worst nightmares is that it is really hard for humans in general to accept responsibility for something. Capitalism is the only system on earth that lets people support or doom their own nations as a collective while using their own individual genius to better both society and themselves. This nation has a GDP (essentially a buying power) of $16 Trillion. Use it for Chris Christie's sake!

If we stopped buying foreign, sure, our cost of living might increase a little, and we might have a few less gizmos around, but we would keep a strong sense of national unity and restore our manufacturing economy. If we let the Chinese pass us in economic strength, they will be able to break free of our buying power and sustain themselves as the most powerful nation on earth. That's something I don't think any of us want to see, but apparently those $100 cellular phones that can access the internet and that cheap price on a child's toy are all worth the collapse of a nation. This is the stage of complacence that the British Empire went through in the 19th and early 20th centuries when it let us pass them by as earth's most prosperous power. Our future is not set in stone! Stop buying foreign. If you don't, the mirror will be the only answer to your questions of, "How did we fall off the tracks?" You control the world economy every time you shop, don't foozle that power.

On the other hand, you have government, which does not have to bend to the people's will to stay alive. "Yes it does, what the heck-fire do think an election is, buddy?" you say? That theory is really nice until you consider that the real government—the bureaucracy and its contractors, which make up an army of greater than ten million unelected officials that seldom changes its policies due to some silly expression of the people's will, actually enforce the law and write the regulations. Is government currently working the way most citizens under its jurisdiction want it to? Not even close.

When 85% of the country disapproves of the job that government's first branch-the legislative branch-is doing in every poll, you have a broken government. Yet, its balance sheets show no hint of pain from shareholder sales. The government's customers are locked into the plan, so government officials don't have to worry about product quality, only about looking like they're trying to clean up the mess around election times. Every place around the world where the functions of a society have been entrusted to a centralized collective body, the situation has either not improved or deteriorated. The truth, whether you like it or not, is that we have much more control, as a society, over what a large corporation does than over what our monster of a centralized government does.

The central concept to understanding liberty is that any centralized power, whether private or public, is a threat to its continuance. Any conservative economist, especially the more individualist ones, would tell you that they are troubled by the rise and dominance of multinational corporations. Margaret Thatcher, Milton Friedman, and Ronald Reagan, all central figures in the capitalist revival of the 1980s, commented at some point or another about how businesses were growing too large not to be a threat to individual freedom. The ultimate goal of the Founders was to prevent government from being the same way, and trusting the people to protect their own economic interests. We have failed on both accounts (thus far).

Keynesian economics relies on one fundamental principle that has been disproved again and again in real-world economics: that the government spends and invests capital more efficiently than the private sector. At its root, what is Keynesian economics' premise? The premise is that the level of demand in an economy is what the government should work to correct, adding demand with stimulus spending in times of crisis and taking demand out of the economy by raising interest rates in times of economic growth. Now, this theory presumes that the government can spend money or tax it without constricting the productivity of a society, which is simply not the case. Government can essentially spend money in three ways: it can print the currency, borrow the currency, or tax the currency. All three of these propositions have economic consequences beyond their purposes, and constrict the economy like a Green Anaconda.

If the government taxes the funds that it wants out of a certain group that is politically easy to attack, like, say, the "top 1 percent," investment capital is taken out of the economy at large, and people lose their jobs from a lack of business capital. Some of you may be saying, "Trickle-down economics doesn't work; this last recession proved that beyond a shadow of a doubt." I'd have to disagree with you; what failed in this last recession was a combination of easy-money policies propagated by Alan Greenspan and Ben Bernanke, the greed of America's largest corporations, and the speculation that ran wild on Wall Street for two decades before the crash of 2008.

Capitalism is free trade and free enterprise, not the government-supported oligarchy that continues to rule America through the Federal Reserve and every financial institution. Let's take a specific example of the effects that taxation has on the U.S. economy.

Let's say that I own a building business with a 10% profit margin that amounts to $5,000,000 out of the $50,000,000 in total revenues that my company brings in. We have fifty employees that make $40,000 each and have another $10,000 of payroll taxes and healthcare costs attached to each of them. That means that I am spending $2,500,000 on my employees. Currently, the government takes about 39% of my revenue, because our business is very hesitant to incorporate, which would increase our capital, allow us to get more done, and allow me to hire more workers as an employer. Why am I so reluctant to incorporate my company and attract capital? The top individual/unincorporated business tax rate is 39.6%, while the corporate tax rate is 41%.

So, if I was making $5,000,000 in profit after operating costs and other expenses at the 2011 Bush Tax rates of 35%, the government was taking $17,500,000 of my $50,000,000 in gross revenue. If the taxes on top earners go up to 39.6% (which they did), the government is now taking $19,800,000 instead of the previous $17,500,000, an increase of about $2,300,000 in my expenditures. Although I might not lay off every employee, to offset the decrease in profit margin, and to keep re-investment in my business alive, I will probably lay off at least twenty workers, decreasing the government's ability to collect payroll taxes from me in the future by hundreds of thousands of dollars. Not only that, but, when I lay those people off, unemployment insurance will pick up their incomes for over two years, costing the government $1,600,000 over that two-year period just in benefits, not to mention the unemployment workers that the government has to hire to serve them, the office that has to be maintained by the government, the heating and cooling and building cost on that building, and the bureaucrats that have to be hired above them to administer the increasing size of the program.

When you factor in that my business will be worth much less next year, that my investors lost confidence in the profitability of my company, and the chance that that $50,000,000 in wealth might not exist the next tax season, the government will end up in a losing position. Good thing the government got that extra $2,300,000, or we might not have been able to fund a "Bridge to Nowhere" or a Northern Nevada Cowboy Poetry Festival (I'm actually not joking about the Northern Nevada Cowboy Poetry Festival; Majority leader Harry Reid made a very impassioned speech in defense of the festival's funding amongst the August 2011 debt ceiling debacle). What are the actual facts when it comes to taxation in the United States?

The top 5% of income earners pay over 60% of the nation's taxes according to IRS, while the other 95% of the people pay less than half of Uncle Sam's expenses, and nearly 50% of Americans actually make money on the federal income tax system, despite the fact that the top 5% of earners make about 37% of the nation's income. Is that system unsustainable because we aren't squeezing the rich enough, or is it unsustainable because too many people are living off of the government and have an interest in increasing our ever-growing spending levels? You make the call. When the president talks about making the rich pay their "fair share," every middle class person had better hope that he's not serious about balancing the budget through tax increases, because the "millionaires and billionaires" are already heavily taxed by localities and most states as it is, and the CBO recently guesstimated (take anything the CBO says with a grain of salt; it said that we would spend about $12 billion on Medicare in 1990, when we actually spent over $100 billion) that there is less than half a trillion ($500,000,000,000) left to tax out of that easily attacked group. To put that in perspective, the yearly federal budget deficit that we have been running is around one trillion dollars a year, with this year's budget deficit in Washington hovering around $700 billion, and that number is predicted to jump up to around $800 billion in Fiscal Year 2014 if President Obama gets his new programs through Congress (CBO estimate). In all seriousness, if you raised the top rates to some ridiculous amount, you would drive away investment capital and wealth, probably producing a negative impact on the federal budget situation. What this means is that if the liberals are really serious about balancing the budget with taxes and fulfilling what they view as their "moral obligation" to support the poor, they are going to have to go after where the real money that can't afford a Cayman Island bank account is: the middle class.

What we have been headed toward in this country for a while now, and where Europe already is, is in a system of serfdom to the government in which the society's productive middle class pays taxes that go toward supporting both the lives of the lower classes and the lower corporate taxes of the ultra-wealthy (In France, a classic example of Western European Socialism, the top income taxes for individuals are about 45%, the payroll tax is a suffocating 66%, yet the corporate tax rate is 33.3% to encourage large businesses to locate themselves in France). For those of you saying that lowering corporate taxes is a conservative position, you're missing the big picture here, which is that unless you lower the taxes for individuals and unincorporated businesses that want to hire along with the corporate tax rate, you are guaranteeing an oligarchy of "Too Big to Fail" businesses, a stratified and socially immobile class structure, and an urban proletariat that doesn't care to break free of government.

The truth about taxation is that it stifles the economy, and the government will get less revenue most of the time it raises taxes, while increasing revenues by stimulating growth when it cuts tax rates. This concept is illustrated quite plainly by the Reagan Tax Cuts of 1981, prior to which the top individual income tax rates were 70%. Ronald Reagan, the first true conservative economist to occupy the White House since the days of Herbert Hoover, cut the tax rates of the top earners in society all the way down to 26%, leading many Americans to believe that the government would soon collapse for a lack of funding. In reality, the exact opposite thing happened; Ronald Reagan doubled the federal government's income tax revenues by the time he left office. In fact, the increase in federal revenue was so large that the government was able to spend the Soviet Union into military obsoleteness. For those of you still lost in the woods and wondering how this can be possible, consider one of the most accepted economic theories of our day: the Laffer Curve.

The Laffer Curve is named after Arthur B. Laffer, a conservative economist that played a big part in developing the theories of supply-side economics in the late 1970s. The Laffer Curve states that the revenue that the government gets from taxes increases as you increase the tax rates up to a critical point, the location of which varies along with the economic conditions, after which an increase in taxes produces a decrease in revenue because it discourages investment and worsens economic conditions. The general consensus is that if the economy is more fragile at some point in time, the critical point is at a lower percentage than when the economy is in an extremely prosperous condition. When you think about it, this makes perfect sense.

Imagine that you have $10,000,000 in savings at age 65 from owning your own business. When the economy is humming along, you might be able to put your money in a bank CD that yields 7-10%

per year. That means that you are making $850,000 a year for your retirement. So what if the government wants to tax you at 60%; you'll still have $340,000 to play golf with? This is the reason that Bill Clinton's tax increases really didn't affect the economy's robust performance in the 1990s. As I frequently tell Democrats, "Mickey Mouse could have been on Bill Clinton's Council of Economic Advisors, and we would have still had prosperity."

Conversely, when the economy is in the doldrums, that same retiree is stuck trying to get that really "hot deal" of a 1.01% APY CD because the Federal Reserve is trying to get lending going again. That person is not going to sit by and watch the government tax him at 60%; he's only going to make $40,400 with no access to his principle investment if he does that. If you raise taxes at all in that environment, you are guaranteeing that the retiree will hoard his money, keeping it out of the market at large, and causing deflation on a macroeconomic scale. This is the effect that the much misguided Hawley-Smoot tariff had on the depression-era economy.

Notwithstanding the Fed Reserve that sat by while the deflationary spiral began, the major deterrent for investment and trade in the depression-era economy was the tariff, which helped the depression spread across the globe, and ultimately resulted in a decrease of over 50% in U.S. trade volume according to the Chamber of Commerce and the U.S. Government. All you have to do to understand the implications of over-taxation in a less-than-vibrant economy is to look "across the pond" to the nations of the European Union, which have seen six straight quarters of contraction in their socialist nirvana. There will be those that argue in the next decade that Europe's state of ruin was caused by the austerity measures put into place in the last three years, and those people will be wrong. Why did the governments of Europe put austerity into place? The European nations adopted austerity measures because their budget deficits became unsustainable, and taxation was killing their economies.

Then, of course, comes the eternal problem of government: how do you enforce a law or tax without expressing the bias of the enforcer? This struggle was exemplified by the recent IRS scandal, in which the IRS targeted conservative or libertarian-leaning groups for extra scrutiny. The conservative groups were applying to become tax-exempt before the elections of 2012, and many Democrats feared that these groups would abuse their privileges as tax-exempt organizations. So, to remedy the problem, the IRS asked conservative and Tea Party organizations applying for tax-exempt status what prayers they said and what their reading lists were. The news originally broke in 2011 and 2012, when many Tea Party activists claimed that they were being discriminated against by the Service. In a hearing before Congress, Lois Lerner, the head of the tax-exempt branch of the IRS at the time, danced around questions about the possible targeting of conservative groups, although she strongly suggested that no such targeting would take place within the IRS.

This May, the IRS confirmed the story by way of a staged apology to the American Bar Association in a phone conference. The IRS originally placed the blame on a few local employees in Cincinnati and said the incident was isolated. Lerner was later quoted amid the controversy, when the story was confirmed, as saying that the program was ended in April-May of 2012, when, in reality, lawsuits were being brought forth against the IRS for discrimination that took place in 2013. By the way, for you liberals who assert that the IRS was acting in the spirit of efficiency, how do you explain the fact that, while over 300 conservative groups were selected for extra scrutiny, of which zero were approved or denied, just put in limbo as to their tax status, only 20 liberal groups went through the same process, an they were all turned down or approved. In fact, it was discovered that Lerner herself signed off on many of the letters asking for the personal information of groups seeking tax-exempt status. Although it's beside the point, this is the woman that will be charged, at the time I am writing this sentence, with oversight of Obamacare implementation in the IRS. Should we really be surprised by what happened at the IRS? No; George Washington, James Madison, and Thomas Jefferson sure wouldn't have been surprised. The entire philosophy of the Founders was to have a locally-controlled society with vast individual freedoms and liberties, curtailed by nothing except localities or state governments. We have the complete opposite right now: we have centralized power aplenty. When you give someone power, at some point or another, that entity is going to abuse that power.

The reason that this is not as troublesome for the legislative and executive branches of government as it is for the bureaucracy is that the people still hold the power to vote them out if they become tyrannical, and, beyond that, the people have the option of an armed rebellion if the vote isn't recognized as the ultimate source of sovereignty. However, when you're talking about a bureaucracy, you're talking about people with the power to ruin others, or intrude; to force their own beliefs upon others or coerce; but these people cannot be voted out, and they are very seldom fired. What happened to Lois Lerner after it was discovered that she changed her story, lied, and then took the Fifth before Congress? She was put on *paid* administrative leave. James Madison once famously wrote that if men were angels, no government would be necessary, and, that if angels were to govern men, no internal or external controls on government would be necessary. What is in plain view from this controversy is that we are not governed by angels, and that those non-angels are not very well-controlled. When a top official faces the only mechanism that we can effectively control a bureaucratic agency through, congressional oversight, and uses her Fifth Amendment Rights, you cannot say that we have control over the bureaucracy. As the noted comedian Lewis Black once put it, "You cannot show a video of a cat getting run over by a Land Rover, and say, "Uh, the cat was trying to kill itself"." If the IRS is out of control and about to get larger, how do you fix it? To answer that question, you have to figure out from where the IRS's power emanates.

The power of the IRS does not really rest in its ability to tax, but the complexity of the rules it enforces. The U.S. tax code is currently over 70,000 pages long! That means that the IRS, in a liberal administration, can reward Democratic campaign donors, give green energy companies unfair tax advantages over conventional energy companies, and punish political enemies. In a conservative administration, it can do the opposite. It takes the extraordinarily virtuous president to resist from using his immense executive authority single-handedly. In fact, every president since the end of Gerald Ford's term has put troops somewhere in the world without congressional approval, even though Congress passed the War Powers Act specifically to prevent it. Only the first president, George Washington, was extremely successful in limiting his own power. If he wanted a crown, Washington very well could have become the first King of the United States. However, he accepted the title of president, and declined to be called anything that stunk of monarchy like "Your Highness." George Washington did not step down after two terms because he had to, but because he felt that no man should play such a powerful role in the young republic's governance for more than two terms. It was Washington whom coined the phrase, "Few men can resist the highest bidder." What is going on right now is that we have too complex a tax code for people to refrain from using, because it is the "death star" of the political world. With that document, someone can intimidate or coerce nearly anybody through the might of the government's authority. So, how do you take away that power and stimulate the economy at the same time? Why not institute a flat tax rate of 15% for corporations and individuals alike that still brings in approximately the same amount of money that the government rakes in now, eliminates all disincentives to hire through the elimination of the payroll tax, lowers the death tax, abolishes the marriage tax, encourages corporations to bring money back to the United States to invest and build the economy, eliminates all loopholes and deductions, and stimulates the economy with increased consumer discretionary spending? This system of taxation would take in roughly the same amount of money that the federal government takes in right now: somewhere in the neighborhood of 2.5 Trillion dollars. For those of you doubting the effectiveness of this red tape-cutting program, let me cite an example from the pages of history.

In the 1600s and 1700s, Great Britain (Mother England as we called it then) had a mercantilist economy, meaning that the government instituted heavy tariffs to protect native industries and wanted to make a hefty profit on any trading happening within the confines of its territories. To enforce the tariffs and duties, England had to hire an enormous amount of civil service employees, and political patronage and favoritism often played a role in who got approved for a business license and who didn't or who could trade what. Because of this, many people seeking to trade profitably or set up their own start-up businesses resorted to bribing government officials and smuggling goods into and out of the Motherland. England's reputation was that of a criminal nation out only for money in the 1700s. One century later, however, England was known as the most law-abiding and prosperous nation on the face of the earth (in some respects; in others, the USA had already surpassed Britain economically). What changed? Britain went to a system of laissez-faire, free-trade capitalism, in which someone didn't need a license to start most businesses. If you didn't need government approval to do anything, why would you bribe the government? By the same token, if trade is completely free and unfettered, it's impossible to be a smuggler! You couldn't smuggle if you tried. Milton Friedman once commented on this phenomenon, saying, "The way to create more crime is to pass laws that do not appeal to common morality." Put in other words, everyone agrees that murder is wrong, so that law is pretty Jeremiah Wright GD legitimate. But, when you pass a law that a shotgun can only be used to hunt Geese on a Thursday evening between 7 and 10 pm when the wind speed is between 3 and 5 mph and the temperature is 62.5° Fahrenheit, you're bound to get plenty of law-breakers.

The second way that government can spend money is through borrowing the money, which is part of what America has been doing for the past half-century. Most people think that we owe the majority of our debts to China, when we actually owe most of our debts to . . . . ourselves. Of America's $17,000,000,000,000 in debt, we owe somewhere around $4,000,000,000,000, or 23% of our debt, to China. Other nations hold about 5% of our debts, and the Federal Reserve System (oh, joy), holds the balance.

Why does the Federal Reserve System hold such a large share of our own debts? The Federal Reserve has been in a rush to buy up our own securities to stimulate the economy and reduce the share of currency that we have to send outside of our borders. After all, if we are paying ourselves, aren't we going to help the economy out by having the power to drop the interest rates on our own debt? The argument is dizzying, I know. What the people at the helm of American monetary policy don't seem to grasp very well is that if I owe my friend $10 and pay him $11 to get my debt note and stop paying him interest, it would be eternally befuddling if I came to the genius conclusion that I should keep paying myself 10 cents in interest every month and lose some of that money as it passed through multiple hands and carried out the transaction. Any rational person, upon getting the note of their debt, would readily tear up the note and be rid of the wretched thing. No, no, not us; we've got a better plan. When people say that the Federal Reserve is buying up Treasury Notes (the stock shares that the government issues as public debts), they don't mean it literally, because the Fed doesn't have 10 trillion in cash just sitting around. It would take a hefty sum of time just to print that staggering amount of money. Even if the Federal Reserve could print the cash in an instant, the effect of immediate inflation on our currency and its debt would make it such that the Fed couldn't buy up the notes in the first place. So, what do you do when you have to buy up 10 trillion dollars worth of debt and don't have any cash on hand? You issue a handy-dandy IOU, of course. Some of you may be losing faith in your government right about now.

Why the heck would you issue an IOU if you already owe someone the money? It comes from the theory that increasing the amount of money in the system, while it might drive up the prices of goods and services for people, will stimulate the economy by making credit more widely available and cheap. What is the actual process, you might ask? The Federal Reserve issues ten trillion dollars worth of IOUs, then proceeds to lend the money that it has acquired by lending the Treasury Bills to the Treasury, and puts the Treasury Bills on its balance sheets as debt to be repaid. Once the Treasury Department has the pretend money, it turns it into liquid cash to "stimulate" the American economy. The main thought behind this wrongheaded policy is two-fold: that the government spending money can stimulate the economy even though it will eventually result in hyperinflation, and the thought that lower interest rates will spur more borrowing in a weak economy. You see, when the Federal Reserve buys up the Treasury Bills that were being auctioned off and puts them on its balance sheet, the number of actual bills on the open marketplace declines drastically, driving the price of the Treasury Bills up according to supply-and-demand, and driving the yields (dividends) on the shares down, taking interest rates on American debts along with them. The result of this policy is that the dollar gets devalued, and the debt that the Treasury still owes to foreign and domestic debt holders is more expensive to finance because it has to pass through another set of hands before getting to its destination.

Every year the Federal Reserve sits on the massive debt burden that it has imaginarily bought up, we pay it about a 1% interest fee on the debt; amounting to about 100 billion dollars per year. In addition, we still have to pay interest on the IOUs that we issue to our actual creditors. Basically, it's Keynesian economics at work, which, when it has truly been implemented in cases such as this, have truly resulted in oligarchy and a centrally-controlled economic system. The economic implications of this policy can be clearly illustrated by the recent "recovery" that wasn't. Do Federal Reserve buying tactics actually stimulate the economy in any meaningful way? No, those tactics support the quasi-oligarchy that we have now nearly set into stone. The inflationary result of these policies will be felt by many to come. Beyond the economic ramifications of this action, there is the vast moral issue that underpins it: are you really willing to finance your lifetime's government programs on the good name of your children's work ethic? I think that most of us would answer that question with a resounding no, but that's not what has been reflected by America's spending policies over the past three-quarters of a century. So, for all the banter about America's debt, how bad is the problem?

America's total debt is about $17,000,000,000,000 (17 Trillion), and might be 18 Trillion by the time this is printed. To put that gargantuan figure in some sort of perspective, if I had the amount of pennies needed to pay down that amount of money, the mass of pennies would, at ten feet high, be about 14.5 miles by 14.5 miles (I did that as a practice Fermi question); roughly one-quarter the size of an Eastern county! Put another way, if that debt were spread out over every day since BC turned to AD (or BCE to CE), each day would represent a staggering $23,134,130! Given that the U.S. continues to rack up budget deficits every year, that number is simply unsustainable. With that level of debt, if the U.S. Government were to hypothetically tax every single dollar of income, every dollar worth of corporate earnings, and every single dollar of everything else, we couldn't pay down the national debt. The last time that these United

States didn't have a national debt was before the Civil War. That's not the scary part.

The scary part is that the national debt has been growing exponentially faster than the GDP of the United States for the past two-thirds of a decade now. Anyone who thinks that this problem rests entirely on the shoulders of one political party needs to go back and look at the facts. The Republican Party contributed to our budget deficit with No Child Left Behind in the early 2000s and an expansion of Medicare, the so-called "Medicare Part D" package, along with two foreign wars. That being said, the Democratic Party has managed to rack up much more debt at the helm of the American government in a miniscule five years in power than President Bush did in eight years. The solution to this problem lies in deep cuts and spending reductions, which the majority in neither party is willing to propose or act on. Why the inaction? No matter what political party is in power, the nature of government is always the same: a politician wants to be re-elected. In accordance with that millennia-old principle, he or she will most often do what the majority of the constituents tell him to do. Now, how would Milton Friedman explain this principle? He would tell you the same thing that I'm about to tell you: you might not say it, but the majority of you want inflation. It's true. When you respond to a survey and say that government should cut spending, what programs are you referring to? If you're not referring in some way to the Department of Education, Energy, Defense, Social Security, Medicare, Medicaid, farm subsidies, or clean energy research, you do not support a balanced budget at all.

Now, when the survey gets to the ancient question, "Are your taxes too high or too low?" the great majority of you probably say that taxes are too high, which they are. So, the message your legislator gets is: "Please get more federal money for my Grandma Jenny's Medicare, don't stop handing out welfare and unemployment, but, by Gettysburg, don't raise my taxes." At this point, only a few brave legislators will make the right decision and support free market replacements to government programs. Most legislators, including Republicans, will please their constituents with more programs while taking the money from the Chinese, T-bill buyers, or firing up the printing presses. What does that mean for the debt? That means a ton more debt in the future, and completely unsustainable levels of deficit spending. For those of you whom are currently saying to yourself, "The deficit is shrinking, we're fine," think again.

It is true that the budget deficit that Washington has been running has shrunken over the last year faster than expected, with yearly deficits projected to be less than 3% of GDP by 2015 (assuming that the economy keeps humming along and tax revenues keep coming in at better than expected levels; stats provided by the CBO). Before you break out the confetti and party hats, let's consider what is expected to transpire in the years after 2016. That year is the year in which U.S. deficit-to-GDP ratios are expected to bottom out around 2% according to the CBO (again, take the cheery projections of the CBO with a grain of proverbial salt). After that, the aging population of America is going to eat up a much larger chunk of the federal budget, especially when you consider that the price of healthcare is going up even faster than expected under the new national health care law.

By 2030, the CBO expects the federal deficit to be catastrophically large, with the projected tax revenues (assuming continual growth, when's the last time that happened?) only being able to cover the "Big Three" (Social Security, Medicare, Medicaid). Not only is this a huge problem, but a potentially much larger fly in the ointment lies in our own hopes. The CBO is counting on the economy to rapidly rebound for the American deficit to shrink to around 2% of GDP by 2014. However, what also comes with a better economy? Eureka, higher interest rates! Since the world economy was so horrendous for so long after the crash of 2008, interest rates are still about 1% on speculative and other stock market loans, with yields on U.S. T-Bills in the gutter. That means that borrowing a Trillion dollars doesn't hurt very much right now, because it will only cost you about ten billion dollars a year to finance that huge amount of cash.

When the economy improves (if it improves), investors will start gambling more liberally with their capital, the volume of investing in U.S. T-Bills will fall through the floor, causing yields to go north of three or four percent. Just what does that jargon mean? Currently, we pay around $250 billion to service our debts. If interest rates shot up in a boom economy to three, four, or five percent, another $750 billion dollars in expenses would automatically be put on the federal government's budget. At that point, we had better have 10% GDP growth and very compliant citizens as far as taxes go if we want to have a country beyond the year 2025. In this respect, Keynesian economics has served as a one-move self check mate for the American economy. On one hand, if the economy pulls a Reagan-era miraculous turnaround in spite of liberal economic policies, the nation would be practically bankrupt overnight. On the other hand, if the economy continues to go through yearly cycles of semi-recovery and anemic growth or "double-dips" into another recession, federal tax revenues will fall even further while federal payouts to the unemployed rise. In the long term, however, our entitlement programs are going to skewer us. So, what with Social Security and Medicare, the so-called "third rail" of American politics?

As for Social Security, I think the way that the program is currently carried is not only un-economical, but it is detrimental to the poor and lower-middle classes. Think about this: who has to go to work first to pitch in for their family, a poor child or a rich child? The poor child does. Let's suppose that this particular child goes to work at age fifteen at a low-wage position. The rich child, whose parents make over a million dollars between them, will probably go to school to become a doctor, lawyer, or businessman. Odds are that the rich child won't enter the workforce until around twenty-five. Since Social Security taxes come directly out of their respective paychecks, the poor child will contribute more of his productive years to Social Security, pitching in for a full half-century before receiving any benefits (assuming that the fund remains solvent long enough to pay him anything).

The rich child, in contrast, is going to receive benefits after contributing to the system for forty years. That's not the worst part. The worst part is that the rich man is going to retire with a huge wad of cash to pay for medical procedures and healthier food, leading to a life expectancy of around 80 or 85 years old, while the poor man probably will be on a government insurance plan with plenty of holes in it and a bad diet. In all likelihood, this man will die right around age 70. What's the end result here? Well, the rich man worked for 40 years and got 13ish years of benefits, a work-to-benefit ratio of three years of work for every year of benefits, while the poor man worked for 50 years and got a scant five years of benefits, a ratio of ten years worked for every year of benefits received. What the program does, because it is not means-tested, is to re-distribute the wealth that should have been gained by the lower and lower-middle classes to the upper and upper-middle classes! This is a great example of the unintended and counter-intuitive results of government policies.

So, the perception that Social Security is there to take care of old, sick, poor people is simply not true. The wisdom of such a system will be up for debate shortly, but before politicians defend Social Security like the Holy Grail that protects the helpless, let's at least make it a means-tested program (If you make over a certain amount of money, you don't benefit from the program). As far as what the best solution to our little debacle is, the best example lies south of the equator in Latin America: Chile.

Chile's retirement system is one in which the government gives each citizen a choice between the government-run retirement system and putting their retirement fund taxes into a private retirement account that compounds annually in safe investments. The result is that the average Chilean retires on much more money than the average American! A nation that was undeveloped a mere century ago, considered third-world, has bested the United States in giving its aged citizens a standard of living! If that's not a wake-up call, I don't know what is. So, what else can the now prospering nation of Chile teach us? As former Secretary of Labor and Social Security for Chile José Piñera said in an <u>Investor's Business Daily</u> interview, "For the first time in history, we allowed the common worker to benefit from one of the most powerful forces on earth: compound interest."

What's more is that America's current system gives the government a darn strong incentive to have a rapidly growing population of workers and future workers to support the elderly. The only way to sustain such a system is to have exponential trends in population growth, which will invariably put pressure on the environment and our infrastructure. In Chile, the government has absolutely no interest in maintaining a larger population to support the elderly, and citizens have a vested interest in making sure that the government has a sound fiscal policy and taxes the dollars it wants to spend instead of printing them, and wants to spend very few dollars. The reason for this incentive is that a portfolio is always diversified (at least a good portfolio is), and a large portion of any diverse portfolio will be tax-free municipal and national bonds, which are directly effected by monetary and spending policies. If half of every working citizen's retirement was in U.S. Treasury Bills and municipal bonds, I think we would have a much more pro-market, pro-capitalist, pro-fiscal sanity populace. In implementing this system, the Chilean government told new workers that they had to go to the new system, but offered everyone that had already heavily invested in the government system their retirement through the State. Although this was a painful period for Chile, the long-term impacts of this decision for Chileans have turned out to be positively stupendous. Here, as in every case in which it has been tested, the risk in trusting your earnings to political volatility and stupidity proved to be less than the risk of trusting it to the risks and long-term steadiness of market forces. America could have its average retiree retiring on as much as four times as much as they do now in twenty years, and still manage to fulfill our promises to older Americans, if we followed this model.

There are those left-wing economists and philosophers (pseudo philosophers if you ask me) that will argue that government spending is not the problem that is driving our debt crisis, but that a lack of solid revenue is. Those economists are either brainwashed, intentionally deceptive, or haven't looked at a federal balance sheet lately. America's spending has increased much faster than the rate of inflation since the JFK administration, with entitlement and social spending leading the way.

In 1961, we had a budget of about $98,000,000,000 (98 Billion for those of you who are decimally impaired) according to internal government statistics from multiple departments. Today, that figure stands north of three trillion dollars per year, an increase of well over 3470%. In that same time, the GDP went from 530 billion dollars to about 16 Trillion, an increase of only 3000% (most of that GDP increase occurred in the earlier part of this period, while most of the exponential growth in the federal budget occurred in the later period).

In the Fiscal Years 2010 and 2011, the government spent about 23% of the U.S. GDP annually, well above the historic average. Revenues sat only slightly below the traditional average of 19-20%; around 18.5%. In a down economy like this, the Laffer Curve would dictate that if we raise taxes, the amount of revenue that the federal government receives will probably remain stagnant or go down. If revenues go up (consistently, not for one quarter of good growth like we have seen at the outset of 2013), it is a sign that the economy has recovered, but is definitely not a solution to the spending problem we have.

When you're spending trillions of dollars every year with budgets that grow on a yearly basis regardless of economic conditions, you do not have a taxation problem, you have a spending problem.

Saying that America has a taxation problem is like saying that a man making $50,000 and spending over $75,000 a year is going in debt because his boss won't give him that pay raise in hard economic times, not withstanding the fact that this man gambles his earnings and takes out loans for new cars that he doesn't need. In all of this, it is important to remember what happened to Rome with respect to government spending as described earlier.

Critics of cutting government spending call it "austerity," reference the current economic anguish of the European Union, the really, really, horribly painful sequester cuts that have been recently implemented, and ask if we really want to go down the path of Europe (the irony might kill a less cynical reader right now).

First of all, conservative economists and conservatives in general have been pointing at the EU for decades as exhibit A to refute socialist and quasi-progressive policies. The reason that the EU is in deep trouble with a contracting economy and shrinking population is not that it has gone to conservatism and free-market economics, it is because that continent abandoned free trade and capitalism for the better part of a half century. A government does not cut its own pay for the fun of it; it does it because it has to in order to avoid complete financial ruin. Why was Europe on the brink of economic destruction? Most nations in the EU have overreaching cradle-to-grave government assistance programs, stiflingly high taxes, and a collectivist attitude. Spain's government stands out as a particularly good example of the harm that liberalism can inflict upon a nation. In the late 1990s, under an already strained socialist economy with a full welfare state, the Spanish government set strict limits on how much electricity could be used by power companies, basing its dictum on a need to save the planet from deadly greenhouse gases. Today, the Spanish government is bankrupt, the unemployment rate in Spain is well over the 20% mark according to the EU and the Spanish government, and the economy of that jewel of collectivism is in a constant contraction, with power output constantly declining.

What do you know, people actually like to keep some of what they earn and not see government throw it away on theoretical science; who would have thought? If the Euro zone nations teach us anything, they should teach us to run back to free markets and away from the expanse of big government.

As for those unbearable, awful sequester cuts, where do I even begin? I guess I should start by explaining what a "cut" means to a government department. Government bureaus have built-in budget increases of some set percentage. When the sequester cuts went into place, only one department was really cut: the Department of Defense. The rest of the agencies affected by those cataclysmic, draconian cuts actually had a reduction in the amount of future increases in spending. If this all seems abstract and incomprehensible, let me use an analogy that Rush Limbaugh once used to explain this government accounting trick.

Let's say that I weigh 300 pounds, and I have been eating like an absolute pig lately. I project, in my annual weight assessment, that I will gain 100 pounds next year. My doctor then tells me that I can only gain 25 pounds the next year. Upon carrying out the doctor's modest request, I brag that I have lost 75 pounds even though everyone is telling me that I'm getting heavier. It's absolute madness; there's simply no other way to describe it. At the outset of 2013, the White House was warning us that if the sequester cuts were passed, the subsequent decrease in government spending might send us into another recession. Here we are three-fourths of a year later, and still no Armageddon. In fact, the perceived decrease in government spending has had a positive impact on this economy if it has had any effect at all, with GDP and real estate numbers looking rosy this spring. The bottom line on the sequester cuts is that a decrease in a proposed future increase does not equal a cut, and that government spending is not a stimulant, but a retardant. Although some military programs have become collateral damage (no pun intended) in this whole political mess, I think that real conservatives will see, in the end, that along with Newt Gingrich's now infamous 1990s shutdown of the federal government, the implementation of the sequester was a key event to show the public that Calvin Coolidge was right all along about the uselessness of an intrusive federal government.

For those of you who disagree with my assertion that the Federal Reserve's printing and buying tactics will create hyperinflation, what are you basing that opposition on? What you're basing it on is what you see in stores around you: prices are only going up at a moderate pace. Inflation is still outpacing wage growth by a country mile every year, and the only reason that we did not see immediate hyperinflation in the printing and borrowing craze of 2008 and 2009 is that the U.S. dollar is still the World Reserve Currency, meaning that it is still viewed as the safest option for riding out an economic storm out of all the earth's currencies.

Once the economy recovers, however, all of the money that the Federal Reserve and the Treasury put into circulation will produce massive inflation as investors sell off mountains of bonds in U.S. currency and debt, driving the price of T-bills lower, the yields higher, the price of just financing the interest payments on the debt well north of one trillion dollars per year, and the prices of everything up. This is hyperinflation, and if you're in disbelief over it happening to the United States, I suggest you re-read Chapter Two. The effect of hyperinflation like the kind we had in the late 1970s, as Milton Friedman described it, is just another tax on the American people in a different form. In fact, the tax is probably much more painful than a traditional tax increase because it effects every dollar that we spend, not just the amount that government decides to confiscate; I meant tax. Inflation drives the price of goods and services through the roof, which inevitably leads to employees wanting to work for larger salaries. When a business's revenue is falling because fewer and fewer people can afford its ever-more expensive products, it will be less and less willing to hire new employees, driving a vicious cycle of inflation. As goods get more and more expensive, the only people able to afford them are the rich, or those with investments in tangible goods that can be sold to keep the owner's buying power in the midst of inflation, like land. As, once again, the great Milton Friedman put it, "The most effective hedge against inflation is high living." Here again, the best intentions of government to stimulate a floundering economy can easily end up harming all in it except the privileged, whom politicians profess to detest. When, inevitably, we lose our World Reserve Currency status or the economy turns around, we will have to pay the piper and suffer through inflation.

The central theme of Keynesian and progressive economics is that a centralized power will be able to make smarter decisions with regards to finances than individuals, and that the government will be able to re-distribute much of the upper classes' wealth to the lower classes. This argument just simply does not hold true. Anytime the government tries to make society a more ordered and fair place, it gets more and more unfair, as we saw earlier. Another example that has recently come to light is the hot topic of farm subsidies, a now decades-old tradition of passing pork so we can get cheap pork (or that's what we're told).

Just a few days ago as I write this, the U.S. House and Senate Agriculture Committees have passed a "farm bill" that spends about one trillion dollars between now and 2018. Actually, Congress should have called the bill the "Food Stamp Bill," because that's where roughly 80% of the funding provided is going to go if the representatives and senators vote on final passage. Regardless of that fact, what do farm subsidies actually do? Well, as we discussed earlier, most of America's farmland is now owned by corporate entities and farmed by a few guys watching a screen to make sure the automated tractors don't crash and the water systems stay up and running. So, when we pay farmers not to farm, we're usually not paying Uncle Joe with a few acres down the lane; we're paying ADM, Riceland, and the like.

In fact, the majority of farm subsidies go to farms that have annual revenues of over one million dollars. These farms get an average payout of about $55,000 a year according to the USDA. Meanwhile, only 20% of farms that have annual revenues of under $100,000 get farm subsidies, and those that do get a pittance. The average subsidy to one of these farmers is about $4,000 (also USDA). If you have the resilient urge to burn this page for the sake of getting it out of sight, I don't blame you. The stupidity that our government shows in every situation imaginable is quite depressing indeed. So, you may be wondering, why do we even have farm subsidies?

The thinking is that if we pay farmers to farm, they will be able to sell their products at a lower cost to the consumer. The other line of thinking is that the government should also pay some farmers not to farm, because this will keep the price of American agricultural exports high on world markets, bringing more money into the country. I'm not sure what economist the government consulted before instituting this line of incoherent and inconsistent thought, but, whoever it was, they need to have their degree revoked.

The latter notion flies in the face of every fundamental economic truth ever known to man. If I have one million pounds of corn on the market, the value is some amount set by the level of demand in relation to the supply present, let's say it's $2 a pound in this hypothetical situation. That means that my overall revenue is going to two million dollars. Let's say that I decrease the supply of corn to only a half of a million pounds with the same level of demand. Sure, the price is going to double, but the amount of corn that I'm going to sell gets cut in half. That means that I'll make the same amount of money! It's just like the minimum wage debacle.

If some amount of capital is chasing goods, the total amount of money spent, and, therefore, total revenue, is not going to change because if more goods are available, the price goes down, more goods are bought, and the same amount of money is spent. If the amount of goods on the market drops, the price goes up and the total amount spent is constant. The best way I can illustrate this principle to my fellow science enthusiasts is to say that this is just the equation for the speed of an electromagnetic wave with different variables. For those of you who are unfamiliar with this equation, it states that frequency and wavelength are inversely proportional to each other (if one doubles, the other gets cut in half), and that the product of those two variables always has to equal the same speed-the speed of light. No matter how you alter one number in that equation, your final value will always be the same thing. I guess we don't have many physicists on the hill, because Washington seems to think that altering one side of an equation is going to change the total amount of wealth created by some magical process currently unknown to economics. In fact, this first type of farm subsidy is an entirely losing proposition for the United States, because even if we somehow broke the laws of economics and got a little richer from this reduction in supply, that gain would be more than offset by the government having to tax the economy to pay the farmers that aren't farming. So, you have to ask yourself, why are we paying people not to be productive if we aren't going to gain?

The second type of farm subsidy is just general aid to farmers in the form of crop insurance (the bulk of farm aid) and payments to farmers. So, the thought behind this one is the exact opposite as the thought underpinning the previously mentioned type of farm subsidy. The economic line of thinking here is that if we pay farmers and reduce the cost of production by taking care of their insurance for them, they will be able to provide the American people with "cheap food n' fiber," as a Nebraska farmer would undoubtedly describe it. That's not exactly how things actually work. As previously stated, most of the "aid" that we give goes to large agricultural operations that don't really contribute to our economic productivity, because those largely automated farming operations really don't hire anybody. The money doesn't come out of thin air from the government, the government have to tax it (please don't think to yourself, "Oh, just print it." That's a different form of taxation-inflation) from somebody. Well, they tax it from you. The effect of this is that the smaller efforts of millions of people go to a few thousand people in larger sums, allowing those people to produce cheaper goods. But, what's the cost?

Since the money has to pass through multiple hands to get to the farmers, Edison's rules of DC electricity apply, and we lose some of the money to "friction." That means that the reduction in the price of our food is more than offset by the amount of tax money that we hand over to farmers. The American consumer (by the way, I loathe the term "consumer"; I prefer the term "citizen" in most cases, because that's what we are) would be better off to keep that portion of their taxes and pay a little bit more for their "food n' fiber." In addition, the whole idea here is that a little payment from everyone is amplified when it is paid out to a few. Is that really a good thing? American agriculture is becoming increasingly centralized, so this effect is going to be amplified. Do we really want to waste money propping up ADM when agricultural prices and productivity are both at all-time highs? I'd hope not. How is an average farmer supposed to compete with a corporation that can sell its goods for 30%, 40%, or 50% less because that corporation has lobbyists in Washington? Here too, the work of a supposedly well-intentioned and benevolent government is to create an oligarchy and squeeze out smaller businesses and farmers. The free market encourages individual innovation, independence, economic growth, lower prices, and a fair environment much more effectively than a bloated government can ever hope to.

The last economic issue that I am going to touch on (you just sighed a sigh of relief, I know) is unionization. If you talk to a hard-line conservative, they will tell you that a union is a big, corrupted machine that does nothing but contribute to Democrats and tries to grow its membership. If you speak with a dedicated liberal, they will try to say that the union was God's gift to planet earth in the 19th century, and that, without unions, we'd all be making twenty-five cents an hour in some slaughterhouse in Chicago. In reality, neither of these people have an accurate read on what unions are. Unions can be a force for good or a force for over-paying employees and reducing productivity depending on the time period that you study and the line of work that you look at. For example, I am pretty sure that I would not want to go into a West Virginia coal mine without a union to negotiate for health benefits and a few not-so-trivial safety regulations for me. In contrast, if Apple unionized its workforce, they probably wouldn't do so well. In Apple's line of work, a union is pointless. The only adverse health risk that working at Apple comes with is the possibility of carpel tunnel, and the entire business plan is based on innovation. In the coal mine, not a whole lot is being innovated; you pick up the shovel, dig the coal, load it on to the machine, and the machine puts it onto the railroads. The most glaring problem with unions is that they don't seem to recognize the value of putting time into the job; unions seem to only value seniority.

In a conventional union, the pay scale is based solely on how long the employee has been working, not on the quality or amount of work. The other troublesome thing about unions is that they don't take into account the level of education needed to take a position, or the investment needed to get into that job. For example, in the 1990s, when the economy was just humming right along, the unions got sort of greedy. People turning lug nuts on assembly lines were making $25 an hour, and people driving forklifts for the UAW were making $30 an hour with a full pension and great healthcare. That's great, except that those workers are in completely unskilled positions, and that is not really sustainable. The only time a menial worker can get paid like that is when the economy is in a bubble like it was in the 1990s and early 2000s. When you can make $30 an hour coming right out of high school, why would you go to college?

Am I saying that there's anything wrong with the UAW negotiating a great contract for its workers? Nope. I'm just asserting that when school bus drivers are making almost as much money as the AP Biology teacher, it's a pretty good sign that the economy isn't going to stay headed in whatever direction it's headed for very long. The bottom line is that everything goes in cycles. In the 1800s and early 1900s, employers could abuse their employees and pay them horribly (I'm not going against free-market economics, the government helped suppress workers), and unions grew as institutions that could ensure survival, and life past another five years in the factory. Instead of having the children going into the really dangerous machine to fix it while it was still running because they were the only ones who could fit, maybe the machine had to be shut down for a few minutes thanks to the union's negotiations. As time crept by, union membership grew rapidly, and so did union influence. Today, unions are declining because most workers see that they will get paid just as well with or without a union, and that they can usually do better if they rely on their individual merits. Over 90% of American private-sector workers today don't want unions. However, the tables will turn eventually, and the other side, the business side, will get too greedy, just like the unions got too greedy, and we'll repeat the whole thing. If people want unions, they'll have them, and if workers don't, they won't. We don't need a Card Check program to help unions hold unfair elections and coerce, they'll come back in their own sweet time.

Moreover, in questioning what is right economically and what will help people, whether or not we should have a European-style cradle-to-grave society that models what "Julia" went through (Obama campaign narrative; look it up), try to consider why people flee that socialist paradise, and fled Cuba's communist paradise, and Haiti's totalitarian paradise, to come to the free soil of the United States. People don't want to be taken care of their whole life, they want to take care of themselves; Americans don't want to be governed, they want to govern themselves. If I decide that 65 years of eating fast food is better than 95 years of being a vegan, that's my decision;

stay out of it! What has made America that shining city on the hill that she is is not the government control and collectivism that enrapture the rest of the Western World, it is the lack of it and the "opportunity society" that we embrace (or at least used to embrace).

CHAPTER 14

Coming to the Summit: The Resource Peak and Environment

F or all the liberal clap-trap about humanity expending its resources and destroying the planet, for all the skewed statistics and fouled-up (or fraudulent, depending on your level of cynicism) UN reports, for all the hype about immediate population control needs, there lies, somewhere between the ocean of deception and the sea of spin, a few facts and deep questions that we need to ask ourselves about our energy and environmental future. You may think that we are living in the first time period to have problems with strained resources and population growth. You are, as Jim Carey would say it, "Wrong-o." In fact, three peoples before us have had serious environmental problems that lead to extreme economic woes, and two of them are not around to talk about it today, not to mention the issues that the ancient Chinese had with the over-harvesting of timber. Civilizations in Africa, Europe, and Oceania experienced some of the same issues that we are going to be forced to confront very soon.

Great Zimbabwe was an empire that was situated along the Indian Ocean coastline of Africa in what are today the nations of Tanzania, Kenya, Somalia, Mozambique, and South Africa. These people existed in this past millennium, and formed a vast trading empire within what came to be known as the Indian Ocean Trade system, just in case you never read a world history textbook. This trade system encompassed everything from the Straits of Malacca in Indonesia to the Iberian Peninsula when the Portuguese entered the trade route. The empire assimilated along the coastline with the people of the Arabian Peninsula, Indian subcontinent, and the Red Sea.

The people of Great Zimbabwae traded ivory, metal products, dyes, and their vast supplies of wood from the mesic (well-drained) forests of East Africa. In addition to that trading economy, the more traditional Zimbabweans lived slightly inland, practicing a method of agriculture commonly referred to today as slash-and-burn. This is where a farmer burns the vegetation off of a plot of land to get to the soil, farms on it for a few years, and moves on when the soil loses all of its nutrients. Great Zimbabwe built an empire that was extremely wealthy compared to most nations in the Indian Ocean Trade Route. As the trade continued, the trade volume increased, and the empire continued to trade away more and more of its timber, until the rate of wood harvest outpaced the rate of new wood growth. As the empire grew and grew, and the citizens on the trading coast got wealthier, the supply of wood continued to dwindle, along with the supply of arable farmland that had not already been used for slash-and-burn.

At some point, Great Zimbabwe hit what economists generally call "peak production," which is the phenomenon that occurs when someone is pulling out a natural resource as fast as it can possibly be pulled out, while demand keeps going past the supply. When this critical tipping point occurs, you can expect the price of the product to go through the roof in some kind of hurry, because the demand is outpacing the supply. Due to this incentive, the producer inevitably wants to keep pulling out the product as fast as possible to turn a humungous profit (except in some cases where the market controls itself, like crude oil). Therefore, the empire kept pulling out trees and elephants (for ivory) faster than they could be replaced to maintain its now urban, coastal lifestyle. Combine the lack of trees with a point of critical mass with its farmland situation, and Great Zimbabwe simply imploded, as it ran out of resources to keep up its lucrative trade.

Easter Island has a similar but more isolated and horrifying story. The people of Polynesia colonized the island by sailing their canoe-like ships to the island from the west, moving with the general direction of the entire civilization. When these people settled the island, they found it to be a very inhabitable and hospitable place, with plenty of coconut trees, seabirds, and fish for food. The colony started to grow in both land size and population (we can determine all of these things via archeological evidence on the island, especially in the caves that the islanders used for shelter).

As the population grew and more food was being taken from the forests that once covered vast portions of the island, fewer and fewer people had to participate in agriculture. Near the height of the Easter Island civilization, it had a sufficient sum of people to build the giant Easter Island heads that the island is known for today. However, with a population in the hundreds of thousands on an enclosed island, things started to go askew rather quickly. We know this because the quality of the food that the islanders were eating slowly declined in the archeological records that we have found in the island's caves. Seabirds started to make up a larger portion of the islander diet, then the bark of the trees remaining, then the smallest fish, and, finally, each other. In a few hundred years, Easter Island's civilization had gone from a people building monuments to its gods that even today's humans marvel at the craftsmanship of, to a shrinking population that was cannibalizing itself into oblivion. How did this happen? It's quite obvious really.

The population grew and grew without end, leaving the islanders to cut down more and more of the forest every year, exhausting the supplies of coconuts on the island, increasing the rate of soil erosion due to wind on the agricultural land that was developed in the wake of the forest. If anyone knows anything about soils, you know that a sandy soil like the one that would be present on a South Pacific island will drain very easily, and will have virtually no nutrients. The layer of topsoil on the island that was produced by the forest would be eaten up in no time at all. A huge population that puts its waste on the land and drains it into the ocean has to overfish the populations of aquaculture organisms off the coast, and will drive many of them off with pollution. So, without the fish, the seabirds had no incentive to stay near the island, and left for areas that still had fish. Without those organisms, without a forest, and without a good agricultural system, the population of Easter Island resorted to cannibalism. Thus, all but a few of the islanders disappeared, and a once prosperous and contemplative civilization disappeared into the pages of history, save for the few people who survived the calamity to live like barbarians for hundreds of years.

This story is one powered by many factors that we are currently experiencing in modern times, and is explainable by the most fundamental pattern in all of life: bubble and bust. What applies to the housing market and the health care industry applies too to our energy supplies, population levels, and food resources. This cycle is repeated by every living organism on the face of the earth, from the smallest bacteria and paramecium to our own species. The crises that we face in the semi-near future are maybe the most important that human kind has ever been forced to face. Three principle problems face humanity as it relates to a large population in the coming years: strained food resources, strained water resources, and depleted energy stores.

Every species on the face of the earth reproduces at a rate faster than the death rate when it has not hit the carrying capacity of its natural environment yet, which is defined as the maximum number of organisms that the land can support. When the species goes over the carrying capacity, the population starts to shrink due to a lack of resources. So, the big question a plethora of people have been asking lately is: "What is our carrying capacity?" There is some debate about exactly where the human carrying capacity is, as we are the only species in history that has changed our own carrying capacity.

In Paleolithic times, humans were nomadic, and had to live from hunting and gathering. In that type of environment, the human population remained very low, perhaps fewer than ten million, near the carrying capacity. Since then, we have obviously come up with much more effective techniques for getting food out of our surroundings. When humans invented agriculture in the early Neolithic period, we were able to grow around one hundred times as much food per unit area than we were able to gather in Paleolithic times, increasing our carrying capacity dramatically.

In early European times, farmers invented what we call today the two-field system, in which nutrients are put back into the soil by leaving one field out of two fallow (devoid of crops), enabling the human population to increase to around five or six hundred million. At this low population level, relative to today's populations, the people of Europe were starving by 1300. It was said that any child born into 14th century Europe could expect to go hungry at least a few times in his or her lifetime. After the Black Death plague, which temporarily and tragically solved the problem, the three-field system was developed, and it is still in use today by many farmers around the world. As the world population passed over the one billion mark in the 19th century, there seemed to be plenty of resources available to sustain the growth. Innovation in pesticides that eliminated nearly all insect issues and increased crop yields by fifty to seventy percent in some cases, in addition to new ways to fertilize the soil, cleared the way for the modern period of population growth. Although our carrying capacity might continue to increase, we will not be able to outpace it forever. Currently, scientists disagree on what the carrying capacity of humanity is. Some put it at two to three billion if everyone consumed like Americans, and some put that number closer to six or seven billion. If all of humanity lived like the average human being, our carrying capacity would be between eleven and twenty billion. Right now, we are at about seven and one-quarter billion people. The problem is that nearly 90% of that growth has come at an ever-increasing rate in the last two or three centuries. Over 50% of that growth has occurred just since the middle of the 1960s, when the earth's population was approximately three billion people.

The bottom line is this: without a major innovation that increases our carrying capacity fast, or a slowdown in population growth, we are going to hit that number within the next century. With that in mind, please take into account that Westernized nations are not contributing to this growth in any meaningful way. Although the Chinese population, which is currently the largest on earth, will level off, it will be more than made up for by growth in Nigeria, and Eastern Africa. The population growth of the United States is entirely from immigration (legal and illegal). Without that, our population would be very slowly contracting along with the modernized nations of Europe. This situation, combined with our agricultural land, puts America in an enviable and unique position in the next century.

The Great Plains of the American heartland are often called the, "Breadbasket of the World," because this region supplies an inordinate amount of the world's foodstuffs. When you add in California's fertile valleys, Florida's farmland, and the farms of the Eastern region, the United States produces enough food in an average year to feed itself at least five times over. Now consider that the population of the United States is only going to hit about 400 million by 2050 at current rates (an increase of around 32%) at current growth rates, and we have the world by the tail (no pun intended).

China, India, and other nations with rapidly growing populations will be willing to pay much higher crop prices in the not-so-distant future. In last year's drought, an early test of the corn crop's strength in commodities markets, prices hit all-time highs easily, and nearly pushed nine dollars a bushel. For some perspective on what the heck that means, the average price per bushel for corn in the 1990s and early 2000s was between $3 and $5 a bushel. Anything over five and a half dollars a bushel was simply unheard of. Many of the top firms in commodity markets are starting a new trend: opening up ETFs focused on the raw corn, soybean, and wheat markets on the Forex floor, allowing traders to capitalize upon droughts in the short term, and the rapidly growing human population in the long term.

America stands to make tens of trillions in the coming peak food production crisis. We could even possibly use that leverage to get our national debts forgiven in exchange for cheap or free food exports to nations in need of it. This position also carries an obvious danger with it: the danger of military action. If India doesn't feel like starving, and it doesn't feel like forgiving our debts, it might elect to stage a coup on a world stage. In addition to a growing world population, we have aging pesticides to contend with. In the Great Plains, some insects are already developing resistance to the broad-spectrum pesticides. The application of more advanced pesticides would be more expensive, and increase food prices. If insects were to completely resist pesticides in the future, crop yields already widely sought after decrease back to 1940s-era levels. So, we have to hope for new innovations in farming fast, as we are going to run out of new land for agriculture in the very near future, especially with governments around the world trying to protect more of their wilderness areas. My point is that when I see an article saying that if the earth's population levels off at only eleven billion, that is too low in Newsmax, I really wish that this particular publication would check its facts along with its sanity. Although a decreasing or leveled off population can put stress on retirement systems and manufacturers of baby products, I would much rather live in a world with food but not as much money than in a world with more money but not enough food; call me crazy.

The facts cannot be a partisan issue, or we are in some trouble as a civilization. What that crazy ideology preaches is that infinite growth in demand is just fine, because it means infinite growth in profits and share prices. What that idea fails to factor in is that the resources aren't there! I once heard a saying that made me stop and think that might apply here, "Anyone who believes in infinite growth in a finite world must be one of two things: a madman, or an economist." We probably won't hit peak food production for a while, but the lowest grain and corn reserve levels ever recorded should probably tell us something. When that happens, we had better have a plan ready at a national level for defense and capitalization, because the whole world is going to want farmland like America's.

Then there's the peak in world energy production. This bubble-and-bust cycle could prove to be the death of the American economy as we know it if we aren't prepared for it. The term that is most commonly used to describe when we will hit this critical stage is, "peak oil," meaning a point in time when the world is pulling crude out of the ground as fast as it can to keep up with demand, but we can't increase our rate of extraction. This point in time will have grave consequences for the world economy if we hit it without an alternative energy source. Nearly half of all the energy that the United States consumes is crude oil, even though less than 2% of electricity is generated using oil. That means that because of our heavily consumer/luxury-based economy, most of the energy we use is energy for transportation.

First, let me explain what will happen if we hit peak oil, about when we will hit it, and what it looks like on a graph. If you look at a graph of oil production and consumption for a given country, Mexico, for instance, you will notice that after oil is discovered, it is being pulled out at a rate that far exceeds that of the nation's demand, and that the production line is exponentially growing, while the demand line is just starting to increase. The gap that you see between the lines is what the nation pulls out but does not consume. That gap constitutes that nation's crude oil export in any given year. For a time, extraction keeps increasing faster than the demand. But, after a nation starts using more gas or oil-fired machines due to their cost-effectiveness, the demand for oil starts to increase exponentially, even while new land for resource exploration is running short. Eventually, the line representing extraction will level off entirely. It will not decrease, but level off. This means that oil is being pulled out as fast as humanly possible, and that supplies are going to be depleted very quickly. The demand line will not go down, however; it will continue to increase exponentially. When this happens, you have less oil than is in demand, and you can expect the price to easily quadruple, increase six-fold, or even go up ten-fold in a hurry.

Mexico has already hit this point as a nation. The Mexican people now do not have enough oil to meet their own demand. Only a few decades ago, the Mexicans were exporting oil to the United States and Europe. Another troubling trend is that the Middle East appears to be approaching this point. Oil is currently nearly $100 a barrel. The Saudis and Kuwaitis should have as much incentive as possible to pull out more oil and get it to market. However, Saudi Arabia's oil production has increased at rates that are lackluster at best for the past decade, even with record oil prices. Repeated promises by the Saudi royal family in the 2011 oil boom during the "Arab Spring" to increase oil output have been largely abandoned. The only silver lining here is that the Middle East does not use very much oil at all; it will be able to export for some time to come regardless of a production peak. There is only one possible answer to this quandary: the Saudis are running out of oil.

Now, don't panic quite yet, that idea is what sparked the great oil boom of 2008, in which oil shot up to around $149 a barrel, the highest it has ever been. When world production flat-lined in 2005 and 2006, some on Wall Street thought that the world had hit peak oil. However, discoveries in other regions have brought the oil market back to earth, along with a Great Recession. The oil productions of three countries previously thought to already have hit their peaks are on the rise once again. Those nations are the United States, powered by the Bakken Shale boom, Canada by the Alberta-Saskatchewan oil sands (which is powered by American innovation), and Russia, which is still discovering oil deposits in Siberia. Some of you are probably screaming at the book right now, saying "Why don't we just import all of our oil from Canada until we hit peak oil, and have a switch ready?" Good question.

Let me explain how the Canadians are currently getting their oil out. There is a reason why Canadian oil deposits are called, "oil sands," and it's because the oil literally looks like sand when it comes out of the ground raw, and you have to burn the sand to separate the oil from the silt and sand. Wait a minute, you say; won't it take energy to burn that oil out? If you had that thought, bingo. In fact, it takes more energy to get the oil out of the sand than we actually get from burning the oil. So, why would anyone want to perform an energy-negative procedure? Here's the catch: because of an American innovation called hydraulic fracturing (or hydro-fracking) in which water under high pressure, along with chemicals, are shot at bedrock to release vast reserves of natural gas, the supply of natural gas has increased exponentially in the last half-decade.

Think back to that economics 101 course now; what happens to the price when we dramatically increase the supply of a certain product? The price goes down, and fast! That's just what has happened in the natural gas market. Historically, natural gas prices have been between $7 and $10 a cubic foot adjusted for inflation. However, natural gas prices hit a 2011 low of about $2 a cubic foot, and have only rebounded to the $3 per cubic foot range. So, what the Canadians are essentially doing is selling oil drilling in their home country as a good idea to the residents of the largest energy consuming nation on the face of the earth, which just happens to be a rich next-door neighbor. Then, the Canadians lose energy in the process of exchanging an energy product that is $3 a cubic foot for one that is sitting in the $90-$100 range. Ten years ago, the Canadians would have lost money burning their oil sands with natural gas.

For every 35 to 40 years of oil supplies that the Canadians extract from the Alberta tar sands, they use up 45-50 years of natural gas energy from the United States. The only reason we can't use that natural gas for our own use at such cheap prices is that you have to get a fuel tank very, very cold for it to be able to use natural gas, unless you can liquefy it, which takes a ton of energy itself. So, when people oppose Canadian oil imports, ask them why. If they oppose it because we are wasting energy and handing Canada money and energy that will be valuable after the peak oil crisis, don't rag them out. However, if those friendly uninformed people say that they oppose oil drilling because of environmental damage, they haven't studied their facts, so give them a few. Reindeer and other mammals in Alaska coexist with the Trans-Alaska oil pipeline without issue, and are often observed running under it and near oil drilling sites.

The production of these nations will probably keep the earth out of the peak oil situation until around 2030 or 2035, although new discoveries of oil in deepwater areas could push that back to 2040 or 2050. However, we have four factors on Wall Street that should be keeping oil prices down. The first is the anemic U.S. economy, which is the largest consumer of crude oil (we grew at 0.1% in the last quarter of 2012). The second is the dramatically increased production of the three above mentioned nations. The third is the recent slowdown in China's economy, which is now growing at around 5%. China was growing in the seven to eight percent range just a couple of years ago. The fourth is the dramatic slowdown that we are seeing right now in India, which is growing at around 4%, as opposed to its 8.8% growth rate in the midst of the 2009 recession. With the new production in North America, and the slowdowns in the Asian economy (which was a driving factor in the 2008 and 2011 oil booms), oil should be much lower than it is right now; maybe $40 or $50 a barrel. However, a weak U.S. dollar caused by Federal Reserve Quantitative Easing policies and instability in the Middle East are causing prices to stay high. According to the CEO of Exxon

Mobil, the largest publicly traded oil company on earth, instability in the Middle East is putting a premium of about $15 on a barrel of oil. That puts our oil range at about $55-$65. Now factor in the inflation that has already taken place in relation to other currencies as a result of printing, and you're not quite to $85 a barrel, but you're close. The extra $10 to $20 a barrel that we are seeing priced into the market is a product of speculation.

Speculation is not a dirty word; it just means that someone thinks that the product they are buying will be worth much more in the future than it is right now. So, what would make speculators feel that way about oil? What is driving market speculation is the fact that we are rapidly closing in on peak world oil production, with an economic recovery imminent that will revitalize the rate of growth in demand for fossil fuels. When we hit peak oil, every firm knows that it will be able to double, triple, or quadruple its money on a barrel of oil that it bought for $95 or $100 a barrel years prior, or turn an even larger profit on a leveraged oil ETF (Exchange Traded Fund). For those of you who don't know what the heck leveraged means, it means that your investment is more volatile.

The investors' losses or gains are compounded by a multiplier attached to the ETF, as if the investors are playing a high-stakes game of pinball. For example, if I buy shares in a 5X leveraged oil fund based on the price of WTI (West Texas International) crude oil, and oil goes up 10%, I make 50% on my investment. However, if oil goes down 10%, I lose 50% of my investment. On paper, when you buy an ETF, what you are buying into is the entire world supply of oil. So, on your piece of paper, you own trillions of barrels of oil. Anytime an ETF opens like this, it makes it look like demand for actual barrels of oil for delivery is humungous, which drives the price of the commodity up through the supply-and-demand law. So, what does all that gobbledygook mean?

I hate to sound like one of those "It Could Happen Tomorrow" shows on the Discovery channel, but hitting peak oil is not a question of if, but a question of when. Now imagine the economic consequences of oil going that high. At first, it seems like such an aloof and distant problem. Sure, oil is going to go up, but how will that bring devastation upon us? Well, let me ask you this: where do you buy your groceries? It seems like a personal question, but think about it for a second. If it's Wal-Mart, Kroger, Sam's Club, Costco, or any shop, this applies. If you get your household goods at Lowe's, Home Depot, or any hardware store, this applies. If your home is not within three or four miles of a major employment center, this applies. I feel like Jeff Foxworthy going through the "You might be a redneck if" list right now. Anyway, here's how the ripple effect would shake out.

First, we hit peak oil production, pushing oil prices up to about $400 a barrel, and gas prices to around $20 a gallon (adjusted for inflation). All of a sudden, that Wal-Mart truck won't be crossing the nation carrying goods from HQ in Bentonville, Arkansas anymore, because the fuel in the truck would be worth just as much if not more than the goods it would be carrying! Your profit margin after all the other expenses would be well into the negatives. No moron would stay in business in that climate, they would cut their losses. At that point, if you're not either growing your own food or prepared to pay six or seven times as much for it, things get pretty dicey. We're talking about a pre-Industrial lifestyle coming back here. After that, $20 a gallon gasoline would mean that anyone living greater than five miles from either a major agricultural, Industrial, financial, or mining place of work will be bankrupt for lack of money to commute. The suburbs will be completely gone, along with all of the plazas, supermarkets, and consumer luxury jobs that come along with them. Remember that statistic about over 83% of America's workforce being in some sort of service?

That statistic becomes really important and gloomy right about now, because there would be a major run on the banks under these conditions, and the government would lose 83% of its revenue, along with 83% of America's private sector workers losing their jobs. From there, the economic shockwaves would hit Industrial production sectors that need investment capital to keep running. Steel and automotive plants would close down as the demand for automobiles rapidly disappeared. There goes another 10% of the workforce. With such a decrease in tax revenue, the federal, state, and local governments would be forced to lay off most of their bureaucratic employees, including those that are contracted. That group makes up pretty much the rest of the American workforce except for agricultural workers. From there, only one other sector is left: the electric sector.

This sector would sustain a major hit despite its viability as the nation's population fled the infrastructure-rich suburbs for the major cities and the rural agricultural areas. This sector might or might not survive the peak oil crisis, as the resources for its existence would still be there, but the existing infrastructure to deliver electricity to such a dense yet spread out population would not be. If we had some way to run cars on liquefied natural gas or electricity efficiently, the economy might be saved from the energy crisis, as our nation is rich in both coal and natural gas from hydraulic fracturing. However, if not, this sector might easily succumb to its financial woes and disintegrate. If this sector went, we would be right back to a 1800s-style agricultural economy in a New York minute. Under these conditions, crop yields would decrease as investment in new pesticides and farming techniques collapsed and fertilizer manufacturers shut their doors. The world's entire infrastructure would have to be rebuilt from the ground up.

When this crisis inevitably hits, whether it is in 2025 or 2045, we will have to have some sort of alternative to oil ready, or at least well-researched. There are a few ways to go for this one, but only a few of them are permanent solutions. Before I start, I would like to make clear that buying an electric car is not a solution at this point, unless you have a magic electrical outlet. Believe it or not, that electricity has to come from a power plant, and that power plant is probably burning natural gas or coal, both fossil fuels, and one is responsible for most of the acid precipitation on the North American continent. Save the stupidity, and only buy an electric car if you actually want one.

One possible short-term (by short-term, I mean about 100 years) solution to our energy kerfuffle would be to fully embrace hydraulic fracturing in the Marcellus Shale region (Eastern Ohio, Pennsylvania, West Virginia, Southern New York, Western Maryland, and Northwestern Virginia), along with natural gas drilling efforts in the West. It is important to consider what we are actually putting in the ground and how well it is going to be contained before putting it there, however. Aside from water, the main component in fracking fluid is a chemical called benzene, which is a hydrocarbon functional group. What the heck does that mean? Nothing, except that about one milliliter (one drop) of benzene can make between 100 and 1,000 gallons of drinking water non-drinking water very quickly. Now consider that the average hydraulic fracturing operation uses upwards of 1,000 gallons of benzene (.1% of the one million gallons of total fracturing fluid that an operation uses). That's enough benzene to make about two billion, with a b, gallons of water undrinkable! I'm not trying to scare anyone here; if the benzene is removed (the average operation recovers only 50% of the fluid) or contained properly, it is completely harmless to the environment and the drinking water around it.

This new innovation could make America the "Saudi Arabia" of natural gas if managed properly; and it has the ability to bring in tens of trillions of dollars in revenue. The other benefit of natural gas is that it is extremely clean in comparison with the other fossil fuels, namely coal. After President Bush got the United States off of the Kyoto Protocol Plan (and rightfully so), America's emissions skyrocketed because our main source of growing consumption was coal, which made up close to 60% of our electricity consumption in the mid-2000s. In 2012, America's share of electricity from coal-fired power plants dropped to about 37% according to the Department of Energy (DOE), largely because of the hydraulic fracturing boom. Because of these forces of free-market economics, not government stimulus and investment, the emission levels of the United States are the lowest that they have been since the early 1990s, and are dropping rapidly. Once again, it is quite an enviable position that the United States finds itself in on the world stage. We are going to be holding the proverbial "keys to the kingdom" in the next century as far as food and energy go, but the big question is, are there any brazen key thieves in the room?

That's just the natural gas question, however. Even our one hundred years' supply of natural gas will eventually run short, and we will need some sort of alternative. There is always the possibility that hydraulic fracturing proves to be unsafe as well, although it is a rather remote possibility. At that point, we would have a few options. First of all, let's get what are not good options out of the way. Solar, wind, and hydroelectric are only minor substitutes; these sources will never power any significant portion of an industrial economy like that of the United States. This is a product of a simple fact: not enough energy is present. I like to think of everything in mathematical terms, so, here it goes. We have burned through roughly one-half of the earth's oil reserves in a period of about one hundred years. We built that supply of oil up from the decaying plant and animal matter of about a 300 million year period. For those of you who think the earth is 6000-odd years old, think what you will, but don't try to convince me of your convictions, because I have proof, not a book that was not meant to be fully literal. That means that we are burning through roughly three million years of oil deposits every single year! That equates to about 8,000 years of oil deposits per day that we use! At its root, what is oil? What is coal? What is natural gas? All of these sources are referred to as fossil fuels because they are made up of the remains of prehistoric organisms. Where did those organisms get their energy that they had in life? That's right; those organisms had to either get energy from the sun, if they were plants, or get it indirectly from the sun by eating plants, or eating something that ate plants. So, we're using prehistoric solar energy in using fossil fuels. With that in mind, how the Holder are we going to get all the energy that we need in one day from the sun when we are currently getting 8,000 years of sun energy per day?

We can't is the short answer; that was a purely rhetorical question. Any science-oriented reader may be thinking right now, "We get oil at a much lower efficiency rate than direct sun energy." You'd be right, however, even when you factor in how much more efficient direct solar energy is, it would still be unable to power more than about one-ninth of our energy needs. What about wind and hydroelectric energy? Well, what is the cause of wind? Here we go again, you say. Yes, if you answered that wind's principle cause is the uneven heating of earth's surface by the sun, you're right. Hence, wind energy can be called another form of solar energy, and can't power more of our lives than solar, even if we covered America in windmills. As for hydroelectric power, it's a great semi-clean source of energy, but it doesn't have the sheer quantity to power a modern economy. Why is this? What is the root of hydroelectric power? Water flowing downhill, you say. Correct, but where did that water come from? Uphill, wonderful, where did it come from before then? That's right; it rained in the high country. The rain came from a cloud, which condensed after evaporating from the low country. How did that water evaporate? By the power of the sun! Now you can plainly see that although these energy sources are great for minimal production ventures and substitutes, they are never going to power America in full.

What most of America supports, as I do, is frequently referred to as an "all of the above strategy" on energy. This strategy, I believe, will also have to include geothermal and nuclear energy. The reason that I mention geothermal and nuclear energy as great options is that these are the only two sources of energy that do not depend in any way on the power of the sun.

Geothermal energy, for those of you who don't know, is a form of energy obtained by drilling down to the layer of magma that permeates the earth's mantle and pumping cold water down to it. When the water reaches the magma, it evaporates and comes shooting up the opposite pipe with great speed to turn a turbine, which turns a magnet inside of a copper coil, thus producing electricity. The problem with geothermal energy is that to get down to magma, we have to drill down nearly twenty miles in the average area, making this type of energy currently practical only in nations with a large amount of volcanic activity close to the surface, such as Iceland, or regions like that, such as the Hawaiian Islands. Right now, the deepest that humans have gone is just over seven miles with a miniscule drill bit. However, if we could find a way to get down fifteen or twenty miles, we would have a supply of energy that is literally unending. As long as we have a planet with a molten core, we will have geothermal energy, even without the power of the sun.

We need to have a JFK moment here and try to devote our best minds to finding a way to access that infinite energy supply. The government should play a purely scholarship-providing role in this effort and not use it as an excuse to over-reach its bounds in the entire energy sector by propping up certain companies. The nation of Iceland runs its entire economy on just a few geothermal power plants, which never have meltdowns or run out of supplies. With Iceland's population, and assuming that the United States would use about two to three times as much energy per citizen as Iceland, you can set up a proportion that calculates how many geothermal power plants the USA would need to power itself. The answer is that we would need about 3,200 power plants (I really had too much time on my hands). These plants would cost in the neighborhood of fifty million dollars a piece to set up at current metal prices if we could somehow find a cheap way to get that deep into the earth. Fifty million times 3,200 is about one hundred and sixty billion dollars ($160,000,000,000). Although that number may initially jump off the page at you, take this into account: we spent about four times that amount of money just in bank bailouts, and well over one trillion dollars of the U.S. GDP goes to energy every year.

However, the odds of us figuring out how to drill down two times farther than we've ever gone is, well, slim. So, in addition to natural gas and geothermal, we can capitalize on solar, wind, and hydroelectric (privately), coal, biomass, and nuclear power. As far as energy overall, what will fix our crisis is not a government overreaching into the sector with investment capital. We saw how that worked with Solyndra, where the government loaned a failing solar power company money in hopes that the capital would save the company. Before long, the company went under.

The private sector is fully capable of carrying America through the energy crisis with incentive from the consumer. It's very simple math: nobody can afford gas that is $30 a gallon without going broke. If gas prices are that high, the oil companies will go bankrupt along with the gas stations as the American economy shrivels up. Every energy company on the face of the earth has ample incentive to find feasible alternatives to our current consumption system and to recruit employees to find it. This can be plainly seen today with the example of Exxon Mobil, a company that has been investing heavily in education of scientists and engineers, in addition to paving the way to an alternative future. When the government gets involved, it obstructs, delays the production of any energy sources that it doesn't like, and dithers. Just to give you an example, the EPA recently tried to shut down a North Dakota oil drilling operation because the operation accidentally killed a few Mallard Ducks (the most common ducks in the Western Hemisphere).

The whole coal industry is under intense fire from the EPA, and coal-fired power plants are closing across the Western Appalachians and the Lower Midwest (Ohio, Kentucky, West Virginia, Tennessee,

Indiana) due to overbearing regulations. America hasn't built a new nuclear reactor since the mid-1970s (ironically the same time that the movie *China Syndrome* was released), yet we complain about an aging fleet of reactors. We might as well have a Department of Energy Restrictions for crying out loud. The Department of Energy takes in the money of five behemoth oil companies every year in its budget, and it has yet to produce a lump of coal, a gallon of gas, an acre of corn, a barrel of oil, a cubic foot of natural gas, a megawatt of electricity, or a new energy idea. The private sector will come up with a new and feasible energy alternative well before the peak if it is possible. All these solutions are meant to take on a private sector purpose, with the government maybe playing an educational role at most, paving the way with only a few billion dollars at the maximum. To take it a step farther, why don't we leave it to the states to decide what kind of alternative energy they are going to develop?

As for nuclear energy, a plurality of Americans today are increasingly scared away from nuclear energy by the recent Fukishima scare in Japan, in addition to concerns over where to store spent U-235 fuel rods. Currently, America's best plan is to store all of our fuel rods in a very dry Nevada mountain called Yucca Mountain. We use Uranium that is never above 10% purity, usually in the 5% range. Just to give some background on nuclear power, which few Americans understand, I will briefly summarize the process. U-235 fuel rods are suspended in water while inside a graphite block, and a neutron is shot through the nucleus of one of the Uranium atoms, causing a chain reaction that would quickly spiral out of control if it weren't for control rods made of Boron that keep the neutrons from continuing the reaction by absorbing them, as Boron's nucleus is too small to undergo fission. When the power plant wants to create more energy, it pulls the boron control rods up out of the graphite block so that the reaction speeds up, giving off more heat and boiling the water faster. When the reaction starts getting to hot, the Boron rods are simply lowered back into the graphite block, and slow down the reaction.

From here, the process works just like any other way of generating electricity: the heat from the nuclear reaction heats the water around the fuel rods, which turns into steam, which quickly flows through a pipe, thus turning a turbine, which turns an electromagnet inside of a copper coil, thus producing some kilograms per meter squared divided by seconds cubed (also known as electric power). The problem comes from two places, the first being the least worrisome of the two. The first problem is that sometimes a plant may experience inclement weather, say, a tornado, a thunderstorm, or a giant tsunami. If the power in a nuclear reactor goes out for a protracted period of time, it will not be able to control the rate of the nuclear reaction with the Boron control rods if those rods are not in place. Safety precautions can be taken to avoid this, of course, such as leaving the control rods down in case of inclement weather, even if it means lower electricity production. In addition, there is always the fear that water levels inside the reactor core will get too low during such an event, which can also be curtailed by the Boron rods stopping the reaction. However, the second set of fears is a little bit more substantial. After we burn all of the usable energy from the U-235 and it becomes Thorium, there is still plenty of radioactive decay going on, including gamma ray emission. Right now, we take all of those fuel rods to Yucca Mountain, Nevada, and store them in steel containers that are designed to last in the neighborhood of 10,000 years. The obvious problem is that the radioactive waste will be decaying for hundreds of thousands of years, and that the remains of the fission reaction are highly dangerous to life in any form, as gamma rays can cause cancer, or even incinerate someone. The nuclear power industry would tell you that the odds of us finding a cheap way of getting rid of only a few thousand containers (a little Uranium goes a long way) within the next few thousand years are extremely good, and I'd be inclined to agree with them. Nuclear power, if executed safely, can definitely play a part in our energy needs being met. On a completely related side note, if we can find a way to safely harvest the gamma ray energy that is put off by the uranium for hundreds of thousands of years, we'll have plenty of energy; and someone will get very wealthy.

For those of you who view ethanol as the truly "green" way to go, I hate to burst your bubble. E-85, the most common form of biomass fuel, is a mix of 85% ethanol (an alcohol group that is derived from corn) and 15% gasoline. Some of you are currently wondering why this is not eco-friendly. First of all, when I say that ethanol is not eco-friendly, the word eco has a double meaning: environmentally and economically.

On the economic front, if we replaced all of our oil consumption (20,000,000 barrels/day) with ethanol use, corn prices would skyrocket. Some of you may be thinking that the price of one crop doesn't matter, because it's just one crop. The next time you buy a candy bar, read the ingredients, because high fructose corn syrup will be one of them. Some experts in the agribusiness industry have said that the price of corn could easily double if we switched in earnest to ethanol. Now, thinking in common sense terms, what usually happens to the economy when the cost of foodstuffs goes through the roof? What happens is that consumer discretionary (free) income falls through the floor, and the base of a consumer economy is crippled, as people spend much less on their wants to make room for their needs. In addition, increased use of corn for fuel would take away from how much valuable foodstuff America can sell overseas in the midst of a growing world population. In other words, ethanol is by no means a permanent solution to our energy problems. The world is not going to sit idly by, starving; watching us use corn to get ourselves from the drive-thru to or vacation destinations. At some point, we will be forced to use that corn for food anyway.

Let's wander back to our not-so-common sense for a moment: when the price of a good goes through the roof, what is the incentive for production? Think about it as oil. The incentive to pull out oil when the price is high is much higher than the incentive is when the price is down, because the producer is going to make more money on the same amount of product than normal. The same thing holds true for corn. If the price of corn doubled from a conversion to ethanol fuel, farmers would want to get as much corn harvested as possible and line their pockets. That means that any land not currently set up for agricultural use in the Midwest or Upper South would be cleared of timber to make room for cash crops. This is where the environmental aspect of eco kicks in. What kind of nature-lover wants the remaining forests of Illinois, Southern Indiana, the resurgent forests of Southern Ohio, the whole of rural Northern Ohio, and most of the Eastern Great Plains plowed over and planted with a desert of corn?

Here in my native Great Lakes state, we have what we call the, "Great Corn Desert," as we call it in the naturalist community, in the center of the state. Although mammals make use of this terrain, nearly all reptile, amphibian, and fish life is adversely affected, and it is nearly impossible to find a woodland mammal in this portion of the state. You may say, "What the heck does corn production have to do with fish populations?" The answer is a bit complex. As corn prices hypothetically skyrocket in our ethanol-based Americana of the future, farmers would likely stop planting less profitable crops like soybeans, wheat, and hay. To understand the significance of this, you need to understand a very valuable nugget of agricultural information: the use of nutrients by crops.

Corn crops quickly use up nitrogen in the soil, which can only be replaced by an alternate crop for a year, or at least a growing season. For farmers that don't want to plant an alternate crop that would do that, such as wheat or soybeans, they can either wait a few years for nitrogen to naturally come back, or they can use fertilizer. The problem with doing that is that fertilizer does not just stay where you want it to take effect. Rain washes the fertilizer into low-lying areas and water sources. So what? When huge amounts of nitrogen get into a water source, algae grows really quickly, and you can get an algal bloom. One of these events took place last summer in Western Lake Erie; the algae took up hundreds of square miles. Why does the alga matter? Algae blocks out nearly all the sunlight that fish and aquatic invertebrates need to live, and decreases the oxygen content of the water, causing massive fish die-offs and the disappearance of reptiles and amphibians, as these organisms are rendered unable to breed. Not only that, but a beach covered with algae or a trout stream coated in it is not exactly a big draw for tourism. In my home state, as in other states across the union, the tourist economy makes up a large part of the state's GDP (Uh-uh, Florida).

As if all this wasn't bad enough, algae, especially a species called *Cladophora* is a known sanctuary for bacteria such as botulism and E. coli. No problem, you say, we won't switch over to ethanol in the foreseeable future, and it isn't costing us anything right now. Well, nice try, but the state of Iowa is pretty much won and lost on the issue of federal ethanol subsidies in presidential Elections, and Iowans once again went with the man promising the cash for the crops. Your tax money is subsidizing the ethanol industry to the tune of tens of billions of dollars every single year. What do we get for those tens of billions of dollars every year? We get utter failure on the cost-efficiency side of the dilemma, a fleet of cars unprepared to take ethanol, and a host of economic and environmental problems if the program does succeed. Essentially, what we get is the assurance of an easy election call for the pundits in Iowa. Once again, the government's attachment to the most self-centered parts of human nature leads it to bad ideas for no other reason than a pencil on paper at a ballot box. So, as for ethanol, don't think that you're helping the environment one bit if you run your car on it.

In light of this, I would like to take a minute and ask you if you think that the government is an effective steward of the American environment. Most of you would say, "Yes. I might be a conservative, but Exxon is not exactly going to preserve the land." To you, I would present a chilling story that recently got the energy world in a fuss.

In its infinite wisdom, the expansive government of the English socialist paradise said that its nation is using way too much coal from its Midlands region, and is burning too much fossil fuel overall. To incentivize its energy companies to switch over from those dirty fossil fuels to renewable fuels, the British government put into place refundable tax credits. Not to miss out on a terrific opportunity to rake in a few hundred million British Pounds (multiply by roughly 1.6 to get the value in U.S. dollars), the factories of Drax, a major British power company, are promptly switching over to renewable fuels. Environmentalists were happy to hear this news, until they heard what renewable fuel the new reactors would be burning: firewood. Check your eyes by reading this sentence clearly. Nope, you did not hallucinate; Europe's government is pushing its energy production back into the Stone Age! That's not the worst part. The worst part is that this plan is environmentally, economically, and scientifically unsound. First off, Europe does not have much forested land to begin with, so it is importing it. Guess who's exporting. We are.

English power companies are buying up huge tracts of forest in the hardwood forests of Eastern North Carolina and South Carolina. The method of cutting down trees that these timber companies are employing is widely known as clear-cutting. I thought that this term went out of style in about 1920 in this country, but apparently not. Beyond the scope of the environmental damage being done to North America's most pristine Eastern forests (when you clear-cut, everything dies or moves and mudslides become unstoppable), the economics of this move are unequivocally befuddling. Europe is not burning raw firewood, but wood pellets. To make wood pellets, a company has to ship (using diesel) trees to a pelletizing plant that uses heat from fossil fuels to make the wood into pellets. From there, the pellets have to be shipped across the pond using diesel fuel. From that point, the pellets are shipped by way of diesel-powered truck to the power plants of England. That's an immense amount of fossil fuels to be spent in order to not expend fossil fuels. Now that the wood pellets are at the power plant, they are burned, where they release nearly twice as much CO2 per unit burned than natural gas, which is cheap and abundant in North America, and more easily shipped. Here's the kicker: wood pellets cost over three times more to produce electricity than natural gas!

So, for all that effort and government-sponsored hoopla about going green, what we accomplished was to kill a forest of thriving trees, make sure that those trees stop absorbing carbon and emitting oxygen (which really isn't driving a cycle of global warming; we'll get to that next), use an inconceivable amount of diesel and natural gas to transport the fuel, emit more carbon than by burning coal or natural gas, and raise the price of electricity for the consumer, thereby stifling the world economy. Government is great at this "protect the environment" stuff, isn't it?

As if that wasn't enough to convince you that the government isn't a good environmental steward, just ponder how the National Park Service operated in the 1950s. Today, the park service is a venerable and admirable agency worthy of a constitutional amendment, but it wasn't back then. The Great Smoky Mountains National Park, my favorite national park (or just favorite place; my version of heaven really), is known for its mountain landscape, natural beauty, rugged terrain, and mountain streams. In the 1950s, the National Park Service had much different plans for Abrams Creek, a large stream that runs through Cades Cove.

The National Park Service wanted to dam up the creek and create a huge lake for "recreational purposes" that would cover up the most historic part of the park, kill wildlife, and wipe out mountain habitat for miles around. The lake was to provide "fishing opportunities" to the park's visitors. In accordance with this plan, Abrams Creek had gallons of poison dumped straight into it by the park service, killing off many native trout, and claiming countless Hellbender Salamanders, which are now an extreme rarity in the park. Would something like that happen today in a national park? No, probably not. But, if nature should have taught us anything by now it should have been that we know very little about its inner workings.

I'll take a private conservancy of nature enthusiasts purchasing land for preservation like the Sierra Club, Southeastern Cave Conservancy, or National Wildlife Federation over a bureaucrat looking to get new funding for a new project any day of the week and thrice on Sunday to protect the environment. People forget that the government is a very volatile agency, and that it is not always on one side or another. There was a time in this country when the Department of the Interior was essentially a logger's clubhouse. It took the efforts of private individuals like hunters and hikers to form agencies like the aforementioned and many more to preserve this nation's precious wilderness. If we left it to government in the late 1800s and early 1900s, every square inch of this country would have been cut. This country's most ardent naturalists tend to be hunters, who tend to be conservative or libertarian. I cannot tell you how many times I've talked to someone in passing while hiking to discover that they are not very fond of government, but love the environment.

To the point of global warming, nearly no one in this nation seems to know that the temperature of the earth has been falling for the last three years, and ice caps have actually grown in that time. In fact, the earth stopped warming up right around the turn of the millennium, much to the chagrin of climate activists. It is true that many of the hottest years on record have come in the very recent past, but the years have not been getting consistently hotter as many scientists predicted. First, a little background about how our earth is supposed to be volatile would be helpful.

We are all familiar with the fact that the longest days and the hottest days are in the summer. If you ask someone why this is, they will probably say that it is because the earth is the closest to the sun, in all likelihood. That's dead wrong. The earth is at its closest to the sun sometime around January 4th right now, but we are also tilted away from the sun at this time. With this in mind, now consider that the earth does not have a circular orbit, but an elliptical one that runs on a 26,000 year procession. This effect is often referred to as the earth's "wobble." This means that every generation or so, the day on which we are closest to the sun will shift forward one day. As the earth gets physically closer to the sun when it is more tilted toward it, its temperatures will rise pretty dramatically. Let's just say that I'm glad I won't be around to see the height of the cycle when, in about 12,000 years, we are at our closest to the sun in June or July. On that day, you had better break out the SPF 10,000 sun lotion.

The truth about our climate is that we don't really affect it that much. The majority of climate change is caused by outside factors like the activity of sunspots (when sunspots disappeared in the Middle Ages, it created the Little Ice Age and facilitated the spread of the Black Death Plague), the orbit of the earth, and oceanic temperature shifts. For those of you who are still clinging to a belief in Al Gore's theories, explain this: between 1915 and 1945, the earth heated up like crazy in the midst of the Industrial Revolution, then cooled down between 1945 and 1975 when the post-war boom pushed up fossil fuel usage exponentially, prompting the "global cooling" scare of the 1970s and 1980s. That's inexplicable.

With that said, do we contribute to global warming? Probably, because CO2 is a greenhouse gas, but the quantities that we are emitting have a very, very small effect. Our influence on the climate is dwarfed by that of other forces that we cannot control. In fact, a warmer than average summer could produce a vicious cycle of global warming much more easily than carbon could. This is because water vapor is four times better a greenhouse gas than CO2. So, if global warming from human emissions really is real, the environmentalists had better hope that we never invent water-powered cars. Just for your information, the reason that we have been cooling off for the past three years (here in MI, global warming lost some supporters when we got a week of 40 degree weather in June a few years ago) is that sunspot activity is declining extremely rapidly. In fact, it has all but disappeared. We could be headed for another Little Ice Age. So, what's my message here? The biggest reason to worry about energy is not emission-based, but economically-based. You're just along for the ride on this tumultuous earth.

Anyone who tells you otherwise, like, say, that global warming caused Hurricane Sandy, has either an ego to put an actor's to shame, or hasn't looked at a historical hurricane map lately (In the 1950s, over half a dozen major storms of Category Three or more tracked up the Mid-Atlantic and New England coasts). All we're going to do believing that global warming junk is to surrender our energy independence and go back to an import economy in full. Just for those of you who haven't picked this up, nations that rely on imports to run their ways of life usually don't last very long.

All of our energy problems and faked climactic problems pale in comparison to the issues that we are going to have in the next century with finding a place to put our waste and finding more drinking water. Currently, most of America's waste goes into landfills, but we are quickly running out of space. Most states will completely fill up their existing landfill space in the next decade. There are a few ways to remedy the situation. The first is to incinerate all of our garbage, but that means that hazardous gases within the waste would be released into the atmosphere. If we burned only our paper waste, this would be a good solution, as nearly half of our waste is just paper, and the heat of burning the paper could be used to boil water and create electricity in the process, effectively injuring two birds with one stone. It shouldn't be a partisan issue that we currently use a completely unsustainable amount of disposable products. That's just a fact. Once our landfills are filled up, we will have nowhere to put the tons upon tons of garbage that we produce every day. For those of you currently saying, "Mr. Author, I thought this book was supposed to be about America's fall; we've wandered into a tangent like a Trigonometry student," this completely relates; don't worry.

One of the reasons that Easter Island collapsed was that it ran out of places to put its waste, and began using surrounding forests and agricultural areas for this purpose, which slowly decreased its crop yields and polluted its residential areas, driving away much of the ocean-going food that the Easter Islanders relied on. Currently, to deal with our overwhelming garbage problem, some of our garbage is dumped in containers straight into the Atlantic Ocean, especially off the coast of the Northeastern United States. The hope and expectation is that the trash will stay well-contained at the bottom of the ocean, and that may well be the case. However, if any hazardous waste leaks out, or any large amounts of trash start floating freely in the North Atlantic, you can expect America's aquaculture industry to flounder (see what I did there). Most of our fishing (especially for Cod and Tuna) occurs off the coast of New England and the Mid-Atlantic States. The destruction of that fishing industry would have dire economic consequences for the Northeastern states.

By the same token, waste on land not contained in a landfill could leach into the groundwater and agricultural soil, reducing our ability to get drinking water and food. My community sits adjacent to a landfill that has been in use as long as anyone in town can remember, and it is un-affectionately referred to by many as "Mount Trashmore." In the 1980s, the landfill had a breach, and some of the leachate (reddish liquid that accumulates at the sealed bottom of landfills, resulting from the combination of food waste, paper waste, occasional hazardous waste, and rainwater) leaked into the soil of a nearby farming community. For a few years, the farmers in that community couldn't drink their water, and they couldn't farm a thing. The obvious solution to this problem is to start using things that will erode back into the soil, called bio-degradable. A few years ago, I marveled at a glorious invention by the private sector that reflected everything dandy about free-market capitalism. The invention was that of the bio-degradable bag by the Sun Chips company. Once you used the bag, you could literally put it straight into your garden as compost and watch it disappear within a few days. What a genius idea. What happened next was the opposite of the invention, an event that screamed ignorance and luxury-economy gone wild: Sun Chips stopped making the bio-degradable chip bag because customers were complaining that the bags made too much noise! There can be no greater symbol of the ridiculous binge that we are engaging in than this. But, people get what they deserve, I guess.

Then, there's the biggest conundrum that humanity faces: water. You can't live for more than three or four days without it, and many states and countries are beginning to run very low on this precious resource. States in the desert Southwest have begun a bidding war of sorts, and the object of the bidding is the right to have Michigan and other states bordering the Great Lakes ship their water to the Southwest. Nevada, for example, is experiencing rapid economic growth in the Las Vegas area, partly due to the sunny climate, and partly due to new development. However, Nevada's main water source, Lake Mead, is being used up faster than it can be replenished by the Colorado River, which is also the water source for towns downstream like Yuma. The water from the lake is being used ever-faster as the state continues to be developed, with water levels currently about half of what the historic levels are.

Unlike Nevada, Texas has the benefit of the Gulf of Mexico, and can use desalination plants to separate the halite (salt) from the drinkable fresh water, an investment that Texas will be able to easily make with its growing economy. However, Arizona, New Mexico, Utah, Nevada, and even Colorado will not be so lucky. Like all problems, this one has a solution. In most communities in the East, towns use a sewage treatment system that recycles all used water and returns it into the environment cleaner than it was found in the lake or river. With this method, a town is not using water; it is merely recycling water as it goes. The problem is that most nations around the world are not going to be able to get a large amount of water from desalination, and sometimes you can't recycle the water fast enough to keep a constant supply.

Once again, the United States, or at least the Eastern portion of the United States, is in a rather cozy position as far as this resource goes, thanks in large part to the glaciers that deposited the Great Lakes. The Great Lakes system has approximately 20% of the world's fresh water, quite a large chunk for just a few American states. Now consider the vast reserves of spring water that flow out of the Appalachian Mountain range just west of the Atlantic coastal plain, and America is sitting pretty when it comes to water. Some people drastically underestimate the problem that many of the Asian and African nations will have with water, and dismiss is as very long-term.

Let me ask you this, how does a nation like Nigeria, that has an exploding population, decreasing amounts of farmland, a precious little coastline to desalinate in, and hardly any fresh water resources, continue to expand with its current infrastructure? Those nations can't sustain what they're doing. The Chinese are completely trashing the Yangtze and Yellow (Huang He) river valleys with heavy metal pollution, and are rapidly developing any pristine mountain springs that they have yet to tap. Their population will not level off below 1.4 billion people, and the Chinese dump nearly all of their garbage straight into the East and South China seas. How are they going to provide themselves with water?

One day, you'll wake up, flip past CNBC, see the commodities ticker, and wonder to yourself when water became a tradable commodity, because it's going to take on gargantuan importance in the decades to come. America will be able to bring in a grotesque amount of revenue from selling our water in the years to come, if we can capitalize on it smartly.

All of these problems, I believe, stem from a completely apolitical problem in our society: our disconnect from the land we live on.

Look around any high school in America today outside of the few desolate areas in our nation, and you will see a multitude of devices: I-pods, I-pads, Kindles, Laptops, Smart phones, I-thing-a-ma-jiggers galore. The problem is not the technology itself, but the attitude and ignorance that the excessive use of it brings. Men and women have inherent respect and reverence for what allows them to live; it's basic psychology. How ever a society makes its living, that's what the religion and culture will be based on. Take the example of the Mesopotamians versus the Egyptians in ancient times.

The Egyptians made their living along the Nile River Valley, which floods like clockwork every year. Since the life of the Egyptians was so easily planned out; because the flood and the life-giving waters that accompanied it were so easy to predict, the Egyptians had a fairly stable religion and society; their livelihood was reflected in their religion. Because of their easy lives, the Egyptians were respectful toward the natural world that gave them their wealth, embalming crocodiles with pharaohs, and worshipping gods that were modeled after animals as benevolent providers.

The Mesopotamians, on the other hand, lived along the Tigris and Euphrates Rivers in what is today Iraq. The Tigris and Euphrates flood, but both of those rivers flood very irregularly and change course often, making timing up when to plant and harvest any crops in that region all but impossible. This instability was reflected in the Mesopotamians' religion and society. The Mesopotamians' gods were hectic, unnatural mixes of animals, and the society was violent. Perhaps the most ordered society that man has yet found is that of an agrarian society based on law instead of brute force, the system that the Western World has been living under for the better part of two millennia now. The truly troubling thing about today's society as it relates to our livelihood is that, for the first time, most people don't know where their wealth originates, and they don't respect what's around them, or really care to understand it. As we become more wrapped up in technology and more preoccupied in our time, we become less and less vehement in our beliefs, thoughtful in our discussion, deep in our thought, and less based in religion.

Throughout the later part of the 20th century, while Europe was experiencing decreasing church attendance and spiritual activity, America's spiritual community remained relatively strong. In the last fifteen years, America's churches and synagogues have been seeing decreased attendance. I believe that this is partly due to the proliferation of technology that detaches us from all but the electronic world. Ask anyone to tell you the difference between a lizard and a salamander, ask them to distinguish between a Blanding's Turtle and a Spotted Turtle, inquire about what a Sassafras tree smells like, or ask them where the nearest national park is. The average American won't be able to answer one of these questions, and, unless you get an aspiring naturalist or extremely aware youth to answer your questionnaire, not one person under the age of twenty will have a clue.

Thomas Jefferson, my favorite Founding Father and author of the Declaration of Independence, was also a naturalist and land surveyor, and actually studied wildlife for a period of time. He was repeatedly quoted as saying that the world is a gift that we cannot take for granted. Benjamin Franklin proposed the Wild Turkey as America's national bird because of the heritage that it holds for the connection that Americans in the East once had to the land and the forests of that region. Our Founders were all men deeply rooted in nature via the soil, respectful of the land, and deeply faithful in whoever the land's creator is. That is something that we've lost, particularly in the last half century. When fewer than 2% of the people grow over 90% of the food, and a few people own most of the wide open space, your society is not going to respect the land that provides it with life, because it is too wrapped up in what humans create in a virtual world. Has there ever been a society that collapsed for this reason?

Not in the sense that we know, but the Romans went through a tremendous period of urbanization before their republican system of government fell into disarray. The overall point here is this: if the average teen hasn't seen a national park, a national forest, or an endangered species, what the Lucifer's fiery lair do they care about protecting them for future generations? If the next generation has no idea how certain environmental factors impact human life at some point or another, how is it going to manage the nation's resources? In a broader non-environmental sense, how is America's youth going to learn much of anything while addicted to cell phones and technology? How many people will know how their lights get lit, understand where our energy policy is headed, or know when it is a good time to buy a house? In short, are we to know our land, be enlightened, truly live our lives, or are we to be the "consumers" of a great economy based on air and credit, driven by our impulses, living in Huxley's *Brave New World*, with nothing real to hang on to, with what we do collectively effecting every earnings report and leveraged buyout, but what we do personally being miniscule and serf-like in nature? I hope you choose the former, but, for now, most of my fellow Americans choose the latter.

CHAPTER 15

The Roots: Hamilton vs. Jefferson and Madison

Throughout the course of this book, I have been quoting James Madison and Thomas Jefferson, without really taking the time to explain who these men were and what they stood for. In stark contrast to them were the views of the Northeastern banking and merchant class, led by Alexander Hamilton and John Adams. These two political forces divided the nation into two loose camps from the start of the Constitutional Convention all the way up to today. Many of the political and philosophical questions that arise in today's political discourse can be traced directly to the days of Hamilton, Jefferson, and Madison. Although George Washington was a colossus of his day, and set the precedent for the executive branch of government, these three men were the drivers of America's great political divide, and thought up and debated the principles that came to found the American Republic. Perhaps no part of American history is as crucial to understanding it as the period from 1770 to 1810, when nearly all of our precedents and constitutional interpretations were set, some of which changed drastically with the Industrial Revolution, the Great Depression, and World War II. However, the rifts that inevitably appeared in our society in the earliest days of the republic are still visibly with us today. Usually libertarians, economically moderate Democrats, and freedom-minded conservatives sit on one side of this rift, and hardcore liberals, statists, and entirely national-security-minded and pragmatist conservatives sit on the other.

Thomas Jefferson was a planter from rural Central Virginia (what was rural at the time). He was also a land surveyor and an avid naturalist. He was in favor of a much decentralized republic that gave most of the powers of governance to the states and localities, and would have liked a great many of government's powers to not exist at any level at all. He was in favor of every single one of the amendments in the Bill of Rights (all of the original 12), and founded the Democratic-Republican Party after being an Anti-federalist in the time of Constitutional Convention (he was actually in France as the Constitution was drafted). Jefferson favored the system that we had under the Articles of Confederation, and wanted the military to be a militia only.

He feared a standing army, especially one under the direction of the Chief Executive that formed permanent alliances with other nations. Thomas Jefferson was for an agrarian economy with support from small manufacturing and "cottage industries." As far as his philosophy on economics and nature went, he thought that a republic would function much more efficiently if its people were knowledgeable with respect to the land and were closely tied to it. He favored a system of free trade across the globe, and didn't want any protective tariffs for the Northeastern merchants. Jefferson was maybe the first politician to be for the "common man," as his political philosophy taught that everyone is equal in political power, that is to say, voting power, and that the most important people in society are not the elites, but those that feed the elites and everyone else in the country.

Although he believed in political equality, he was solidly for free-market capitalism, teaching that every man got what he worked for, and that you must earn everything you get. His motto on luck was simple: "I'm a great believer in luck; and I find, the harder I work, the more I have." He wanted the poorest among us to be cared for by private charities like churches and community organizations, feeling that the closer to home the organization is based, the more efficient and less intrusive the help given would be. He was very generous and nature loving, but somewhat paradoxical and hypocritical at times.

He preached against the institution of slavery his whole life, but he decided not to release his slaves upon his death, while James Madison and George Washington did. Jefferson was a very strict person on the interpretation of the Constitution, and understood the importance of the Rule of Law in keeping order in the society. He was a deist, and believed that God created the earth, but he was not sure that he believed in the book of Genesis, thinking that science was just as valid as religion, and that God was not an interventionist God, but that we are responsible for all that happens on earth. He was in favor of a republic that constrained swift action, but he wanted the republic to be much more democratic than his federalist adversaries, and he wanted us to be very distinct from the civilizations of Western Europe. Above all, he wanted the America he knew of small-scale farmers and self-sufficient citizens, with its necessary freedoms and liberties, to live on.

James Madison was a planter who lived fewer than ten miles from Thomas Jefferson, but had many differences in ideology with him. Madison believed strongly in states' rights as they pertained to items or actions not enumerated in the Constitution, whereas Jefferson originally did not want a national government at all, or a national government that was nothing more than a glorified confederation. As Madison put it in one of the *Federalist Papers*, "The powers granted to the national government are few and defined. The powers of the states are numerous and indefinite." Jefferson thought that the government closest governs best, while James Madison favored decisions being made on a national level for things mentioned in the Constitution. Although he went away from his former beliefs during his terms as the fourth president of the United States, when he wrote the Constitution, he held the belief that a large, diverse republic such as the United States would have so many small religious, economic, political, and social (don't worry AP World students, a compare and contrast essay is not following that infamous five-word phrase) interests that the possibility of one or two factions taking over the United States government would be next to nothing. To make sure of this, Madison used the Constitution to spread power around throughout three branches of government, which he thought would not intermingle.

In addition, Madison inserted the Tenth Amendment of the Constitution into the Bill of Rights. The idea was that power would be spread in so many places that no one faction could obtain an inordinate amount of power. Madison never really made clear what kind of economy he preferred for the new nation, but he probably concurred with Thomas Jefferson that farmers were the most important people in the society. Madison was a believer as Jefferson was in the Rule of Law governing the justice system. Madison became more and more of a strict interpreter of the Constitution as he got older. Politically, he wanted everyone to have a relatively equal say in who represented them in government as Thomas Jefferson did, although he was slightly more cynical toward human nature than Jefferson. Madison did not seem to favor one system of foreign trade over the other, probably thinking that that decision should be left to future generations to iron out. James Madison was the primary author of the United States Constitution, while Thomas Jefferson wrote the Declaration of Independence, which may explain some of the reason for Jefferson's obsession with philosophy and moral ideals, and James Madison's brutally pragmatist thought process and lack of vocal ideals. Madison was originally a non-partisan leaning toward the Federalist Party, but he switched over to the Democratic-Republican Party before becoming president.

Alexander Hamilton was the complete opposite of everything that James Madison and Thomas Jefferson stood for, save for Madison's early belief in a strong national government. Hamilton was a social climber in Northeastern business circles. He favored a national bank, wanted the economy to be based on financial services and manufacturing, and wanted America to get a sense of nationalism and national unity like that of most European civilizations. He felt that the descendants of the English in the Northeast had a right to collect on everyone else's productivity and speculate on the land in the frontier regions that had not been bought up yet. While Thomas Jefferson famously remarked, "A national bank is more dangerous to liberty than a standing army," Alexander Hamilton believed in a national government with the power to commission both of those things.

Hamilton believed that the old alliances of people to their states or local areas had to be broken in order to create a society that functioned almost entirely from the national capitol and had a very centralized power structure, much like the nationalist, centralized governments of Western Europe. Hamilton was what we would call a snob in modern times for sure. He had a much different definition of the word, "republic" than Jefferson or James Madison. Hamilton wanted only people that were entitled hereditarily or by having a certain amount of money (a very large amount of it, no less) to be able to vote. In fact, he wanted most males to not have the right to participate at all in the political process, and was basically proposing a quasi-oligarchy supported by the new national government. Alexander Hamilton had an unusual craving for power and high-level connections, and thoroughly disliked the average American subsistence farmer. He wanted the banks and financial houses to run a heavily regulated economy, and draw huge profits from it. He also coveted a nation that made amends with Great Britain, the main trading partner of merchants, shipbuilders, and shippers in the Northeastern states. Due to the heavy industrial production of the New England areas, Hamilton wanted to put protective tariffs in place and restrict free trade.

This belief in the power of a trading and banking class tangled up in foreign business deals led Alexander Hamilton to want America to enter into permanent alliances with nations that would protect our business interests overseas (the re-emergence of this belief would lead the red, white, and blue into the Spanish-American War a century later). Perhaps Alexander Hamilton's scariest and most telling idea was his theory of a "ruling class" that would be eligible to hold office, and run most of the nation's major functions, in addition to have guaranteed voting rights. His political party became known as the Federalist Party, and had a wide base of support in the New England states and parts of Pennsylvania. The party drew support from the merchants, shippers, and businessmen of the newly formed nation.

The other major division between the two political parties (if you can call them that) was what the two camps thought the Constitution meant. The Federalists, under Alexander Hamilton interpreted the Constitution to mean that the federal government could do anything that was not specifically banned in the Constitution, and, that in certain extraordinary or unusual circumstances, the government could even do the forbidden stuff. This view led Alexander Hamilton to successfully lobby for the creation of a national bank, and John Adams to pass the Alien and Sedition Acts while waging an undeclared war with the French Navy in the Caribbean, which flew in the face of both the First Article of the Constitution, which specifies that Congress alone has the power to declare war, and the First Amendment.

The Federalists (the most inaptly named political party in the history of political parties) felt that the state governments were made completely and utterly subservient to the national by the National Supremacy Clause, which makes no such allusion, actually stating that the National government is only Supreme in such matters as are enumerated in the document itself. Thomas Jefferson, and, eventually, James Madison, and the Democratic-Republicans argued that the Constitution gave very limited powers to the national government, and left innumerable rights to state governments with the Tenth Amendment and the National Supremacy Clause itself. The Anti-Federalists, at least in my mind, had much more credibility than the Federalists, because they had, on their side the main author of both the Constitution and the Federalist Papers. The Federalists developed what we today call a "loose constructionist view" of the U.S. Constitution, based heavily on the Necessary and Proper (or elastic) Clause, which states that the Congress can issue any laws it pleases for the purposes of pursuing its constitutional power. Well, that says it all, doesn't it? The Clause only allows Congress to pass laws in pursuance of its constitutional Powers. Given that the author of that clause fell on the Democratic-Republican side of that debate, I'd say that that clause was intended to block state objections to clearly constitutional pieces of legislation passed by the national government. The people on Jefferson's and Madison's side believed that the government in D.C. could do only what it could clearly do via the parameters of the Constitution, a view that has come to be known as "strict construction."

The battle between the Jeffersonians and the Hamiltonians can be summed up by looking at perhaps the most vitriolic battle in American financial history: Andrew Jackson's bank war. Andrew Jackson was a fervent states' rights advocate and strict interpreter of the Constitution. One of his main objectives was to abolish what he saw as an abomination to the republic: the National Bank of The United States. In the case of McCulloch v. Maryland just about a decade earlier, the Supreme Court ruled that states did not even have the right to tax an enterprise of the national government like a normal institution, because, the Court said, that tax would violate the National Supremacy Clause. This ruling predictably came down much to the chagrin of Democratic-Republicans (which were, at that time, becoming the Democrats).

Andrew Jackson tried to introduce motions to abolish the national bank upon becoming president, and, in response, bank President Nicholas Biddle raised the interest rates on the national government's deposits to bide time for the bank. Jackson and Biddle proceeded to have a war of words over the next few months, with Jackson saying that the National Bank held too much control over the nation's economy, and that the bank's existence violated the Constitution, as it never specified how Congress was to coin money. Biddle retorted by saying that only an intelligent group of people could plan the interest rates and loan amounts for the economy and manage the nation's industries; even implying that the Northeastern hereditary elite has an inherent right to make money on society's productivity. Andrew Jackson eventually won the bank war by simply withdrawing the federal government's deposits of both precious metals and paper currency from the National Bank and putting them in hundreds of community-owned banks called, "pet banks." The resulting economic shock helped send the USA into the Panic of 1837, although land speculation, which the National Bank was embracing before it became defunct, played a large role as well. After that, the economy went through a boom the likes of which had not been seen on the planet. Capitalism without central planning lasted for nearly 100 years, until Woodrow Wilson's administration set up the Federal Reserve System that we currently have.

When you take a closer look at what Jefferson, Madison, and Hamilton stood for, two things dawn on you rather quickly. The first is that these three men embodied three fundamentally different visions of where America would be today. Thomas Jefferson, although rightfully fearful that the government would quickly gain ground at freedom's expense, as shown by his remark, "The natural progression of things is for government to gain ground, and for liberty to yield," would want an America today of subsistence and small-scale farmers with traditional family values, a strong work ethic, and a strong belief in community unity and free markets.

Apart from Jefferson's isolationist foreign policy attitude, the America that he envisioned still survives today in rural Southern Ohio, rural Pennsylvania, and most farming areas of America. The isolationist policies and pro-individualist side of Jefferson's philosophy are reflected in Appalachia and the Inter-Mountain Western states, where libertarian philosophies are common, more than anywhere else in this country. Thomas Jefferson's vision, however, is dying out quickly as states and localities lose both their sovereignty and distinct culture. James Madison's ideal republic has been gone for awhile. If you take the republic that Madison wanted as president at the outset of the 19th century, it is very close to Jefferson's, and that ideology still survives in most rural areas, although its political influence has been declining in the face of politicians promising goodies or running on valence issues that appear to be pragmatists. The constitutional system that Madison foresaw has so many holes in it that it's now an ideological fortress of Swiss cheese. Alexander Hamilton wanted an oligarchy dominated by the banking industry in which the government and financial sectors colluded and provided a net to those who failed. He foresaw an America that went to war overseas to protect its business interests and made formal alliances with everybody under the sun, an America in which a common culture wiped out any state or local loyalties, where social values slowly faded away, and life was good enough with a consumer economy that we are all content to live in utter serfdom.

Aside from the technological differences that separate us from the late 18th century, the world we are living in right now is the one that Alexander Hamilton wanted. Take the Federal Reserve, for example. This Federal Reserve System is made up of the former heads of America's largest financial houses. This institution is the one that decides what interest rates are in any given quarter, and what measures will be taken to stimulate the economy, along with printing the nation's money supply. Here's the catch: the Federal Reserve buys up most of the debt that it creates through printing money. So, this body of former bankers has the power to literally print money (devaluing the currency for everyone else) and collect 1% interest payments on this debt. The Fed cannot be audited, for fear of sensitive economic data leaking out, despite the will of about 90% of America that wants to audit the Fed. They secretly buy up and sell of shares of certain securities with nearly infinite buying power through printing and borrowing. So, we have no idea how much of the stock market is actually supported by the Federal Reserve and how much is real economic activity.

This is not a free-market model of capitalism, it is a monopolized market! It's the model of mercantilism that the British Empire used for centuries to combine the largest corporations in its nation with the British government. The British government in the 17th through the early 20th centuries would go to war to protect its corporations' interests, and force upon its own citizens increased prices due to protective tariffs (which Alexander Hamilton favored) and economic manipulation through currency printing (a.k.a. a National Bank). Every European nation that acquired a national bank in the Industrial Revolution and trading periods of the 16th, 17th, 18th, and 19th centuries had a middle class that lost money by way of higher prices on goods and a devalued currency (think Holland).

Britain is maybe the best example of this mismanagement and collusion. The British East India Tea Company nearly controlled the British government for a full century, leading the British to take land in Brazil and Northern South America for a short stint of time. This unholy alliance eventually brought itself down, and the British Empire went into a period of slow decline. We are doing the same thing as the British by bailing out the banks and allowing them to heavily influence our government. The British government backed the financial status of shares in the East India Company much like we backed the shares of our largest banks in 2008.

In a free market, Goldman Sachs, JP Morgan, and Morgan Stanley would have gone down in 2008, leaving room for community banks to rise up and expand. That's the way the system is supposed to work. If you take too large of a risk and lose, that's what happens, you lose. You got too greedy if you hedged such a large bet that it was sufficient enough to bankrupt you. Sorry, that's free-market capitalism. After that, one or two big banks will survive, and the rest of the market will be taken up by smaller banks that are still community-oriented and customer-centered, because the demand for expansion will exist. Every bank that survives the crash, in this system, would be very cautious toward large risks and subprime lending, and another major crash would not occur for at least a half a century. But, no, the government has a much better idea about how to handle a crisis. We bail out every bank that took huge risks to "save" the economy; we "abandon capitalism to save it," and expect that those banks will stop taking risks. Then we proceed to pass a "Wall Street Reform" bill under the guise of ending the "too big to fail" doctrine. But, the fly in the ointment is that the bill actually locks in the bailout ideology, and makes lending so difficult that any community bank start-up would go bankrupt just hiring lawyers to interpret the law. All this is added to the control of the Federal Reserve. Now, I ask you, do you really think that the solution to this problem lies wholly within the bulwarks of one political party? If you answered yes, please go check yourself into the nearest insane asylum. Both parties are bought off by these special interests.

To give an example, General Electric, the largest corporation on the face of the earth, was given a tax break by the Democratic-controlled Congress when Cap and Trade was thought to be on the legislative fast track. How big was the tax break? GE paid exactly $0 in U.S. taxes in 2010. President Obama's biggest general election donor in 2008 was the Goldman Sachs Group, and the Republicans caved on the stimulus package in 2009 and the later bailout packages of 2008. Mitt Romney got the party's nod after saying that the Wall Street bailouts were just fine and showing apathy about social issues. As is plainly apparent, the Hamiltonian ideology has survived quite well since the 1820s. Do you think that you are living in Jefferson's republic, or Hamilton's oligarchy? Another aspect of our lives that Alex Hamilton would be thrilled with is how our economy is organized.

Currently, over 60% of the American workforce is in the service sector. Let me repeat that stat; it bears repeating. Over 60% of the American workforce is in the business of servicing other people's needs. The average age of an American farmer is about fifty-seven, and that number is still rising. We produce more physical education majors every year than agriculture majors. Only 20% of the U.S. economy is now based on manufacturing, with that number still dropping. Don't forget, there are plenty of services that aren't related to finances, like car washes, teaching, day care, fire protection, police protection, television services, and internet services. All told, almost ¾ of America's GDP is based on some sort of service. That's how over 70% of us earn our living. Quickly ask yourself one question: how sustainable is that?

The short answer is that it is not sustainable at all. That type of economy is exponentially more volatile than an agricultural or industrial economy. If everyone were rooted in the land like they were in the 17th and 18th centuries, prices of goods would be much more stable, because we would all have a value in relation to working the land, and a credit-based consumer economy would never blossom in that type of society. The stock market would have more small investors, and a smaller quantity of people in the speculation business, as nearly everyone would have an interest in the actual delivery and sale of the product that they were producing. Free-market economics would still be very applicable, and more people would have a sense of individualism in this lifestyle, with a relatively constant source of wealth. In an Industrial economy, the economy is slightly less stable, as people are buying shares on Wall Street based on a company's ability to sell a product to someone else working in industry, but the economy is still stable in this system compared to the market we have, because the wealth being created still only takes a few steps to get back to the agricultural base, and the wealth created in industry is still based on something tangible: making something for use. This theory makes sense at its base due to its sheer economic principles. It's like playing operator, the more people and professions the money has to get passed through, the less to be had at each level unless the first person in the chain can create ever-more resources, which usually happens through centralizing and expanding something.

This theory also held true in the Great Depression of the 1920s and 1930s. In the 1920s, America developed a consumer economy based on credit. In the late 1920s, that system collapsed in on itself. As the shockwaves slowly spread throughout the global economy, aided by the ill-fated decision of the government to institute the Hawley-Smoot tariffs, the nations with simpler agricultural economies stayed more stable, while nations with complex consumer and Industrial economies felt the brunt of the economic downturn. A prime example is Russia: even though the economic downturn hit Britain and France like a freight train full of bad earnings reports, the simple economy of Russia withered the storm just fine, with low but stable growth rates persisting right through the 1930s. Some conservatives might be wondering why I just used a communist nation as an example. Good question.

It's not that communism worked, when you look at how much undeveloped, arable land Russia had in the 1930s, and the rate of population growth that Europe was experiencing between World Wars, a simple economy like Russia's could have been growing at an annual rate of over 10% if it weren't for communism. It just goes to illustrate the point that a nation with that simple of an economy is much more stable than one like, say, ours. Just look at how this last recession has been playing out. Latin American nations grew at solid rates straight through the recession, posting numbers above 5% rather consistently. Now look at our economy. If Apple puts out a bad earnings report, short sellers from the pits come in like sharks, drive the stock price down 15%, and, by the end of the day, the Dow Jones is in the proverbial gutter and the Fed is talking about extending Quantitative Easing.

Think about this: as mentioned earlier, my father is a public school teacher. He is providing a service. His salary is paid at the expense of the taxpayers of Michigan. The average Michigan taxpayer is about 45 years old, makes $50,000 a year, and works in a service-based business. Let's say for all intents and purposes that the taxpayer we're looking at is an employee at a Citigroup Bank branch. His salary is paid by the bank from the interest on the money of the depositors and the profits that the bank makes on the investments it gambles with on Wall Street. What does the bank gamble on in NYC? Most likely, the bank invests a big sum of it in its own stock to drive up the share prices and collect modest dividends. It probably also gambles with leveraged commodity ETFs when it thinks that it knows where the raw materials market is headed, and probably uses the rest to short sell its competitors' stock. Where does the bank get that money? That's right; no more Glass-Steagall Act is in place, so the bank gets it from its depositors. Where do the depositors get the money? The depositors get the money from their employers, who are most likely service businesses themselves. The point you should be getting is that in a typical situation, it takes a long time to trace the money back to where it was actually created; when someone farmed something, made something, or extracted something.

We have a powerful national bank that can print money to its heart's content, and banks that own 90% of the nation's assets between them. Most politicians are beholden to their donors, which are the largest banks and financial houses for both sides of the political aisle. Hamilton's vision of a highly centralized government without regard for real Separation of Powers or the Tenth Amendment is being realized bit by bit as we whittle away at the Constitution. The Executive branch is gaining power quickly, and collusion and takeover of the government by a single faction of American society are getting easier and easier as the productivity of America gets funneled to a single locus of power in Washington, D.C. Social values are declining in our society as we become more permissive of everything from abortions to gay marriage and drug use. Even some Republicans are going this direction.

Mitt Romney is a prime example of how Hamilton's America is the predominant vision right now. If you can remember the GOP primaries, Mitt Romney didn't have any dazzling debate performances, any new ideas, many conservative principles, or a strong sense of direction. The reason he won the primary is because he got hundreds of millions from Wall Street and Northeastern elites that no other candidate got. Mitt Romney only won the small, Hamiltonian faction of the Republican Party by any convincing margin. He even supported the bailouts. How many conservatives do you know who wanted to bail out either Wall Street or General Motors? I know very few of those people. Romney used his Super Pac money to pound Santorum and Gingrich into submission with negative advertising. Take the state of Ohio, for instance. In the primary, Gingrich and Santorum won nearly every rural county by wide margins, including every single Republican stronghold. Romney won that state by cashing in on the votes of Cuyahoga County, Franklin County, and Hamilton County. Jefferson's America lost that primary along with Rick Santorum. What worries me is not that Mitt Romney won the GOP primary when every conservative could have told you he was not going to win; it is when Mitt Romney won that primary. If a moderate to liberal Republican with Hamiltonian leanings can win after the Tea Party movement and the 2010 Republican Stampede, when is a conservative ever going to win?

Hamilton's America is also being realized in another sense: the way we operate overseas in relation to our economic situation. If you recall, Alexander Hamilton wanted a military that made alliances to protect the business interests of the Northeastern merchant class.

We do just that. How else would you explain alliances with Saudi Arabia and Qatar in the Arabian Peninsula when both of those nations have kings? The reason that we are allied with those nations is that they have a very strategic position as it relates to the crude oil market, which is heavily speculated upon in America.

We allied ourselves with Hosni Mubarak in Egypt even though he was a brutal dictator because the vast majority of Europe's oil comes through the Egyptian-held Suez Canal. The Jeffersonian economy also disappeared right around the middle of the 20th century as small farmers started selling their land to larger corporations and moving to the suburbs and cities. Currently, the United States economy is the spitting image of what Alexander Hamilton wanted it to be.

Banks and financial institutions make more money than anyone, and collect interest on nearly everything we purchase or take a loan out on. The people that actually produce the society's wealth (small farmers, manufacturers, miners) make the least amount of money save for the urban proletariat. Actually, check that, with the welfare state growing exponentially, the members of the urban poor may soon be making more money than family farmers in Indiana or coal miners in rural West Virginia. We don't put very much emphasis on working on the land or making things right now, but more on gambling on the stock market or providing a service to someone else.

Hamilton's vision of a middle class and common population that was content enough with the standard of living and creature comforts to power a consumer economy and live under serfdom has come to fruition in the last century as technology has advanced ever-faster. America's economy is not even a consumer economy powered by real, tangible money; it's powered by deficit spending and credit cards, which is essentially a purchase being funded by a bank or insurance agency that makes its money from interest and investments. With only 2% of the population growing over 95% of the food supply, and farming and energy production becoming more and more monopolized by the large financial houses themselves, the American economy has become Hamiltonian in every way imaginable. We can take any political question that comes up in today's society and look back at how Alexander Hamilton, James Madison, and Thomas Jefferson would interpret, and see how the demographics in America today still reflect many of the same rifts that were present in 1790 or 1800.

For now, say goodbye to Jefferson's Republic and Madison's constitutionally tamed beast, because you are definitely entering the era of the Hamiltonian oligarchy, in which no control over the government exists, and liberty is a thing of the past. Put on the shackles; welcome to serfdom. We all work for the government and to pay off loans from the banks now. Say hello to MERS and a collusion of the government and the largest businesses on a scale never before seen. Much like the feudal lords of old Europe, the biggest businesses in America are teaming up with their government to ensure their eternal economic survival, in addition to making sure that they can provide for their employees' financial needs, while taking away their free spirit, innovative capacity, and liberty; for the common people are too uninformed to make their own decisions or live their own lives in their minds. Though it is much easier to control a public corporation than a government, make no mistake, they are both currently destroying our liberties. Welcome to regulated oligarchy.

CHAPTER 16

I don't Get it: Summary

E verybody takes something different from what they read. The main point of this book was pretty straightforward, or at least I hope so. The bottom line is that America is headed down the wrong track in a hurry; a path that was blazed for us by the Roman Republic and Roman Empire, and contributed to by the environmental follies of Great Zimbabwe and Easter Island, the inflationary mistakes of the Ming Chinese, Mongols in Russia, Germans, and Yugoslavs, the speculative mistakes of the Tokugawa Shogunate and the Dutch trading empire, and the ruling class experiments of Britain, Rome, and Western Europe in general. We're positively coming apart at the seams, and we're losing much of our old spirit and wisdom.

The Road to Serfdom is plainly in front of us, staring us in the face, yet we continue on our current course. Is there still time to turn around? Absolutely, but that time is running out very quickly. I don't expect many people to agree with everything that I said in this book, and I don't really want everyone to agree with everyone. Come to think of it, that would be a pretty boring world. But, we do need to come together as a nation and agree on what reality is, look at what's worked in the past, and look at where we're going with a little more urgency than Harry Reid, who mourns that poetry festival that I won't give the honor of mentioning again. Both parties need to stop worrying about who wins and start worrying about the well-being of the nation. But, above all, the message that you should have gotten is that only one person can fix America and enlighten you: you. If America does not enlighten itself, does not come together, doesn't become a community-oriented society with strong convictions again, all the deregulation in the world will mean absolutely nothing, and all the military power in a ten trillion dollar budget won't re-polarize our broken moral compass.

Find your own set of values that makes sense and argue it; don't just take my word for it. No one political party is about to fix our problems, and no one set of values reigns supreme over all issues. Just voting is not enough, especially considering where the Republican Party has gone recently; talk to your neighbors and co-workers, and to your family, about more than just the usual status-quo prevailing wisdom on issues. Try to convert somebody, argue your cause, and get the free marketplace of ideas that is the United States alive with them again.

Don't let your ideology dictate the facts;
let the facts dictate your ideology

About the Author

Nathan Richendollar is a conservative-libertarian teenager who also has a passion for science, the natural world, poetry, and music in addition to his political viewpoints. He frequently uses Founding Fathers' quotes in arguments, as the astute reader has no doubt found out by this point.

He enjoys looking for salamanders and other amphibians and reptiles in his spare time, and is constantly out in the woods. Appalachia is his favorite place, with a special emphasis on the Smoky Mountains, the Nantahala National Forest, and the wilds of Southern and Eastern Ohio. He has found thirty-six species of salamanders as of his writing this, and will have more soon.

It should be noted that Nathan's great-great-great grandparents on his mother's side, the Trouts, were good friends with John Muir in Canada; friends enough that the esteemed naturalist spent a few years at their humble abode. Thus, his family attributes his love of national parks and the wilderness to ancestry as well as intrigue.

Richendollar is currently 16 years old, and participates in a wide array of activities at his school. He is a member of the Ocean Bowl team, Science Olympiad team, Quiz Bowl team, Book Club, Football Team, and Envirothon team. He devotes much of his time to writing poems about the natural world or human nature, and also thinks up puns and plays on words frequently. He hunts, fishes, plays sports, does Fermi questions, does math, plays chess horribly, invests small-scale in commodities and general stock, and debates liberals, statists, progressives, and creationists for fun.

His brother is the consummate birder, and the author has recently commenced to participate in the chase of avian species. The author also plays the Blues, Bluegrass, Folk, Southern Rock, and Rock guitar. His favorite TV shows are *ALF* and *Monk*. But, above all, Nathan's most peculiar trait is his tendency to write about himself in third-person terms in the "About the Author" sections of his own books.

"I believe that banking institutions are more dangerous to our liberties than standing armies."

-Thomas Jefferson

Sic Semper Res Publica describes how America is following down the road of the Roman Republic, Ming Chinese Dynasty, Tokugawa Shogunate, and many other fallen civilizations. It was written by a sixteen-year-old AP student from Michigan who wrote it to preserve his sanity as he observed what happened around him in the past decade. It discusses the Founders' idea for a republic, the threats we face from oligarchy, socialism, corporations, government, and a lack of morals alike, and stresses the need for self-enlightenment and honesty in society. Learn how to stop America's demise and fight for our experiment in republican democracy!

WestBow
PRESS
A DIVISION OF THOMAS NELSON